The Existential Self in Society

The Existential Self in Society

Edited by

Joseph A. Kotarba

and

Andrea Fontana

The University of Chicago Press
Chicago and London

JOSEPH A. KOTARBA is associate professor of sociology at the University of Houston. He is the author of *Chronic Pain: Its Social Dimensions* (1983) and coauthor, with Jack D. Douglas and others, of *Introduction to the Sociologies of Everyday Life* (1980).

ANDREA FONTANA teaches in the department of sociology at the University of Nevada, Las Vegas. He is the author of *The Last Frontier* (1977) and coauthor, with Ronald Smith, of *Social Problems* (1982).

THE UNIVERSITY OF CHICAGO PRESS, CHICAGO 60637
THE UNIVERSITY OF CHICAGO PRESS, LTD., LONDON
© 1984 by The University of Chicago
All rights reserved. Published 1984
Printed in the United States of America
93 92 91 90 89 88 87 86 85 84   5 4 3 2 1

Library of Congress Cataloging in Publication Data
Main entry under title:

The Existential self in society.

   Includes bibliographical references and index.
   1. Sociology—Addresses, essays, lectures.   2. Existentialism—Addresses, essays, lectures.   3. Self—Addresses, essays, lectures.   4. Identity—Addresses, essays, lectures.   I. Kotarba, Joseph A.   II. Fontana, Andrea.
HM24.E86   1984   301   84-166
ISBN 0-226-45140-2

Contents

Foreword

Stanford M. Lyman

A risen spirit is haunting American sociology: the self. I say "risen" rather than "new" because the idea and problematics of self are older than the discipline and have affected its development from the beginning. What has revitalized the self as central to sociology is its emancipation from second-class citizenship as a dependent variable, its recognized autonomy as an independent phenomenon and topic for investigations into the social construction of human relations. The self is now conceived *existentially*, in terms of its contingent, assembled, changeable, and precarious modalities. Autonomy and emancipation entail a reconceptualization of the relationship of the self to mind and society, a rewriting of the hoary thesis that animated the social psychology of the pragmatists and found its near-iconographic expression in the eponymous book of George Herbert Mead and in the subsequent writings of his colleagues, interpreters, and critics. The existential self is free-floating, or nearly so, like Mannheim's idealized intellectuals, who, having been liberated from ideological constraints and utopian fantasies, might construct and reconstruct the world. What happens to thought and to social institutions is, thus, much less determined by external material forces and far more problematic with respect to the positivists' promise of prediction and control than ever before.

How the existential self appears and assembles itself in society is a topic of the present book. The authors of course cannot give a closed, determinate, and predictive picture of this process or of its product. To do so would violate the very premises of their perspective. Existential sociology is postpositivist and postfunctionalist. It leaps beyond the overthrown paradigms that promised sociological seerdom and social scientific hegemony. It returns sociology to an *unprivileged* position in its relation to human activity. Whereas general social science and, more particularly, conventional sociology have opted for its Baconian elevation above the suspect reasoning capacity of ordinary humans, existential sociology follows the admonition of Pico della Mirandola to place the human studies side by side with their subject, sharing the latter's attributes, deriving their concepts from an acceptance of *man* for what he is and treating sociology as *his* expression.

It is thus that in the pages to follow we meet characters who are simultaneously familiar and unorthodox but never "deviant": victims, ex-nuns, homosexuals, wheelchair runners, organization men and women, and a host of secure, insecure, formed, and forming selves in various states of becoming, persevering, transposing, and dying. Because we are all part of this universe, this is but a small segment of the entire population of existential selves. However, small and unrepresentative as it is, it provides a portraiture and a description of some of the most salient processes, dilemmas, conflicts, and contradictions in which the self both participates and observes its own and others' participation. In the existential world we are all simultaneously ethnographers and subjects of ethnography.

This new sociology takes its departure from the uneasy relationship between experience and meaning. The former has the character of being-in-itself, the truly empirical; the latter, of being-once-removed. Yet, experience is, in and of itself, without meaning; it belongs to the world of the absurd. Meaning is given to experience through language. A sociology of the absurd becomes, then, an existential phenomenology, the discipline that examines how the raw experiences of everyday life are sociolinguistically constituted as parts of the ever reconstructed comprehensible world. The land of the absurd is a labyrinthine limbo where few care to live. Language is the Ariadne's thread that winds each Theseus out from the dangers of Minotauran meaninglessness.

The nonabsurd world and the existential self are created within the perimeters of time, place, manner, and power. Although seemingly "out there" for every person, each of these is subject to individual and collective interpretation, reconstruction, counterdefinition, and manipulation. Time retains its Augustinian mystery as *durée*, while its man-made forms appear, inter alia, as history, evolution, event, memory, term, hours, minutes, seconds, and the terminable or interminable future. The spaces on the earth are *territorialized* through accomplishment of human dominion over them and exist under such forms as established, contested, or soon-to-be-sovereignized regions, states, provinces, or colonies; as places for public or private activity; as interactional or obstructed trajectories of communication; and as what the philosophers call "extension," i.e., nature's construction of the fleshly limit of the human body. What is peculiarly human has its pristine character, but such is the distinctiveness of each individual's or group's understanding that personality, group identity, idiosyncrasy, inheritance, culture, and situation are said to modify—or mollify—its appearance. And standing over duration, space, and the mannered self is the protean phenomenon of potency, the capacity to secure compliance in the face of resistance. If we were to look for the sociological concept that expresses the unity of time, place, manner, and power within a single individual or a collective entity of awesome personification we would find it in *charisma*, acting as form and force, the instrumentality of true social *change* rather than mere historical *passage*.

*

The existential self has something of the character of Simmel's stranger: it is ever with us but mysterious. For some, e.g., "primitive men," its mystery as well as its existence goes unnoticed as self remains an undiscovered and inarticulated aspect of a collective humanity. One historian of the individual, Colin Morris, speaks of the emergence of self-referencing in the West in the twelfth century, and surely he is right to point to its intimate connection to the European rediscovery of Latinate humanism. But the existential self had earlier origins in Yahwistic religion, as Max Weber's study of *Ancient Judaism* certainly suggests, and a later development as a consequence of the Protestant ethic. Yahweh was the self-chosen god of the Hebrews, who were admonished to have no other gods before him and to enter into a contract (covenant) with him for mutual benefit. Yahweh and the Hebrews had constantly to work out, reinterpret, and renegotiate the terms of that contract, and the Hebrews were enjoined to open continuous discussions and debates with Yahweh through their representatives, the prophets. The prophets, as Weber pointed out, were not officeholders, bureaucrats, or priests; rather, they were men who lived on the edges of Hebrew civilization, who would assert their authority as negotiators and spokesmen charismatically, and, by this very process, they suggested an individuation of mankind. Moreover, the covenant with Abraham, especially after its renewal with Moses, was one of laws, and it adumbrated a *politicized state* as the appropriate social organization. The search for a Christian *community* of believers, conjoined in faith, is a later Pauline development, introducing a respecification of the powers of Yahweh and the weakness of man and requiring a mystifying obscurantism to replace the no longer negotiable terms of man-god relations. When Calvinism reopened the question of faith and fate once again—this time in relation to a god who was declared to be omniscient, omnipotent, and absolutely prescient—man was left in a fully determined but absolutely incomprehensible world, granted the free will to choose his path but always ignorant of his ultimate destiny. The recognition of an absurd condition takes its point of departure from the human condition after the Reformation. The Puritans invited each man to seek his calling within himself, to plunge into the unfathomable void of this world in the hope of obtaining a sign of his place in the next.

The existential self is poised precariously between the two philosophies of absurdity that distinguish, in opposed argument, the relations between world and meaning. For the first, all that exists meaningfully is language, while the world is a dark cave of shadows and appearances; for the second, the world is an obdurate but solid mystery, possessed of its own intrinsic character, while language is a pale and ephemeral producer of its illusions.

For man, then, the future of an illusion also could mean an illusion of the future. The unarticulated and unwritten word might yet be its most potent element; language consists of "language games," as Wittgenstein reminds us. But we are all in what Nietzsche called the prisonhouse of language and cannot escape to the freedom of existence-in-itself. When the epigoni of the Frankfurt School call for a new emancipation of communicative conduct, they do not call for a liberation *from* it. It would appear that we are all Vladimirs and Estragons, living in a Sartrean world from which there is no exit—we cannot depart from our anxiety-provoking waiting room; we endlessly converse, while the time for our appointment with Godot seems always to be postponed.

The existential self is also ambiguously located on two of the dualities that derive from the critique of Cartesianism: embodiment-disembodiment and articulation-ineffability. The self seems to be embodied within the anatomical frame that nature has given to man. Moreover, the self is said—or desired—to be just that, i.e., singular. For each human there is, supposedly, but one self. However, contained within a body, this self has organic characteristics. It evolves, develops, grows. And it separates its essence from its appearance. A single body for each human might seem to require a single embodied self, but there are problems inherent in this requirement. The comprehension of the development and presentation of this self within the same body makes it difficult to discover it empirically and to classify it analytically. The self is surely essentially more than and different from its appearances ("roles"), and by its possessor it is perceived at any given moment as fully formed rather than in process—as "being" rather than "becoming." Yet its appearances alone are visible, and its brute existence and state of motility are not available at all to the observer. These must be inferred. An unbridgeable gulf separates the experience of the self by its possessor from the apprehension of it by its observer.

Moreover, the self is disembodied even as it is supposedly limited by human extension. For the self finds its singularity encompassed within a collectivity that transcends its fleshly limits. Typically, we see ourselves as members of historically and socially constituted sodalities. The pronominal "I" defines itself as a member of a plural "we." Asked "Who am I?", the individual is likely to respond categorically: I am a black, an American, a professor, a homosexual, a cripple, etc. The "I" seems to require a reference *group* that owes its own claim to recognizable existence to the social constitution of collectivities. "I am I" is not an answer that anyone, even I, will respect. Thus we all disembody and socialize the self in the very act of claiming its singular embodiment and individuality. An individual becomes a person, and a person exhibits his or her personification of the social self-referencing group.

Moreover, if disembodiment connects the bodied self to other bodies in space, it also links it to collectivities in time. The disembodied self partakes of history, memory, hope, or dread. To say "I am a Jew" is at the very least potentially to identify with the Yahwist, Elohist, or secularizing conceptions of that people's past, to dredge up to consciousness the recollections of one's own ethnic group life, and/or to connect one's persona to the dreams or nightmares of the always problematic future that the cunning of futurity holds out to Jews. The disembodied self can be referred to predecessors, contemporaries, consociates, and successors in a single synthesizing phrase: "I am we." For this apparently inescapable singular plurality the problematics of the "I" are great. Its very "I-ness" is at stake. It struggles against becoming submerged completely in the "we-ness" that gives it its unique identity.

The existential self also seems to depend on language for its own confirmation and for its affirmation of or conflict with the world around it. The conversation of gestures, so basic to symbolic interaction, is vernacular in character: the sign becomes a symbol. The world around us is subdivided into an *Umwelt* and all else that is beyond it by the juridical rules of action and the jurisdictional rules that tell us where the action takes place. These rules are articulatable, although for most socialized persons they need not be spoken or written down. Hence, a major project of the ethnomethodologists has been to introduce an archeology into symbolic interaction and to plumb the depths of the juridical and jurisdictional knowledge from which every person's *Umwelt* derives. Although much of this work appears to be microecological, it could herald the social scientific reconstruction of civilization itself. Language in its expressed forms and in its deep structures provides the means by which the existential self finds, defines, and reorders its place in the world.

However, the existential self and its students are also troubled by the limits of language and that which is beyond language—the unutterable. Again we must turn to Yahwistic thought to grasp some clues to this phenomenon. To the ancient Hebrews, and to religiously-minded Jews today, their god's name was unutterable and symbolized by letters that were not pronounced. He was the "the lord," "our god," the one "who brought us out of Egypt." Understood through his commandments, contractual arrangements, punishments, and rewards, he nevertheless remained ineffable. Identification with him did not permit his name to be spoken. Rather, it was silently understood by all who were members of the covenanted agreement by which his sacred authority was established. By a dialectical process the very essence of membership in the covenant became itself unutterable, so that a constituted sacred peoplehood revealed its awesome roots precisely by being inexplicable to outsiders. The bases for identification with the sacralized we-group became an insoluble mystery to outsiders at the very moment that its unspeakable character formed the ground for an in-group understanding that required—indeed, demanded—no words.

The existential self owes a part of its existence to the supraexistential soul and to the reference groups with which the soul identifies. The soul, it seems, belongs to a soul group. The soul is disembodied at death but remains immortal, finding its place, in accordance with different eschatologies, in transmigration, paradisiacal reward, or hellish torture. The mundane existential self of modern secular man has its own intimations of immortality. In its relation to the sacred reference group to which it refers for guidance and self-definition it transcends both embodiment and life. Nowhere is this more revealed than in the selves that find their inspiriting source in ethnicity and its descent, in what Max Weber recognized as the mystery of blood, a primordial irrationality that forms both the taproot of collective ascriptive solidarity and a source for referential individual identification.

The ethnic self constitutes one instance in which silence confirms identification at the same moment that it confounds comprehension. Ethnicity can conventionally be depicted in terms of color, culture, and condition, but these act only as mediating shibboleths for the unutterable covenant that binds together every member of an ethnic congregation. A most telling example—one that harks back to ancient Hebrew sources and the dialectical desublimation in which the ineffable character of Yahweh was transformed into the unutterable basis for individual and group identity—is that of "soul" among America's blacks. Although the soul idea among American Negroes can be traced back to the transmigratory, disembodiable, and shadow-casting soul complex of West Africa, its special character in the United States is that of something uncommunicable, ineffable—something that cannot be transmitted to or adopted by outsiders. Afro-American "soul" can be experienced by blacks but not explained to whites. To share in the ethnic legacy of "soul" is also to become a part of the silence that accompanies rightful descent. By contrast, to demand a verbal explanation of "soul," or—worse—to claim the right to partake of it without possessing the appropriate ascriptive credentials is to signal one's fundamental ignorance of its sacred and inexpressible nature. This tacit estate of ethnicity is an ineffaceable source of ethnocentrism.

A sociology of the existential self must take as its topic the irremediable marginality of that self. For the existential self is the product of both experience and the language used to render that experience understandable, but it is a member of neither the brute society of experience nor the reconciling community of language. Ethnolinguistics has rightly emphasized the importance of speech communities; but if it is to be faithful to the nature of its subject matter, existential sociology must recognize man as the creature who is never fully realized as a participant in his word- and symbol-using world. Always there is a striving for that emancipatory self-realization that would translate the self into its irreducible individuality; always there is an agonizing search for recognition and response that, when granted, pulls one back into the collective identity.

Acknowledgments

Although assembling this collection of original essays has been a labor of love, the labor involved was made much easier by the assistance of many people, all of whom we would like to acknowledge. Our colleagues at the University of Houston–University Park and the University of Nevada–Las Vegas afforded us their organizational, emotional, and intellectual support. The Center for Public Policy at the University of Houston provided much-needed clerical and secretarial assistance. And, finally, Polly Kotarba and Tina Fontana have given us more love and have demonstrated more patience with us and our work than we have any right to expect.

We dedicate this book to our children—to Christopher Joseph and Jessie Marie Kotarba and to Nicole Marie Fontana—for whom the self is a joyous adventure.

J. A. K.
A. F.

The Existential Self in Society

Introduction: Existential Sociology and the Self

Andrea Fontana

> When a new *paradigm* appears in the world, you may know *it*
> by this sign, that all the dunces are in confederacy against *it*.
> > With apologies to Jonathan Swift
> > and thanks to John Kennedy Toole

> The chief merit of the name "relativity" is in reminding us that
> a scientist is unavoidably a participant in the system he is studying.
> > Nigel Calder

The discipline of sociology was born in the nineteenth century, and to acquire credibility it patterned itself on the natural sciences, which were, at the time, enjoying great legitimacy and success. This is what Durkheim did, for example. However, science has moved onward, while traditional sociology has not.[1] Newton's quest for absolutes has given way to Einstein's understanding of relativity, in which time and space depend on perspective and context. It is not that Einstein's science has abandoned the search for ultimately invariant properties of the universe, but it has acquired a new awareness: that to understand the vast ordering and patterns of the universe one must begin by realizing its utter diversity and complexity. Something as simple as a flash of lightning in the sky can be perceived in totally different ways, depending on the location of the observer and on whether the observer is stationary or moving toward or away from the lightning.

If the natural sciences have changed, why not sociology? Much of sociology is still preoccupied by a Newtonian concern with invariance and formal causes that blinds it to the complexity and uniqueness of its subject matter: human beings. As a result, the sociological quest for understanding humanity tends to oversimplify human behavior by clustering its diversities in oversimplified analytical categories, often chosen with no regard to the variable elements of space, time, and situation. Thus, sociological categories of human behavior tend to be presented in either dichotomous or fourfold choices (see, e.g., Parsons, 1951), stripping human behavior of its complexity and leaving us with a skeletal view that in no way represents the human beings who people the everyday world.

In response to these concerns, a number of alternative models of social life, including existential sociology, have emerged in recent years. All too often, however, these models begin and end with harsh criticisms of traditional sociology, with perhaps a bit of programmatic statement on how sociology *ought* to be accomplished, and in some recent models, like ethnomethodology, theory and substance alike appear to be moving away from sociology's still viable disciplinary scope. The basic purpose of this book, then, is to demonstrate that the promise of existential sociology, especially as articulated in the earlier Douglas and Johnson (1977) work, is being fulfilled. The essays presented here portray the development of a distinctive existentialist theory and the application of that theory to a range of contemporary social issues. Although our ideas are new, we bring them to bear on the further understanding of one of sociology's and social psychology's key concepts: the self.

What is existential sociology?[2] I hesitate to define it outside its empirical usage. The empirical chapters of this book will show the meaning of existential sociology far more accurately than a definition could at this point. However, some guidance is necessary for the uninitiated reader, and a working definition will therefore be provided. Existential sociology is the sociology that attempts to study human beings in their natural setting— the everyday world in which they live—and to examine as many as possible of the complex facets of the human experience.[3] Existential sociology does not discard the topic of inquiry of traditional sociology, the formal properties of human behavior, but it wishes to include other important features. Thus, existential sociology looks at formal behavior, informal behavior, rational elements, irrational elements, genetic dispositions,[4] psychological traits, and social rules; in short, it opens its inquiry to anything that forms the context of human action. Existential sociology pays particular attention to the forgotten elements in the social sciences—to feelings and emotions (see Manning, 1973; Fontana, 1981; and Merleau-Ponty, 1962). To paint a picture of human beings without considering their feelings and emotions is like making a painting of a peacock's tail in black and white.

And yet, this is exactly what traditional sociology has done. Following Durkheim's lead, Western sociology basically has been the study of social rules as these are determined and shaped by society, with the human actor assigned the role of mere performer, following a script.[5] In a metaphorical sense, the human performer in traditional sociology is very much like a musician in a large orchestra, playing his tuba or oboe according to the musical score and the conductor's baton, with little leeway for personal interpretation. In existential sociology, instead, the human performer is like a jazz musician in a small combo. There is a musical theme to follow, but since there is no score to read and no band leader, there is plenty of room for mood, feelings, and interpretation. Life is not quite a jam session, but it certainly requires improvisation. As absolutist social rules break down and lose their meanings, people are forced to be creative in coming to grips with their worlds.

Lest we credit existential sociology with a totally new breakthrough, a few words on its antecedents are in order.[6] Throughout the centuries, most Western intellectual political and religious thinkers have attempted to subordinate feelings and creativity to rationality; yet if we read history well, we see that a great many events were influenced and shaped by less-than-rational elements, too often ignored in post hoc historical accounting. Could we, for instance, ignore Antony's feelings for Cleopatra in analyzing Roman policy toward Egypt at that time? Should we consider only rational elements in examining the Nazis' atrocities against the Jews? More recently and closer to home, who can forget the televised sight of then-presidential candidate Senator Edmund Muskie crying tears of rage in a snow-swept square somewhere in New Hampshire because of publisher Loeb's unpleasant comments about the senator's wife? Those tears dissolved Muskie's rage and also his presidential chances.

The territory of existentialism has been mapped out chiefly by philosophers and by the writers of novels, short stories, and plays. The latter have always been concerned with the total person, and existential philosophy has been a perennial reaction against more rationalistic modes of thought, such as empiricism and theologies; still, over the centuries, it has waxed and waned in influence, more often than not being submerged in a new wave of rationalism (see Dahrendorf, 1968; Koyré, 1958). As science gained enormous credence and momentum in the past few centuries, so did rational modes of thought, epitomized in modern times by the methods of scientists, technologists, and bureaucrats. While sociologists like Georg Simmel and Max Weber gloomily pointed to the inevitable march of an increasingly rationalized society (see Gerth and Mills, 1946; Simmel, 1968), writers like Kafka and Dostoevsky cried out against the vise that was reducing modern man and woman to puny human beings, overbound by rules and constraints (see Kafka, 1956; Dostoevsky, 1970). Existential notions like freedom, authenticity, sincerity, humanism, empathy, and creativity beat in vain against the walls of the crystal palace of scientism (Yalom, 1980). Society became a cage, and we were the rats running its mazes. It is no wonder that many early sociologists turned their attention to society's rules, whose iron grip was strangling humankind at the time.

The golden flight of scientism was temporarily obscured by the dark shadow of the two world wars in the twentieth century. Conformity and rationality grew increasingly meaningless as people died for reasons that were hard to rationalize (see Hemingway, 1940). It was in this period that Jean-Paul Sartre championed the movement that is known as existentialism. He said that man was condemned to be free, condemned to choose his own values (Sartre, 1945a, 1945b, 1945c). Camus was another great exponent of existentialism. His hero, Sisyphus, kept smiling while confronting the futility of existence (Camus, 1955). Closer to home, Ernest Hemingway wrote about and lived a life of freedom, challenge, unrestrained passions, and deep feelings (Hemingway, 1940, 1953, 1957, 1964).

Soon people lost the urge to question. From cars to cameras, pianos, radios, television sets, recorders, tennis rackets, and baseball gloves we indulged in an unthinking orgy of materialism, consumerism, and technologism, under the more-than-ever-powerful aegis of scientism (de Grazia, 1962).

The struggle of literature against an overly rational and scientifically based picture of human beings has created in existential sociologists both a sensitivity to and an awareness of the complex and problematic nature of life, but their discipline is based more on existential philosophy than on literature.

Søren Kierkegaard, who wrote in the nineteenth century, is often regarded as the founder of modern existentialism (Yalom, 1980). Faced with an increasingly unquestioning society, complacently living by absolutist platitudes, Kierkegaard felt the deep *Angst* of searching out the meaning of being. While Kierkegaard sought the meaning of man vis-à-vis his Maker, his basic principle of inquiry was the same as that of existential sociology. Rejecting shop-worn paradigms and frayed explanations, he looked instead at the complexity of life-as-it-is-lived (Kierkegaard, 1957).

Friedrich Nietzsche, also a nineteenth-century philosopher, turned anguish into anger and declared God to be dead. Nietzsche meant to point out that paradigms at times grow old and their roots begin to rot. Yet tradition, sloth, vested interest, deep-seated beliefs, ignorance, and habit often make people go on accepting the existing paradigms—in other words, the unquestioned tenets upon which a particular reality is constructed (Nietzsche, 1968). For example, the astronomers representing the powers-that-be refused to look through Galileo's telescope; they did not wish to be confronted with a universe that did not revolve around the earth (Brecht, 1966). Similarly, famous surgeons, their backs turned to the patient, read anatomy from Galen's books in the operating room, literally refusing to look inside the human body, leaving the surgery itself to lowly assistants.[7]

The ideas of Kierkegaard and Nietzsche are of tremendous heuristic value to existential sociology, but it is in the works of two other philosophers that we find more direct connections with the empirical discipline of existential sociology: Wilhelm Dilthey and Edmund Husserl. Dilthey offers sociology the notion of *Verstehen*, of understanding human beings by empathizing with them. Dilthey intended his ideas to be used for the interpretation of history, yet their message is equally valid for existential sociology: one must immerse oneself in everyday reality—feel it, touch it, hear it, and see it—in order to understand it (Dilthey, 1961).

Dilthey's theory of interpretation was not novel. Schleiermacher and others had already written much about interpretation (hermeneutic understanding),[8] but it was Dilthey's ideas that proved relevant to sociology and influenced generations of sociologists, from Max Weber onward.[9] Empathetic understanding grounded in the concrete reality of everyday life is a basic tenet of today's existential sociology.

Edmund Husserl was disturbed by the lack of scientific precision generated by Dilthey's methodological approach (Husserl, 1965). He therefore sought to create a scientific philosophy to reach the pure essence of beings. He called this discipline phenomenology. Phenomenology is often confused with existentialism, but the two perspectives are distinct in the ways they approach the empirical world. In fact, Husserlian phenomenology is not directly amenable to sociology.[10] To "do" phenomenology requires closing off ("bracketing") the social world, thereby literally eliminating the object of inquiry of sociology.

Husserl sought to discover the essence of human consciousness by reductions, a progressive "stepping back" from human involvement in everyday life (Husserl, 1962, 1964). He hoped in this way to do away with variable elements that relativize human behavior and irremediably tie it to a given situation and context (Garfinkel, 1967). If one "stepped back" far enough, according to Husserl, one would be left with a "consciousness of" some action but would remain uninvolved in it.

Whether a complete Husserlian reduction (i.e., the achievement of pure consciousness) is possible or not is debatable; in any case, it is clearly not easy. Yet Husserl's impact on existential sociology can be seen in the work of Alfred Schutz, who applied phenomenological ideas to the problems of social science. Schutz turned his mentor upside down, so to speak.[11] He ignored Husserl's presocial consciousness and focused instead on what was apprehendable to our senses—on our presence and actions in the everyday world. Schutz developed a set of concepts (Schutz, 1971a) that are very useful as a frame for the sociological study of human interaction, since they point out many of the social links that allow interaction itself to take place, such as "reciprocity of perspective," the belief that two interactants can exchange places and see the world from each other's viewpoint, and the "natural attitude," the pragmatic, utilitarian stance taken by individuals in their daily lives.

Thus it was from Dilthey that existential sociology gained the idea of empathetic understanding, grounded in everyday life. It was from Husserl (via Schutz) that it realized the ways in which human beings share (or fail to share) their universe. And it was from two other students of phenomenology that existential sociology acquired yet another paramount element: the idea that the self is not a reified entity but an incarnate one. Martin Heidegger and Maurice Merleau-Ponty both pointed to the important fact that human beings are single entities: that body and soul are not separate but form an indivisible whole. Heidegger spoke of *dasein* (being-in-the-world) and Merleau-Ponty spoke of *être-au-monde* (being-within-the world);

both terms emphasize that the self is totally enmeshed in the reality that surrounds it and is inseparable from its physical body (Heidegger, 1962; Merleau-Ponty, 1962).

It was from these roots that existential sociology began to sprout. Once sociologists began to realize the complexity of human interaction and increasingly questioned the orderly, yet fictional, world of fourfold tables, the floodgates opened.

At first there was some confusion about the meaning of existentialism and about the way to use it in sociology. Words such as existentialism and phenomenology were used in the same breath, often with little understanding of the differences between them.[12] Some spoke of phenomenological sociology, loosely referring to Husserl and his "stepping back," yet ignoring the important differences between doing phenomenology and being phenomenologically informed.[13]

There have also been efforts to blend existential thought with the predominant sociological paradigm, with variable success. Edward Tiryakian, for example, one of the early exponents of existential sociology, tried to reconcile the work and thoughts of several traditional sociologists with concepts drawn from existentialism. He saw an affinity between Max Weber's argument for the interpretive understanding of social action and the approach used by the existentialist thinkers. Less successful, however, was his attempt to reconcile Durkheim's view of social determinism with existentialism's focus on the problematic nature of social experience (Tiryakian, 1962). Despite the difficulties of finding ties between traditional and existential sociology, Tiryakian persisted in the attempt. Rather than reject the views of some sociologists, he found some value in them. Thus Tiryakian sought to complement and expand the traditional sociological view of human beings.

Other writers pointed to the weaknesses in traditional sociology and sought to replace it instead of stressing possible ties with it. Jack Douglas's seminal work, *Understanding Everyday Life* (1970), clearly differentiated the new sociologies from the traditional ones. However, he did not spell out clearly the fine differences among the new sociologies; phenomenologically oriented approaches, ethnomethodology, and existential sociology are mixed together in this work.

As the new sociologists moved away from polemics and programmatic statements toward detailed research and empirical findings, marked differences became apparent. While phenomenology was a common inspirational source, its new sociological disciples took two different paths. The first was ethnomethodology, which sought to understand the routines that sustain the everyday reality of the members of society.[14] Thus, ethnomethodology's topic of inquiry became those taken-for-granted elements of society that had been the unquestioned resources for studies pursued under the traditional models (see, e.g., Zimmerman and Pollner, 1970).

Ethnomethodology relies on a complex and varied model of social life. It adapts many of Husserl's notions (via Schutz) to sociology, such as routine interactions and the process of "stepping back." However, ethnomethodology does not completely break away from the immediate goal of traditional sociology, namely, to locate the invariant, formal properties of social life.[15]

The second path is that of existential sociology.[16] Existential sociologists take a more patient approach than ethnomethodologists. They feel that it is futile to make claims about invariant social elements before undertaking a close examination of how human beings interact in their natural setting, the everyday world in which they live.

Under the existential approach, sociology has been transformed. It is similar to adding a wide-angle lens to your camera: there is so much more to see. And existential sociologists are beginning to gather data by studying the members of society in total detail, in different settings and in varied circumstances, thus improving sociology's understanding of human interaction. The eventual goal is to be able to trace the recurring common patterns that lie beneath this sea of human variance.

Although existential sociology is a recent arrival on the scene, there are already a number of works representing its perspective, both theoretically and empirically. We have mentioned the work of Edward Tiryakian, who wrote his *Sociologism and Existentialism* as early as 1962. Subsequent works by others presented a general phenomenological/existential approach. Worth noting, among others, is *A Sociology of the Absurd* by Lyman and Scott (1970), which incorporates many of the features of existential sociology, especially its emphasis on the subjective, interpretative nature of social reality, the incarnate nature of the self, and the importance of feelings in human interaction.[17]

Lyman and Scott see life as episodical, as always changing and always being interpreted anew. Thus life is, in the end, essentially meaningless; it acquires meaning only through the actions of social performers. Men and women face the meaninglessness of life and, through this confrontation, both construct social reality and are constructed by it. Lyman and Scott present a conceptual scheme to aid social actors both to understand and to create meaning for themselves and for others.

Peter Manning, in his 1973 article "Existential Sociology," outlined the differences between traditional and existential sociology and explained the basic features of existential sociology. He also pointed out a number of concepts to be employed in sociological research relying on an existential perspective. Seeing the strength of the existential perspective in its awareness that human beings must be studied as whole beings, that is, by considering all of the facets of human nature, from rational elements to emotional ones, from bodily bases to mental states, Manning stressed the paramount importance of studying human beings in their natural setting, the everyday world in which they live and interact. Meaning is the central topic of study of social interaction for Manning, a meaning that is both problematic and situational yet remains a sine qua non in sociological inquiry. Finally, Manning pointed to the reflexive nature of existential sociology, its attempt to understand the nature and relation between the theorist and those who are his or her objects of inquiry, with the understanding that both are human beings *in* the world.

It was not until 1977, when Douglas and Johnson's *Existential Sociology* was published, that we find a book explicitly and completely devoted to existential sociology. This work outlines the philosophical antecedents of existential sociology, its ties with phenomenology, its differences from ethnomethodology, and its reliance on feelings and on the integrity of phenomena. Of distinct importance are the research-based chapters, which illustrate the actual work of existential sociologists. For example, Joseph Kotarba's chapter, "The Chronic Pain Experience," studies chronically ill patients and examines the relation of pain to one's sense of identity and to one's life-world, and Warren and Ponse, in the chapter "The Existential Self and the Gay World," analyze the process of becoming that is experienced by the self vis-à-vis different choices; they also stress the paramount importance of feelings as the foundation of the self.

Existential Sociology was followed by some essays on the nature of existential sociology (e.g., Kotarba, 1979). One of these is found in another work by Douglas and some of his disciples, *Introduction to the Sociologies of Everyday Life* (1981). This book traces the break with traditional sociology and outlines the basic perspective that is common to the sociologies of everyday life. Particular stress is placed on studying social interaction in its natural settings, on observing the way people interact in concrete face-to-face situations, and on understanding the meaning that members of society usually attribute to their actions. The book examines the nuances that differentiate the various sociologies of everyday life and shows the development of ideas among them.

Along with theoretical accounts of existential sociology, there has been a marked increase in the publication of empirical works that rely on the existential perspective.[18] These studies examine social interaction in disparate settings, from nude beaches (Douglas and Rasmussen, 1977) to the Wall Street stock market (Adler, 1981). These studies focus on analysis of specific phenomena as a way to gauge the complexity of human experience, from the meaning of growing old (Fontana, 1976) to that of being a NASA flight surgeon (Kotarba, 1983b). All of the studies subscribe to the basic tenets of existential sociology (as outlined in *Existential Sociology*). At times, however, the existential perspective is only implicit in these works.

In *The Existential Self in Society*—the present work—we have sought to go beyond both the programmatic, theoretical works and the field work that is only implicitly existentialist. *The Existential Self in Society* continues in the tradition set by Douglas, Johnson, Manning, and others, but it represents a step forward in existential sociology; for it combines theory with empirical works that have been explicitly conceived and researched as existential sociology, and, in doing so, it portrays human beings confronting life in its situatedness and staggering complexity.

The Existential Self in Society focuses specifically on the self and its relations with (or rather within) the world.[19] The self is "existential" because it is in an incarnate self, filled with rational thoughts, sudden emotions, deeply felt anxieties, biological urges, and cultural elements. The self is "in society" because it is a self-embodied-in-the-world; therefore, it is studied in its natural settings, in its *interacting* stance, and in its experiential confrontation with society.

The contributors to the book try to understand the meaning and sense of self by examining how we define ourselves, how we change our definitions, what makes us change these definitions, how much we do or can change, how much we are "anchored down" by our bodies and by our sense of social position—all of the questions that pertain to the total sense of that elusive thing we call the self.[20]

Throughout the book some features of the self are implicitly assumed and need to be explicated here. The self is considered to be embodied, becoming, situational, and reflexive.[21] The self is *embodied* because it cannot transcend its physical vehicular unit, and it receives its stimulation to act from feelings and emotions emanating from the body.[22] The self is *becoming* because it is always unfolding, changing, and developing in response to its changing perceptions of the world around it.[23] The self is *situational* because it is always dependent on its immediate contexts for a sense of grounding and belonging.[24] Finally, the self is *reflexive* because it is aware of itself; it is the focal point for the social, biological, cognitive, affective, and interpretive dimensions of being.[25]

The first part of our book provides a theoretical framework for understanding the existential self. In chapter two, Marilyn Lester illustrates the distinctive existential perspective on the self by comparing and contrasting it with alternative perspectives in sociology. In chapter three, Jack Douglas analyzes in great detail the complexities involved in the emergence of our deepest sense of self over the course of a lifetime.

The empirical chapters that follow portray the various ways that individuals experience and express their sense of self in today's society. The relationship between self and society is essentially confrontational, and the battleground on which this struggle is fought is *identity*. Put simply, identity is the perception of self by others, the ways it is defined, controlled, supported, and challenged by the social world. A central theme is that there is wide variation in the degree to which self and identity "fit" or complement each other in everyday life, and the empirical chapters are presented and ordered according to this variance, from the self's virtual acceptance of the identity presented by others to rejections of this societal identity in favor of one more agreeable to one's true feelings of self.

We begin with chapter four, in which Ronald Smith examines how university administrators not only willingly accept the socially expected or normative identity of "administrator" but utilize the vagueness and openness of this identity to justify, rationalize, and carry out their deepest feelings of self-interest.

In chapters five and six we explore situations in which individuals seek or accept a temporary identity in order to cope with critical or problematic experiences of the self. John Johnson and Kathleen Ferraro describe the process by which women finally accept the identity of "victim" both as a way of making sense of certain violations of their self-integrity and as a way of becoming willing to accept help. Wendy Espeland analyzes the mechanisms utilized by blood-plasma donors to protect their sense of self from the stigma that is often attached to this activity by our society.

In chapters seven and eight we explore situations in which a new identity is created in order to accommodate self and other. Helen Ebaugh describes the immense self-work involved in creating the role of ex-nun. David Altheide explores the ways in which athletes and journalists manipulate the athletic identity in the media.

In chapters nine and ten we complete the series by examining how individuals can totally reject socially provided identities by creating innovative social roles conducive to their sense of self. Sheldon Messinger and Carol Warren describe how the "homosexual" self became one woman's strategy for organizing otherwise vague experiences and for shaping courses of action. Dwyne Patrick and John Bignall describe how handicapped individuals substitute the identity of "runner" for that of "handicapped" in order to shore up the sense of a competent self.

In the concluding chapter, Joseph Kotarba describes in detail the theoretical relationship between the self, which is constantly in change and becoming, and social change. As opposed to traditional models of the self, in which it is viewed as a dependent variable in the process of social change, the essays in this book point to a perhaps more contemporary phenomenon, that of the self serving as an active, if not independent, agent of social change. Just as the modern self explores the possibilities of fulfillment and richness, we hope that our book will serve as a stimulus to a fuller and richer sociological understanding of the experience of individuality.

Notes

The first epigraph is paraphrased from Jonathan Swift, "Thoughts on Various Subjects, Moral and Diverting," quoted in its original form in John Kennedy Toole, *A Confederacy of Dunces* (New York: Grove Press, 1981), p. 8. The second epigraph is from Calder, 1979:2.

1. For an excellent critique of traditional sociology, see Douglas, 1971.

2. The roots of existential sociology will be traced later in this chapter. For informative accounts of existential sociology, see Tiryakian, 1962, 1965, and 1968; Douglas and Johnson, 1977; Fontana, 1980; Kotarba, 1979; and Manning, 1973.

3. See Douglas and Johnson, 1977:vii, where existential sociology is described as "the study of human experience-in-the-world (or existence) in all of its forms."

4. It is important not to confuse existential sociology's attention to genetic elements with sociobiology. See, for instance, Douglas's chapter in this book.

5. See Durkheim 1951 and, for an illuminating critique, see Douglas 1967.

6. The following review of literary, philosophical, and sociological works is by no means a comprehensive one. I am mentioning a few important sources simply to provide a contextual frame for this work. The reader interested in pursuing the matter further should consult, among others, Kaufmann, 1956; Barrett, 1962; Dilthey, 1961; Heidegger, 1962; Kierkegaard, 1946; Merleau-Ponty, 1962; Tiryakian, 1962, 1965, 1968; Manning, 1973; Douglas and Johnson, 1977; Fontana, 1980; and Kotarba, 1979.

7. See Ackerknecht, 1955. Galen's medical works are filled with serious misconceptions about the human body.

8. For a brief history of hermeneutics, see Palmer, 1967. Today, hermeneutics is basically divided into two camps. One considers interpretation to be the central theme, since there is no objective reality but only various interpretations, which are the real realities (see Gadamer, in Palmer, 1967, and, for an application of these concepts to sociology, see Blum, 1970, and McHugh, Raffel, Foss, and Blum, 1974). The other camp, led by Betti (1955), is much closer to Dilthey's and our notion of interpretation, which is that there is a substantive reality but that it can be interpreted in a number of different ways.

9. Dilthey and Weber share a general notion of interpretation, but there are profound differences between their specific notions of interpretation. Weber's methodology of interpretation is far more rational and scientific than Dilthey's. On this matter, see Schutz, 1967, especially page 240.

10. See, for instance, Heap and Roth, 1973.

11. See Schutz, 1967.

12. For the difference between the two philosophies, see Kockelmans, 1967; for a distinction between the two sociologies, see Fontana, 1980.

13. For a discussion of this point, see Heap and Roth, 1973. Phenomenology "steps back" from the social world, while phenomenologically informed sociology "steps back" from a social interaction but is still very much *in* the social world.

14. See Garfinkel, 1967. Also see Filmer (1972:203–42), who points to the reluctance of ethnomethodologists to formulate clear definitions. Garfinkel, for example, presents at least three *different* definitions of what he means by ethnomethodology.

15. For a critique of ethnomethodology, see Attewell, 1974:179–210, Johnson, 1977, and Freeman, 1980.

16. It must be pointed out that both ethnomethodology and existential sociology go under different labels. For instance, under the aegis of ethnomethodology we find sociolinguistic and cognitive sociology, while existential sociology is also known as "the sociology of everyday life."

17. See, especially, "Coolness in Everyday Life" in Lyman and Scott, 1970.

18. Most of the field studies done from the Chicago School onward capture some of the spirit of existential sociology in that they study human beings in their natural setting and claim (if not always successfully) to espouse the members' view of the situation. See, among others, Altheide, 1976; Douglas, 1977; Fontana, 1977; Manning, 1977; Warren, 1974; and Kotarba, 1983.

19. See Heidegger's concept of *dasein* (being-in-the-world) in *Being and Time* (1962) and Merleau-Ponty's *être-au-monde* (being-within-the-world) in *Phenomenology of Perception* (1962).

20. With regard to the concept of being a prisoner within one's body, Lyman adduces the case of Cyrano de Bergerac. No matter how romantic and beautiful Cyrano's prose is, his sense of self is dominated by his gigantic nose (Lyman, in conversation, 1972).

21. For a more elaborate discussion of these features of the self, see Kotarba, 1979.

22. Cf. Heidegger's *dasein* and Merleau-Ponty's *être-au-monde*.

23. See Goffman's description of the self as a process in Goffman, 1959.

24. See Goffman, 1959, and also Garfinkel's notion of contextual embeddedness (Garfinkel 1966).

25. See Mead, 1934, and Garfinkel, 1966.

References

Ackerknecht, Edwin H. 1955. *Short History of Medicine*. New York: Ronald Press.

Adler, Peter. 1981. *Momentum: A Theory of Social Action*. Beverly Hills, Calif.: Sage.

Altheide, David. 1976. *Creating Reality: How TV News Distorts Events*. Beverly Hills, Calif.: Sage.

Attewell, Paul. 1974. "Ethnomethodology since Garfinkel." *Theory and Society* 1:179–210.

Barrett, William. 1962. *Irrational Man: A Study in Existential Philosophy*. New York: Doubleday/Anchor.

Betti, Emilio. 1955. *Teoria generale della interpretazione*. 2 vols. Milan: A. Giuffré.

Blum, Alan. 1970. "Theorizing." Pp. 301–19 in Jack D. Douglas, ed., *Understanding Everyday Life*. Chicago: Aldine.

Brecht, Berthold. 1966. *Galileo*. Translated by Charles Laughton. New York: Grove Press.

Calder, Nigel. 1979. *Einstein's Universe*. New York: Viking.

Camus, Albert. 1955. *The Myth of Sisyphus*. Translated by Justin O'Brien. New York: Vintage.

Dahrendorf, Ralf. 1968. "In Praise of Thrasymachus." Pp. 129–50 in *Essays on the Theory of Society*. Stanford: Stanford University Press.

de Grazia, Sebastian. 1962. *Of Time, Work, and Leisure*. New York: Doubleday/Anchor.

Dilthey, Wilhelm. 1961. *Patterns and Meaning in History*. Translated by H. P. Rickman. New York: Harper & Row.

Dostoevsky, Fyodor. 1955. "Notes from the Underground." Translated by Constance Garnett. Pp. 320–419 in Avrahm Yarmolinsky, ed., *A Treasury of Great Russian Short Stories*. New York: Macmillan.

Douglas, Jack D. 1967. *The Social Meaning of Suicide*. Princeton, N.J.: Princeton University Press.

———. 1971. *American Social Order*. New York: Free Press.

———. 1970, ed. *Understanding Everyday Life*. Chicago: Aldine.

Douglas, Jack D., and John Johnson, eds. 1977. *Existential Sociology*. Cambridge, Eng.: Cambridge University Press.

Douglas, Jack D., and Paul Rasmussen, with Carol Ann Flanagan. 1977. *The Nude Beach*. Beverly Hills, Calif.: Sage.

Durkheim, Emile. 1951. *Suicide: A Study in Sociology*. Translated by John A. Spaulding and George Simpson. New York: Free Press.

Filmer, Paul. 1972. "On Harold Garfinkel's Ethnomethodology." Pp. 203–42 in Jack D. Douglas, et al., eds., *Introduction to the Sociologies of Everyday Life*. Boston: Allyn & Bacon.

Fontana, Andrea. 1976. *The Last Frontier: The Social Meaning of Growing Old*. Beverly Hills, Calif.: Sage.

———. 1980. "Toward a Complex Universe: Existential Sociology." Pp. 155–81 in Jack D. Douglas, et al., eds., *Introduction to the Sociologies of Everyday Life*. Boston: Allyn & Bacon.

Freeman, D. Robert. 1980. "Phenomenological Sociology and Ethnomethodology." Pp. 113–54 in Jack D. Douglas, et al., eds. *Introduction to the Sociologies of Everyday Life*. Boston: Allyn & Bacon.

Garfinkel, Harold. 1967. *Studies in Ethnomethodology*. Englewood Cliffs, N.J.: Prentice-Hall.

Gerth, Hans, and C. Wright Mills, eds. 1968. *Max Weber: Essays in Sociology*. New York: Oxford University Press.

Goffman, Erving. 1959. *The Presentation of Self in Everyday Life*. New York: Doubleday/Anchor.

Heap, James L., and Phillip A. Roth. 1973. "On Phenomenological Sociology." *American Sociological Review* 38:354–67.

Heidegger, Martin. 1962. *Being and Time*. Translated by John Macquarrie and Edward Robinson. New York: Harper & Row.

Hemingway, Ernest. 1940. *For Whom the Bell Tolls*. New York: Collier.

———. 1953. *The Hemingway Reader*. New York: Scribner's.

———. 1957. *A Farewell to Arms*. New York: Scribner's.

———. 1964. *A Moveable Feast*. New York: Scribner's.

Hughes, Everett. 1958. *Men and Their Work*. Glencoe, Ill.: Free Press.

Husserl, Edmund. 1962. *Ideas: General Introduction to Pure Phenomenology*. Translated by W. Boyce Gibson. New York: Macmillan.

———. 1965. *Phenomenology and the Crisis of Philosophy*. Translated by Quentin Lauer. New York: Harper.

Johnson, John M. 1977. "Ethnomethodology and Existential Sociology." Pp. 153–73 in Jack D. Douglas and John M. Johnson, eds., *Existential Sociology*. Cambridge, Eng.: Cambridge University Press.

Kafka, Franz. 1956. *The Castle*. Translated by Willa and Edwin Muir. New York: Knopf.

Kaufmann, Walter, ed. 1956. *Existentialism from Dostoevsky to Sartre*. New York: World.

Kierkegaard, Søren. 1957. *The Concept of Dread*. Translated by Walter Lowrie. Princeton, N.J.: Princeton University Press.

Kockelmans, Joseph, ed. 1967. *Phenomenology*. New York: Doubleday/Anchor.

Kotarba, Joseph A. 1979. "Existential Sociology." Pp. 348–68 in Scott McNall, ed., *Theoretical Perspectives in Sociology*. New York: St. Martin's Press.

———. 1983a. *Chronic Pain: Its Social Dimensions*. Beverly Hills, Calif.: Sage.

———. 1983b. "The Social Control Function of Holistic Health Care in Bureaucratic Settings: The Case of Space Medicine." *Journal of Health and Social Behavior* 24:275–88.

Koyré, Alexandre. 1958. *From the Closed World to the Infinite Universe*. Baltimore: Johns Hopkins University Press.

Lyman, Stanford, and Marvin Scott. 1970. *A Sociology of the Absurd*. New York: Appleton, Century, Crofts.

Manning, Peter K. 1973. "Existential Sociology." *Sociological Quarterly* 14:200–225.

———. 1977. *Police Work: The Social Organization of Policy*. Cambridge, Mass.: MIT Press.

McHugh, Peter, et al. 1974. *On the Beginning of Social Inquiry*. London: Routledge & Kegan Paul.

Mead, George H. 1934. *Mind, Self, and Society*. Chicago: University of Chicago Press.

Merleau-Ponty, Maurice. 1962. *Phenomenology of Perception*. Translated by Colin Smith. London: Routledge & Kegan Paul.

Nietzsche, Friedrich. 1968. *The Portable Nietzsche*. Translated by Walter Kaufmann. New York: Viking.

Palmer, Richard E. 1967. *Hermeneutics*. Evanston, Ill.: Northwestern University Press.

Parsons, Talcott. 1951. *The Social System*. New York: Free Press.

Sartre, Jean-Paul. 1945a. *Le Sursis*. Paris: Gallimard.

———. 1945b. *Les Chemins de la liberté*. Paris: Gallimard.

———. 1945c. *L'Age de la raison*. Paris: Gallimard.

Schutz, Alfred. 1967. *The Phenomenology of the Social World*. Translated by George Walsh and Frederick Lehnert. Evanston, Ill.: Northwestern University Press.

———. 1971a. *Collected Papers*. Vol. 1, edited by Maurice Natanson. The Hague: Nijhoff.

———. 1971b. *Collected Papers*. Vol. 2, edited by Arvid Brodersen. The Hague: Nijhoff.

———. 1970. *Collected Papers*. Vol. 3, edited by Ilse Schutz. The Hague: Nijhoff.

Simmel, Georg. 1968. *The Conflict in Modern Culture and Other Essays*. Translated by K. Peter Etzkorn. New York: Teachers College Press.

Tiryakian, Edward. 1962. *Sociologism and Existentialism*. Englewood Cliffs, N.J.: Prentice-Hall.

———. 1965. "Existential Phenomenology and the Sociological Tradition." *American Sociological Review* 30:674–88.

———. 1968. "The Existential Self and the Person." Pp. 75–86 in K. J. Gergen and C. Gordon, eds., *The Self in Social Interaction*. New York: Wiley.

Warren, Carol A. B. 1974. *Identity and Community in the Gay World.* New York: Wiley.

Yalom, Irving D. 1980. *Existential Psychotherapy.* New York: Basic Books.

Zimmerman, Don, and Melvin Pollner. 1970. "The Everyday World as Phenomenon." Pp. 80–104 in Jack D. Douglas, ed., *Understanding Everyday Life.* Chicago: Aldine.

two

Self: Sociological Portraits

Marilyn Lester

INTRODUCTION

In this introductory chapter I shall describe six different sociological perspectives and the way in which each approaches the nature of "self." The
perspectives selected for inclusion are: (1) the normative perspective, (2)
symbolic interaction, (3) the dramaturgical perspective, (4) phenomenological sociology, (5) ethnomethodology, and (6) existential sociology. Providing some background in various sociological and social psychological
theories may enable the reader to better understand and appreciate the
existential view, which is basic to this book.

BIASES

Existential sociology is developing in the United States. It has emerged
partly as a reaction to the theoretical and methodological stances adopted
by American sociologists. To varying degrees, the first five perspectives
covered in this chapter are found wanting by existential sociologists. In no
way does this chapter provide a comprehensive overview of all theoretical
perspectives. For example, Marxist, critical, and otherwise "radical" theories address the significant *consequences* of repressive and oppressive
social structures for the individual, e.g., alienation and false consciousness.
However, a focus on self (or the social psychological level of analysis more
generally) is condemned by radical theorists on the grounds that it contributes to repressive social control. Therefore, it would be extremely difficult to present radical theory in a parallel fashion to the other perspectives
I address. It is excluded from this chapter. So are purely psychological
theories.

THE NORMATIVE PERSPECTIVE

Introductory sociology students often complain that sociology ignores the
individual. This complaint can be heard in two ways. First, unlike psychology, sociology emphasizes *social* processes, not individual ones. Hence,
students' complaints might be disregarded as: "They do not understand
sociology's mission." The complaint can be heard in another way: the social
group and institutional aspects of daily life are emphasized to such an
extent that it is difficult to "see" the individual. Yet, in daily life it is

Alma College
2004 Honors Day
Keynote Address

Robert F. Kennedy Jr.

March 31, 2004

Hogan Physical Education Center
Cappaert Gymnasium

"Our Environmental Destiny"

Robert F. Kennedy Jr., a leading environmental lawyer, is senior attorney for the Natural Resources Defense Council, chief attorney for the Hudson Riverkeeper program and a clinical professor and supervising attorney at the Environmental Litigation Clinic at Pace University School of Law. A pioneer in municipal and governmental responsibility, this impassioned and inspiring speaker reminds us that we have an obligation to protect and preserve the environment for future generations.

Copies of Kennedy's book *The Riverkeepers* are available for purchase in the lobby.

Sponsored by
The Alma College Co-Curricular Affairs Committee
The Alma College Honors Day Committee
Discovering Vocation: The Lilly Project at Alma College

Alma College 2004 Honors Day

Introductions: Mr. James Mueller and Dr. Saundra Tracy

Keynote Address: Robert F. Kennedy Jr.

Questions from the Audience

Book Signing

Major Speakers at Alma College

Past Speakers

March 5, 2003
>Millard Fuller, Habitat for Humanity
>"Building Materials for Life"
>Sponsored by Discovering Vocation: The Lilly Project at
>Alma College

September 25, 2003
>Howard Gardner, Harvard University
>"Good Work in Turbulent Times"
>Sponsored by Discovering Vocation: The Lilly Project at
>Alma College

Future Speakers

September 27-October 1, 2004
>Njongonkulu Ndungane, Archbishop of Cape Town
>Sponsored by Discovering Vocation: The Lilly Project at
>Alma College

January 17, 2005
>Alan Page, Minnesota Supreme Court Justice
>Sponsored by Martin Luther King Day Committee

March 30, 2005
>Richard Leakey
>Paleoanthropologist with the Leakey Foundation
>Sponsored by the Honor's Day Committee

ALMA
COLLEGE

614 W. Superior St.
Alma, Michigan 48801-1599
1-800-321-ALMA
www.alma.edu

individuals, ourselves included, that we experience directly. Frequently, sociology does not seem to reflect persons' actual lived experiences. Indeed, the normative perspective, which is the set of ideas usually presented to introductory students, focuses almost exclusively on the "big picture," on societal and cultural forces that shape social life. Self becomes a logical *consequence* of these forces.

Most sociologists would not identify with the term "normative perspective." I use the term as an umbrella one to refer to the work of a majority of nonradical sociologists who give priority to concepts such as society, culture, social structure, social organization, norms, values, and groups.

Elements of the Normative Perspective

The normative perspective emphasizes the ways in which social structures, social organization, and social processes exert constraint on individual and group action. Two key concepts for this perspective are *culture* and *society*. Culture is the total way of life of members of a society. It includes the *material artifacts*, shared by societal members, that help to forge a particular way of life. For example, automobiles, deodorant soaps, and plastic are part of, and contribute to, life in American society. Imagine what shape our cities would take without the automobile; standards of beauty and cleanliness would be quite different without deodorants; and the invention of plastic has greatly altered consumption patterns. *Nonmaterial culture* includes abstract creations shared by members of a society, e.g., language, technological knowledge, values, norms, and rules.

Culture is shared. Moreover, it is transmitted from generation to generation. While each generation adds to and modifies culture, it does not have to totally reinvent it. The shared and transmittable nature of culture explains the observation that so much of daily life is orderly, predictable, and stable. Members of society are oriented to the culture they share; they internalize it, and they conform to its prescriptions and proscriptions.

Particularly significant in regard to culture is the concept of *norm*. A norm is a shared guideline for behavior. There are norms covering virtually every sector of social life, ranging from public gatherings to behavior while occupying a specific position in society, to life in families, sexual conduct, forms of address, and so on. Particular norms vary in their salience to a society or to a group within society, but, in general, conformity to norms sustains social order. Members are motivated to comply, first, because they subscribe to the general beliefs or values underlying the norms and, second, because conformity is rewarded while violation is punished. The general normative model of behavior is that it is norm- or rule-governed. There are even norms for managing conflict and lack of harmony; e.g., "People should settle their differences by 'talking things out.' "

A *society* is a group of interacting individuals who share a common territory and participate in a common culture. Members of a society interact with one another in *socially structured relationships*. The totality of these relationships constitutes society's *social structure*. Each socially structured relationship is composed of *statuses* and *roles*. A status is a position or "slot" to be filled. For example, "professor" and "student" are statuses when the classroom is viewed as a structured relationship. "Professor," "dean," and "chancellor" are some statuses in the university structure. "Husband" and "wife" are statuses in a marital relationship, while "mother," "father," and "child" are statuses in the family. These examples suggest that statuses are *socially defined* in reference to *particular* socially structured relationships. That is, the status of "professor" means something different in the classroom and in the university as a whole. And, "husband" and "father" are statuses in different structured relationships even though they are occupied by the same person.

The meaning and content of a status is provided by the concept of *role*. Roles are essentially norms for conduct while occupying a status:

> A role represents the dynamic aspect of a status. The individual is socially assigned a status and occupies it with relation to other statuses. When he puts the rights and duties which constitute the status into effect, he is performing a role. [Linton, 1936:114]

For example, in terms of the classroom, professors impart information, convey understanding, and advise and grade students. They can expect to be treated with respect and deference by students and to have their classes attended, etc. As this example suggests, a particular status typically involves more than one role. Merton (1957:369) elaborates:

> We must note that a particular social status involves not a single associated role, but an array of associated roles. . . . This fact of structure can be registered by a distinctive term, role-set, by which I mean that complement of role relationships which persons have by virtue of occupying a social status.

Of particular interest to normative sociologists is the nature of *social groups* and *social categories*. A social group may be defined as a pattern of social positions, the holders of which share a common goal or goals, a sense of group identity, and interaction structured by the expectations attached to their positions. There are many types of groups. For example, a *primary group* consists of a small number of persons who interact on a face-to-face basis. Primary groups are characterized by a high degree of intimacy and involvement (Simmel, 1950). The family is one important primary group. At the other end of the intimacy continuum are *secondary groups*. A secondary group may be large or small (see Bales, 1950), informal or formal. Informal groups include social and recreational clubs, while formal groups often take the form of a bureaucracy—a group marked by a hierarchical structure of authority, formal rules, and job specifications (see Weber, 1946).

A *social category*, in contrast, is a set of persons who are classified together because they share an attribute. However, members do not necessarily interact with one another. For example, blacks, Hispanics, and whites are some of the social categories of race in our own society. But not all blacks, Hispanics or whites have established interaction patterns among themselves, so they are not a social group. Similarly, there exist social-class, sex, age, and occupation categories, and these (along with some other social categories) make up society's *stratification system*.

Self in the Normative Perspective

The earliest sociologists were concerned with carving out a specific domain for their discipline. In particular, sociology had to be carefully distinguished from psychology's emphasis on individual processes. Emile Durkheim's 1950 dictum to "treat social facts as things" was meant to convey the idea that social structures and social processes are as "real" as individual ones and should be studied in themselves. There has been a decided concern in sociology to avoid *reductionism*, i.e., to avoid explaining social facts or social processes on the basis of individual ones (see Warriner, 1962). This has often meant avoiding concepts or phenomena such as "self." Some implications can be drawn from this perspective, however.

The self is seen as fundamentally social. A person is seen to be socialized and to exist in and through the various components of culture and social stucture. More specifically, self can be viewed as the center of a configuration of social categories, social statuses, and social roles. In turn, these are dependent on the larger culture and on the availability of certain categories, statuses, roles, and groups in a society. At the most basic level, culture and society define individuals. And, through socialization, the individual comes to share the culture of a society and the groups within it and to use their precepts both in action and in defining self. I turn now to some examples.

Social categories like race, sex, and class help to define and locate the individual in society. Self-conceptions are often the result of such categories. For example, being white, female, and middle class are social categories that help to explain a great deal about one's life-style, life-chances, experiences, and the like, including self-ideas. A black lower-class male, in contrast, is likely to have a distinctly different set of life-chances, experiences, and self-conceptions.

People are born into groups having certain properties, they are socialized into the ways of these groups, and they live out their entire lives largely in social groups of assorted types. The structure and processes of group life shape the individual's set of values and behavioral orientations. Conformity is exacted through a system of rewards and punishments, formal and informal. More important for social control, the individual *internalizes* group standards and uses them in regulating his/her own conduct. Self is largely a reflection of the configuration of groups in which one participates. So, one might identify oneself as a professor at Harvard, a father, husband, fraternity brother, and a member of the curriculum committee. These group memberships are internalized as one's view of oneself. Since each person's configuration of group memberships is different, each individual and each individual's view of him/herself is different. Moreover, as group memberships change, so do the self-identifications.

Additionally, each individual occupies a distinct set of social statuses and corresponding roles. Knowing these statuses and roles enables the sociologist to predict a great many things about a person. As leading proponents of this view argue:

> The role is a sector of the individual actor's total system of action. It is the point of contact between the system of action of the individual actor and the social system. The individual then becomes a unity in the sense that he is a composite of various action units which in turn are roles in the relationships in which he is involved. [Parsons and Shils, 1951:190]

Even conflict can be explained by the concept of *role strain*, that is, a perceived difficulty in fulfilling role obligations, as, for example, when a parent attempts to fulfill both affective and disciplinarian roles. Two statuses might be in conflict with each other; for example, a teacher who has a son or daughter as her/his student might experience conflict between the statuses of parent and teacher.

In general, the normative perspective highlights the ways in which social processes, structures, norms, and values generate social life as we know it, including conceptions of self. However, self is not a significant concept for these sociologists. When they attempt to focus on that topic, they often employ concepts from the next perspective to be discussed: symbolic interaction.

SYMBOLIC INTERACTION

Symbolic interaction emphasizes the distinctive character of human communication, which allows people to construct meaning and interpretations of physical and social objects, including situations and self. In turn, people use their definitions and interpretations to develop courses of action as individuals, as participants in face-to-face interaction, and even as members of groups that are geographically and temporally dispersed. Whatever the objective characteristics of a phenomenon might be, people's definitions and consequent activity are the critical features for symbolic interactionists.

Most sociologists identify George Herbert Mead (1932, 1934, 1936, 1938) as the central theorist in the development of symbolic interaction theory. An interesting thing about Mead is that he never published a complete statement of his theory. Rather, notes of lectures delivered at the University of Chicago, partial manuscripts, and essays were collected and published after his death. Mead drew some of his ideas from Charles Horton Cooley (1902), John Dewey (1925), William James (1892), and W. I. Thomas (1931). Following Mead, Herbert Blumer (1956, 1962, 1969) has been considered the outstanding spokesperson for this perspective. Today, there are many scholars contributing to symbolic interaction theory and research, including Tamotsu Shibutani (1955, 1970), Ralph Turner (1962, 1968, 1976), Manford Kuhn (1964), Howard Becker (1953, 1963), Bernard Meltzer (1978), and Norman Denzin (1970). There are also excellent collections of readings in symbolic interaction (Manis and Meltzer, 1978; Stone and Farberman, 1981), and Alfred Lindesmith, Anselm Strauss, and Norman Denzin (1975) have written the classic social psychology textbook that relies on this perspective.

Foundational Ideas

For symbolic interactionists, distinctive modes of communication differentiate human association from that of other animals. While insects display cooperative behavior, for example, their form of association is biologically based and consequently remains fixed through time. Meltzer (1978:16) provides a second example:

> . . . when a mother hen clucks, her chicks will respond
> by running to her. This does not imply, however, that the
> hen clucks *in order* to guide the chicks, i.e., with the
> *intention* of guiding them.

In both cases, communicative form and content are fixed. Neither insects nor hens and chicks can redefine their conduct. They must respond directly to the environment in patterned ways. Mead refers to these fixed modes of communication as *natural signs*.

In contrast, human societies are diverse and modifiable. Specific cooperative ventures arise; they often change forms; they may die; they may be resurrected in the same or modified form; they may last for minutes or centuries; they may be dominant or subordinate to other social groups; they may be simultaneously praised and condemned. Biological and genetic structures provide the human being with the capacity for continual flexibility. But they do not dictate specific associative conduct. Unlike the hen and chicks, people respond to each other on the basis of the meaning and presumed intention of a particular gesture. Here, a gesture becomes a *symbol*. Meltzer (1978:17) illustrates:

> Thus, individual A begins to act, i.e., makes a gesture: for example, he draws back an arm. Individual B (who perceives the gesture) completes, or fills in, the act in his imagination; i.e., B imaginatively projects the gesture into the future: "He will strike me." In other words, B perceives what the gesture stands for, thus getting its meaning. In contrast to the direct responses of the chicks and the dogs, the human being inserts an interpretation between the gesture of another and his response to it.

So long as either the participants in an interaction or the members of a group share definitions of symbols, they can communicate meaningfully with one another and engage in concerted activity. For this to occur, one must be able to respond to one's own gestures in the same way as s/he anticipates the Other will respond. Symbolic interactionists refer to such shared symbols as *significant symbols*.

To grasp how it is that a person can respond to his/her own gestures requires the addition of a new concept, *"role-taking"* or *"taking the role of the Other."* In the role-taking process, one imaginatively steps into the Other's place, seeks to understand or anticipate the Other's view of the situation, and uses that understanding for further communication. Role-taking facilitates the probability that the Other's response will coincide with one's own intentions in interaction. To make this more concrete: in a classroom setting, both professors and students engage in role-taking. The professor imaginatively rehearses students' possible responses to a particular presentation, e.g., "Let's see, if I present it this way, they might not understand. If I try this, they will think. . . ." The student meanwhile takes the role of the professor, e.g., "What could s/he mean by this?" In so doing, a person can rehearse alternative courses of action, based on an assessment of the Other's possible reaction and response, and can adjust subsequent action accordingly. Therefore, among other things, role-taking is a problem-solving mechanism for people.

A person does not always take the role of others as they would actually respond. Rather, one takes others' roles as s/he *perceives* they would respond. Indeed, all perception is selectively filtered through acquired perceptions and definitions. W. I. Thomas (1928) elaborates this idea: "If men define situations as real, they are real in their consequences." He went on to provide an example:

> The warden of Dannemora prison recently refused to honor the order of the court to send an inmate outside the prison walls for some specific purpose. He excused himself on

the ground that the man was too dangerous. He had killed several persons who had the unfortunate habit of talking to themselves on the street. From the movement of their lips, he imagined that they were calling him vile names and he behaved as if this were true. [Pp. 571–73]

This example highlights the fact that the *definitions of a situation* and not the objective characteristics of reality are critical in understanding one's own behavior, others, interaction, and selves. To further illustrate: if an individual perceives that someone dislikes him/her, that definition will be acted upon. The person perceiving the Other this way may feel rejected, withdraw from the situation, or attempt to change the Other's perception, etc. In terms of consequences, it is irrelevant whether or not the perception is accurate.

Self

"Self" is both something that one has and something that constitutes a social process for symbolic interactionists. Having a self means simply that one can act toward oneself by relying on the same mechanisms—symbolic communication and role-taking—as one uses to act toward other physical or social objects. Therefore, one can perceive, define, and evaluate oneself just as people perceive, define, and evaluate other things. Charles Horton Cooley (1902) conceived taking the role of others toward oneself as the "*looking-glass self*." That is, we imagine ourselves through others' eyes:

> As we see . . . our face, figure, and dress in the glass, and are interested in them because they are ours, and pleased or otherwise with them according to whether they do or do not answer to what we should like them to be; so in imagination we perceive in another's mind some thought of our appearance, manners, aims, deeds, character, friends, and so on, and are variously affected by it.
> A self-idea of this sort seems to have three principal elements: the imagination of our appearance to the other person; the imagination of his judgment of that appearance; and some sort of self-feeling, such as pride or mortification. [P. 184]

The sense of "having a self" rests on a deeper conception of self as a process. More specifically, self is an interaction process, as Blumer (1969:62) states:

> In short, the possession of a self provides the human being with a mechanism for self-interaction with which to meet the world—a mechanism that is used in forming and guiding his conduct.

This processualization of the concept of self lies in opposition to traditional notions of the self as a fixed object:

> . . . we see scholars who identify the self with the "ego," or who regard the self as an organized body of needs or motives, or who think of it as an organization of attitudes, or who treat it as a structure of internalized norms and values. Such schemes, which seek to lodge the self in a structure, make no sense, since they miss the reflexive process which alone can yield and constitute a self . . . that is to say, acting toward or on itself. [Blumer, 1969:62–63]

Mead, following James (1920), identified two phases of self, which he termed the "*I*" and the "*Me*." The "I" is the knowing subject, the spontaneous actor at any particular moment. The "Me" represents a person's interpretation and organization of others' definitions, expectations, and evaluations. A role-taking relationship and interaction exists between "I" and "Me," as Mead (1964:229) notes:

> The "I" reacts to the self which arises through the taking of the attitudes of others. Through taking those attitudes, we have introduced the "Me," and we react to it as an "I."

When self is the object of attention at a particular moment, the "I" phase of self looks to the "Me" phase, and an internalized dialogue transpires. To illustrate: suppose that three students earn a grade of B on the same examination. What does that mean? In itself, the letter B has no intrinsic meaning. Upon seeing the grade, the first student thinks, "I kept telling Mom I'm no good at this. Now what am I going to do?" The second student says to himself, "Hey, I passed! Now I won't get kicked out of the fraternity." And the third student takes a quick look at the grade and puts the test paper in the class notebook. Clearly, these scenarios are simplistic compared to the reality of the internalized dialogues that take place with regard to self or anything else. However, they illustrate the basic features of self from a symbolic interactionist perspective. In particular, note that the same "objective" situation can result in different self-definitions.

There are also various types of "others" whose role "I" may take in self-definition. The expectations, evaluations, and definitions of particular people or groups may be very important. For example, many people value their parents' definitions, at least in regard to certain domains of life. Alternatively, a spouse and close friend may be the most significant persons. Those identifiable individuals and groups whose definitions and interpretations enter into our own self-definitions are termed *Significant Others*. In keeping with the symbolic interactionist perspective, significant others may change not only through time but from situation to situation. So, for example, if a person perceives that parents put a high value on an A grade and s/he takes their role in the test situation above, that person may define her/his self as a total failure in earning a B grade. If, in contrast, s/he perceives parents' acceptance no matter what s/he does, the B will be a less significant event. Or, if friends value partying over school, the end of the exam rather than the grade may become the critical event if the role of friends is taken.

Sometimes, instead of taking the role of significant others, one takes the standpoint of the larger community in defining self and situations. This is the *Generalized Other*. For example, "I" may feel panic because I don't have the money to pay this month's rent, and "I" may imagine stealing the funds. When "I" looks to "Me" in this situation, "I" may consider the idea that "stealing is wrong." No one individual's or identifiable group's standard is being considered. Rather, the person has internalized general community standards and uses them to regulate his/her own conduct as well as definitions of self.

People are continually in the process of *creating* self as they engage in role-taking in various situations. Many of our self-definitions are fundamentally situational, e.g., the way one feels about oneself "now." One might feel like a situational failure in attaining a poor grade or decide that one looks ugly on a particular day. These more transient self-definitions are sometimes called *self-images*. Some symbolic interactionists suggest that these *situational selves* are primary. Others, however, note that many people have rather fixed self-definitions, ones that they carry from situation to situation. Such enduring self-definitions are *self-concepts*. Self-concepts can result in a self-fulfilling prophecy. Imagine someone who defines him/ herself as a total failure. That person could enter every situation anticipating that others will confirm the definition. The person may act accordingly and then *be* defined negatively. Or the opposite could occur. We probably all know someone we deem to be "arrogant." He or she seems oblivious to all criticism. That person may have such an exaggeratedly positive self-concept that s/he fails to filter in actual negative responses from others. In either case, the actual responses of others are not perceived. Everything is filtered through the self-concept, whether it is positive or negative. Most of us have self-concepts, but they are not overly negative or positive. Moreover, no one concept typically dominates every situation. Thus, we are able to form various self-images according to the situations in which we find ourselves.

The Development of Self

Self requires role-taking. In turn, role-taking requires language competence—at least the ability to share significant symbols. The symbolic interactionists would therefore argue that the infant has the "I" phase of self, the experiencing phase, but lacks the "Me." Learning to take the role of the Other is a gradual process, which begins with "playing at" being an Other. For example, the young child plays at being mom or dad. The child literally enacts that role as well as his/her own role. In this playing at being an Other, the child learns to identify with, and take the role of, significant others. Later, one learns to take the role of the generalized other. Mead (1934) refers to these stages as the *play* and *game*, respectively. To elaborate:

> There are countless forms of play in which the child assumes the roles of the adults about him. . . . In the play of young children, even when they play together, there is abundant evidence of the child's taking different roles in the process; and a solitary child will keep up the process of stimulating himself by his vocal gestures to act in different roles almost indefinitely . . . ; a child plays at being a mother, at being a teacher, at being a policeman. . . . If we contrast play with . . . an organized game, we note the essential difference that the child who plays in the game must be ready to take the attitude of everyone else involved in that game, and that these different roles must have a definite relationship to each other. . . . In a game where a number of individuals are involved . . . they do not all have to be present in consciousness at the same time, but at some moments he has to have three or four individuals present in his own attitude. [Pp. 150–52]

Gradually the ability to take the role of the other becomes more sophisticated, and the ability to treat self-as-object is enhanced.

Changing Selves

For Mead (1934), self is an ongoing process. In effect, self changes each time "I," the experiencer, takes self as an object of attention, i.e., engages in internal dialogue with "Me." In one sense there are as many selves as there are occasions in which self is the object of definition (and evaluation). Thus, the fleeting self-images we have continually undergo transformation as we take the role of various others in specific situations.

The self undergoes continuous change in yet another way. The "I's" experiencing of one moment becomes incorporated into the "Me" of the next moment. So it is that "Me" is changing on an almost moment-to-moment basis. As Mead (1934:229) notes:

> The "I" reacts to the self which arises through taking the attitude of others. Through taking those attitudes, we have introduced the "Me," and we react to it as an "I." . . . I

> talk to myself, and I remember what I said and perhaps
> the emotional content that went with it. The "I" of this
> moment is present in the "Me" of the next moment.

Relatively enduring self-concepts may also change. For example, suppose
that an individual perceives her/his parents to be generally disapproving,
while friends are deemed more supportive. The individual may intentionally
replace parents as significant others with close friends. (When that occurs,
the core of the Me also changes.) Alternatively, one may elect to participate
in situations where desired responses from others can be attained. For
example, a gay person may feel ostracized by the "straight world." S/he
can then choose to limit interaction to a supportive gay community, where
"gayness" is positively valued. Finally, one can alter perceptual schemes.
If one tends to search for negative reactions from others, one can consciously choose to search for positive reactions. Even more likely, if one
displays signs of confidence, others' actual responses can be altered.

In summary, symbolic interaction focuses on cognitive constructions of
definitions of self. As the individual learns to take the role of individuals
and groups, s/he is able to take him/her self as an object of attention for
definition and evaluation.

The Dramaturgical Perspective

The dramaturgical perspective draws parallels between the theater and
life in the everyday world. From the standpoint of this perspective, individuals relate to self and one another as if they were actors playing roles
on a stage. As Messinger, Sampson, and Towne (1975:39) note:

> The theater is a simile, a frame of reference, invoked by
> the analyst to segregate and permit him to analyze one of
> the multiple functions of interaction: its "impressive"
> function.

This social psychological perspective can be traced to the 1930s, when
philosopher-critic Kenneth Burke began to develop a "dramatistic model"
of human behavior (1945, 1965, 1966). However, Erving Goffman's early
work (1952, 1955, 1959, 1961a, 1961b, 1963a, 1963b, 1967) has been central
in developing and solidifying the dramaturgical perspective for sociology.
(Goffman's later works, e.g., 1974, are more structuralist and less concerned with self.) In addition to Goffman, other contemporary sociologists
employing a dramaturgical view include Gregory Stone (1962), Sheldon
Messinger, Harold Sampson, and Robert Towne (1962), Barney Glaser and
Anselm Strauss (1965), Joan Emerson (1970a, 1970b), and Ernest Becker
(1962). Dennis Brissett and Charles Edgley (1975) have edited an excellent
reader.

I must also note the fact that what I am calling the "dramaturgical perspective" is often viewed as part of symbolic interaction and not as a distinct approach in sociology. Rather, sociologists such as Goffman are seen to emphasize certain topics that other symbolic interactionists simply touch on. Goffman and the other sociologists mentioned above do have roots in the symbolic interaction tradition. They are distinguished here partly for organizational purposes and partly for clarity. However, the distinctive emphases of Goffman and others also legitimate and merit separate treatment, the path I have chosen.

Elements of the Dramaturgical Perspective

The dramaturgical sociologist steps away from the stance of the member of society to explore the ways in which social interaction resembles many components of a theatrical performance. It must be emphasized that the dramaturgical view is not usually the social actor's perspective on self and associations with others (Messinger, Sampson, and Towne, 1975). Although many people have episodic insights about themselves and interactions that parallel dramaturgical analysis, this perspective paints too "cynical" a portrait of social life for most people.

One focus for dramaturgical sociologists is the careful description of microscopic aspects of various types of interactional settings, including appropriate participant behavior. Goffman (1959, 1963), among others, has elaborated the intricacies of appropriate role conduct in settings ranging from very public gatherings to meetings among acquaintances to gynecological examinations (Emerson, 1970b). To take one example, people engage in what Goffman (1963a) calls "civil inattention" when passing someone on the street. One must give enough visual notice to demonstrate that one appreciates the other's presence while subsequently (e.g., at about eight feet) withdrawing one's attention. Failure to play a role appropriately can result in losing claims to the role and in ridicule and embarrassment.

To fully understand the contributions of this perspective, it is necessary to describe its particular view of interaction, which involves the reciprocal influence of individuals upon one another's actions when they are in one another's physical presence (Goffman, 1959:15). An interaction includes the roles of *performer* and *audience*. The performer is engaged in what Goffman terms *"impression management."* He/she (or they, e.g., performers working together as a "team") attempts to construct a course of activity that will elicit the desired interpretations and responses from the audience; he/she at least attempts to affect the audience members' perceptions of, and involvements in, the interaction. Here, Goffman's concept of *performance* is critical; it consists of "all the activity of a given participant on a given occasion which serves to influence in any way any of the other participants" (1959:15).

As performers, persons communicate in two basic ways: (1) they *"give* cues," and (2) they "*give off* cues." To give cues involves the conscious and intentional construction and delivery of verbal and nonverbal communication to elicit the kind of response or audience interpretation that is desired. Nonverbal elements include "props" or the material artifacts used in a performance: dress and general physical appearance, speech tone and pitch, eye contact (or its absence), body posture, and general demeanor. Generally, persons give cues to gain control over the interaction episode. However, they also "give off cues," i.e., they unintentionally provide information to an audience. As with cues given, cues given off include both verbal and nonverbal behavior.

The audience is hardly passive during a performance. As Goffman (1959:2) suggests: "When an individual enters the presence of others, they consciously seek to acquire information about him or to bring into play information already possessed." The audience is an active constituent in the construction and interpretation of interaction, performances, and selves. While they use cues given for interpretation, they often search behind those to the cues given off in order to define "the real reality," to ascertain what is "really" symptomatic of the actor. As Goffman (1959:7) states:

> Knowing that the individual is likely to present himself in a light that is favorable to him, the others may divide what they witness into two parts: a part that is relatively easy for the individual to manipulate at will, being chiefly his verbal assertions, and a part in regard to which he seems to have little concern or control, being chiefly derived from the expressions he gives off. The others may then use what are considered to be the ungovernable aspects of his expressive behavior as a check upon the validity of what is conveyed by the governable aspects.

From previous experience as an audience member, the performer knows that cues given off are used as a check on the validity of a performance. Therefore, the performer will attempt to turn cues given off into cues given without appearing to do so. Expressions will be made to look spontaneous while actually they are being carefully constructed and presented. More generally, the actor in daily life seeks as much control over interaction as possible while appearing not to do so. Or, one may wish to appear in total control of a situation when, in fact, s/he is ill prepared for the situation.

While distinguishing performer and audience roles, it is important to acknowledge that in most situations persons alternate playing each role.

One further aspect of impression management is critical. Actors on a stage present a performance to an audience. They become essentially different people when they leave the stage for the dressing room or post-performance party, where they can "let their hair down." So in daily life, members of society carefully divide their *front-region* performances from their *back-region* areas, where there is freedom to "be real."

As one might gather, dramaturgical sociologists view social interaction as a fragile game of giving, receiving, and assessing information about situations and selves. Interpretations are not static. As information flows between participants, the audience's interpretations and consequent responses can alter radically in a short period of time. This, in turn, requires modification or even transformation of the performance. Moreover, discrepancies of many sorts can destroy a performance. For example, conflict or contradiction between cues given and cues given off may occur. The cues given off may be taken as the "real reality" and thus destroy the credibility of the performance. Alternatively, an actor may find his/her front and back regions confounded. A person might believe that s/he is in the back region and behave accordingly, only to discover that there is in fact an audience "making sense" of the actor. As a performer, it is to one's advantage to *segregate audiences* (Goffman, 1959:49). For example, a student is likely to be one person with friends at school and another at home with parents. Should that student take home a friend without "educating" him/her about the cues given to parents, the friend may share the back regions of school life and parents may then reinterpret who the son or daughter "is" in light of this glimpse into a back region. Failure to control props, appearances, and other cues given and given off can destroy a performance and result in a new, often negative, definition of the actor and his/her performance.

Implications for Self

Dramaturgical sociologists have not developed a comprehensive conceptualization of self. However, their primary foci of study lead to some important insights into the nature of self.

People are both performers and audience members. Part of one's self-concept usually derives from perceived adeptness and success in these roles, e.g., "I pulled that one off" or "I sure psyched him out."

Actors are viewed as having, as a major goal of social interaction, the creating and sustaining of others' impressions of who one is. In other terms, performances are vehicles by which self is expressed, sustained, modified, or destroyed.

A particular role can be played deliberately without the actor's *identifying with* it. That is, much of the time people differentiate their "real selves" from their performances, i.e., the performance can be viewed as "not me." Some dramaturgical sociologists have therefore drawn parallels between the performer in daily life and the "con man":

> Inevitably, in watching the swindler take on various roles of respectable society, we are pushed toward the uncomfortable impression that those who hold these roles "legitimately" may have attained their status by procedures not so radically different from the ones employed by him. . . . In one way or another, we are all impostors. [Berger, 1963:135]

> Thus, the "con man" instructs how, in everyday life, without being explicitly aware of it, those who do not conceive themselves as "con men" may sustain another's conception of themselves as "trustworthy" in the face of events which might lead to conceiving them quite differently. [Messinger, Sampson and Towne, 1975:38]

The similarities between professional and lay con men are most apparent when someone consciously devises a performance to manage others' impressions and subjectively views that performance as "not me." An anticipated consequence of successful performances is the preservation of "face." Goffman (1955:214) describes this concept:

> A person may be said to *have* or *be in* or *maintain* face when the line he effectively takes presents an image of him that is internally consistent, that is supported by judgments and evidence conveyed by other participants, and that is confirmed by evidence conveyed through interpersonal agencies in the situation.

Face can be viewed as the coincidence between the actor's performance and others' impressions. In effect, maintaining face maintains and validates one's sense of self. As described so far, performers and audience members are adversaries in a game. Indeed, that is one dimension of interaction. The opposite also occurs frequently, i.e., synergy. For example, participants in interaction often engage in reciprocal face-saving. Each actor is involved in preserving his/her own face, the face of others, and the face of the situation. Essentially, hidden bargains are made among participants to avoid destroying the credibility of one another's face. This is a totally logical characteristic, given the alternation of performer and audience roles in most interactions. We can expect the hidden bargain to be the norm unless there is an explicit reason for adversarialism to predominate or unless the bargain is violated.

Role distance—expressed and pointed separation between the individual and the role performance—can be essential in many situations. Goffman (1961b) provides an example:

> Adults who choose to ride a merry-go-round display adult techniques of role distance. One adult rider makes a joke of tightening the safety belts around him; another crosses

his arms, giving popcorn with his left hand to the person on his right and a coke with his right hand to the person on his left. A young lady, riding side-saddle, tinkles out "It's cold," and calls to her watching boy friend's boy friend, "Come on, don't be chicken."

If role distance is not maintained and expressed when adults ride merry-go-rounds, one's "face" as a full-fledged adult will be severely tarnished if not totally destroyed. When a person must do tasks that s/he believes are beneath him/her, a conscious separation between "self" and "role" will be entertained. The "real self" is sequestered behind the performance so that it will not be compromised. For example, a professor who must type his/her own test or take the garbage out at night may be careful, during these activities, to give cues that say "This isn't the real me." Similarly, subordinates who must act on orders given will simultaneously communicate "I'm not capitulating completely." S/he might play the role of subordinate with irony, sarcasm, sullenness, or other behavior that shows distance between the role and the real self. People who are in some way oppressed are likely to be "on" (i.e., staging a performance), and to separate that performance from the "real" self much of the time (Messinger, Sampson, and Towne, 1975). The wider the discrepancy between real self and being "on," the more the actor orients to "*just* playing a role." For example, blacks and students both exaggerate their deference behaviors to whites and the university, respectively, and thereby achieve separation between "real" and "presented" self. While dramaturgical sociologists do not elaborate the sociological meaning or origination of the "real" or "natural" self, the fact that people often segregate it from their performances is critical to understanding self from this perspective.

However, people do not always separate real and presented self. Rather, people may "embrace" a role (Goffman, 1961b). Embracing requires subjective *attachment* to the role, demonstrating that one is qualified to perform it, and *engagement*, or spontaneous involvement in role activity. "Real self" and "role" merge in these situations. When one embraces a role, s/he is also embraced by it. Front- and backstage, "on" and "off" stage, and "performance" vs. "real self" evaporate when a role is embraced. For example, when a man and woman first meet, they may devise performances to elicit desired responses from the other. If spontaneous involvement with each other emerges over time, self and role-as-lover merge. No longer are the two people "acting as if" they are lovers; they *become* lovers.

For dramaturgical analysts, the self is rather fragile. It can be destroyed in a variety of circumstances, and these have been of great interest to the dramaturgical sociologist. Goffman summarizes (1959:242–43):

> When an individual appears before others, he knowingly and unwittingly projects a definition of the situation, of

which a conception of himself is an important part. When
an event occurs which is expressively incompatible with
this fostered impression . . . social interaction . . . may
come to an embarrassed and confused halt . . . ; when a
disruption occurs, then, we may find that the self-conceptions around which his personality has been built may
become discredited.

If there is a discrepancy between the self-as-consciously-presented and contrary indicators perceived by the audience, one may be denied claims to the
desired role. Shame and embarrassment are common consequences for stepping out of role. Similar consequences occur if one's back region is penetrated or if others play discrepant roles, such as "informer" or "spy." In this
case, audience segregation may be lost as well as positive self-conceptions.

For some people there is an observable discrepancy between role performance and appearance; Goffman (1968) calls this *stigma*. Significant
here are persons with physical differences (e.g., blindness, dwarfism, am-
putation, etc.) who seek to present and have others accept a "normal" self
and performance (Goffman, 1968). Such persons must engage in extreme
strategic manipulations to be taken as they wish to be taken, i.e., as
essentially normal. Stigmatized persons often use what Goffman (1968:44)
calls a disidentifier, which is

a sign that tends—in fact or hope—to break up an otherwise coherent picture but in this case a positive direction
desired by the actor, not so much establishing a new claim
as throwing severe doubt on the validity of the virtual one.

For dwarfs, to take one example, disidentification centers on demonstrating
that they are (1) adults, not children, and (2) fellow human beings, not some
sort of freak (Truzzi, 1968). They use hats, canes, high fashion, and elaboration of sexual exploits to validate their claims to "essential normalcy."

Not every breach of presentation results in self-destruction. The orientation to reciprocal face-saving prevents this.

Origins of Self

The dramaturgical sociologists have not formulated an explicit or distinct
theory of the emergence of self. Many of the elements of symbolic interaction, such as role-taking, learning to share significant symbols, and game-
playing, are implicitly, not explicitly, adopted. What is central to dramaturgical sociology is the notion that each culture provides an intricate web
of social rules for conducting one's self in a variety of situations. The task
of the individual is to learn these rules of conduct. From childhood on,
people must learn to play many roles, to modify the demands of the self
in different types of situations, and to evaluate the performances of others

(Becker, 1962). By learning these things, the individual learns to put forth and sustain self.

Constraint and Freedom

There is one final issue that I wish to address, i.e., the dialectical relationship between constraint and freedom. Many roles that people enact have been scripted by previous performers. Roles are also devised by those who are in a position to control others. For example, staff in prisons and mental hospitals script appropriate roles for inmates and patients. Additionally, the minute rules of social interaction exert constraint and control over the individual actor. Finally, the audience's responses or anticipated responses to actors' performances constrain individuals.

However, the very features of social life that exert constraint can also be used to attain at least some measure of liberation. Manipulating presentations of self is one method people use to escape the tyranny of society (Berger, 1963). For example, Goffman (1961a) provides a rich description of life in *total institutions*—places where persons lead regimented lives, e.g., prisons, mental hospitals, and the military. In total institutions one might expect social control to be complete. Indeed, individuals are stripped of their "normal identities," e.g., street clothes are exchanged for uniforms, and there is a "proper demeanor" for the resident. Behavior in conformity with the social role of "inmate" is called *primary adjustment*. But individuals create *secondary adjustments:* they create an "underlife" in these institutions. Inmates "work the system" to obtain goods, services, and other means to a more normal identity; e.g., they will hoard possessions, use secret manipulations to reap goods and services, mutter discontent, and feign appearances and feelings. By such behavior they resist, at least in part, official definitions.

People outside total institutions also seek relief from social determinism. They may choose to play their roles sullenly or sincerely, with inner conviction or with distance (Berger, 1963). They will consciously create back regions as relief from various front regions. In so doing, they create a margin of freedom from an otherwise constraining world.

As described, the dramaturgical perspective highlights two things: (1) a single major dimension of social life, social interaction, and (2) social selves and the ways in which people devise selves to obtain desired responses from others.

PHENOMENOLOGICAL SOCIOLOGY

Unlike the symbolic interactionist and dramaturgical perspectives, phenomenological sociology does not offer a theory of self. It undertakes a different, more fundamental, task of looking at the ways in which the member of a society experiences the social world in the first place. Describing some of the basic features of the phenomenological approach will lead to an examination of this perspective's *implications* for the concept of self.

It is important to distinguish phenomenology as a philosophical enterprise from phenomenological sociology as a social science perspective. Essentially, the philosophical stance is foundational for application to the social sciences. Edmund Husserl (1962, 1969, 1970, 1973) is undoubtedly the single most important philosopher in developing the phenomenological tradition. Other modern theorists of note include Herbert Spiegelberg (1960), Maurice Merleau-Ponty (1962, 1964), Aron Gurwitsch (1964, 1966), Richard Zaner (1970), and David Carr (1974). In applying phenomenological tenets to the social world, Alfred Schutz's work (1962, 1964, 1966, 1967, 1970) is seminal. James Heap and Phillip Roth (1973), D. Lawrence Wieder (1977), George Psathas (1973), and Maurice Natanson (1970) have also made significant contributions to phenomenological sociology.

The Phenomenological Stance

Edmund Husserl conceived phenomenology as a foundational philosophy, one that establishes the sources or roots of all knowledge. That is, before substantive matters can be addressed (e.g., "What is a home?"), a prior critical question must be answered: "*How* does anyone (including the philosopher and scientist) come to 'know' anything?"

The roots of all knowledge are to be found in one who "turns to an object" through an *act* of consciousness. With this idea phenomenology can be construed as the study of consciousness. Alternatively, it is the study of the way in which the appearances of objects (whether they are physical, social, or merely imaginable) are constituted by an active subject.

To understand conscious activity requires a special attitude or stance for two reasons: (1) consciousness is typically overlooked or taken for granted by human beings, and (2) it is impossible to be simultaneously conscious of something and conscious of the consciousness. Husserl terms this special stance "putting the world in brackets" or "performing the phenomenological reduction." The phenomenologist disengages him/herself from mere membership in the everyday world. S/he refrains from making judgments regarding the "real" nature of objects (see Dickens, 1979) in order to determine how such objects arise (Merleau-Ponty, 1964) and appear through acts of consciousness. Again, the concern is not substantively with any particular object but with how one attends to the world in general. What remains, following this disengagement, is the pure *stream of conscious experience.*

To do justice to the phenomenological analysis of consciousness would require at least a book. A few important features must suffice here.

One critical feature of consciousness has already been mentioned: it is *processual* activity. Additionally, objects are always meant or *intended:* consciousness is always *consciousness of* something. Indeed, intentionality is at the core of one's experience of any material, social, or imaginable object. Self is one social and imaginable object available to consciousness. Like other objects, the appearance of self-as-object progressively unfolds through an interlocking set of conscious acts. Thus, the phenomenologist's interest in self would be in how "it" is intended and appears through intentional, conscious acts.

Phenomenological Sociology

D. Lawrence Wieder provides a cogent description of phenomenological sociology's mission:

> . . . it would be the task of a phenomenological sociology
> to describe and explicate such intended objects as the . . .
> experience ordinarily referred to by way of the concepts
> social role, norm, institution, cultural object, the other
> person, motives, language, and the like. Furthermore, such
> a discipline would describe that which is distinctive about
> the intentional acts which present these objects to con-
> sciousness. [Wieder, 1977:14]

Alfred Schutz provided the clearest interpretation of the significance of phenomenology for the social sciences. He was specifically interested in how the social world is experienced by the member of a society (1962:56). At the core, Schutz (following Husserl) places *the natural attitude:* the "unstated, implicit commitment to, or unnoticed 'belief' in, the world as 'there,' existing independently of us in all of its complex and multiform ways" (Zaner, 1973:35). The natural attitude is a stance taken by the societal member toward both his/her own existence and existence in general. Basically, it consists of a set of untested assumptions that the person relies on to interpret the world and construct courses of action within it.

From the standpoint of the natural attitude, one is born into an "already there" world, a world that is fundamentally organized, objective, and meaningful apart from acts of consciousness and practical activities. Therefore, a significant feature of the natural attitude is that its "work" in sustaining the world "as such" is unnoticed and taken for granted. Moreover, the world is assumed to be an *intersubjective* one. It is not one's private affair. We assume without question that the objects, events, artifacts, ideas, and values, and the world in general, are common to us all. This is referred to as the *general thesis of the alter ego:*

> No motive exists for the naive person to raise the tran-
> scendental question concerning the actuality of the world
> or concerning the reality of the *alter ego.* . . . I assume

everything which has meaning for me also has meaning for the Other or Others with whom I share this, my life-world. [Schutz, 1962:135]

Part of the thesis of the alter ego involves what Schutz (1962) terms the *reciprocity of perspectives:*

I take it for granted—and assume my fellow-man does the same—that if I change places with him so that his "here" becomes mine, I shall be at the same distance from things and see them with the same typicality as he actually does. . . . Until counterevidence I take it for granted—and assume my fellow-man does the same—that the differences in perspectives originating in our unique biographical situations are irrelevant for the purposes at hand. [Schutz, 1962:12]

The member of society has a thoroughly practical interest in the everyday world. And, unlike professional scientists, the person operating in daily life has a thoroughly practical interest in knowledge about the world. S/he acquires what Schutz terms a *stock of knowledge*—a set of what appear to the member as recipes used for interpreting and acting in the everyday world. The individual's stock of knowledge is basically a system of constructs that enables one to *typify* situations, selves, and the world in general (Schutz, 1962:7). The consciousness of persons is a typifying consciousness. This idea is central to Schutz's analysis. He provides the following well-known example and conceptual rendering:

. . . the outer world is not experienced as an arrangement of individual unique objects . . . but as "mountains," "trees," "animals," "fellow-men." I may have never seen an Irish setter, but, if I see one, I know that it is an animal and in particular a dog, showing all the familiar features and the typical behavior of a dog and not, say, of a cat. I may reasonably ask: "What kind of dog is this?" The question presupposes that the dissimilarity of this particular dog from all other kinds of dogs which I know stands out and becomes questionable merely by reference to the similarity it has to my unquestioned experiences of typical dogs. . . . Actual experience will or will not confirm my anticipation of the typical conformity with other objects. If confirmed, the content of the anticipated type will be enlarged; at the same time, the type will be split up into sub-types. . . .

Now, and this seems to be of special importance, I *may* take the typically apperceived object as an *exemplar* of the general type and allow myself to be led to this concept of the type, but I do not *need* by any means to think of

the concrete dog as an exemplar of the general concept
of "dog." "In general" my Irish setter Rover shows all the
characteristics which the type "dog," according to my previous experience, implies. Yet, exactly what he has in
common with other dogs is of no concern to me. I look at
him as my friend and companion Rover, as such distinguished from all other Irish setters. [Schutz, 1962:7–8]

As these statements imply, typifications are not static rules for categorizing
things. Rather, the situation at hand or the *biographic situation* sets the
stage for constantly changing typifications. Schutz (1971:222–23) describes
this idea:

The wide-awake man within the natural attitude is primarily interested in that sector of the world of his everyday
life which is within his scope and which is centered in
space and time around himself. The place which my body
occupies within the world, my actual Here, is the starting
point from which I take my bearing in space. It is, so to
speak, the center O of my system of coordinates. Relative
to my body I group the elements of my surroundings under
the categories of right and left, before and behind, above
and below, near and far, and so on. And in a similar way
my actual Now is the origin of all the time perspectives
under which I organize the events within the world, such
as the categories of fore and aft, past and future, simultaneity and succession, etc.

As one's biographic situation changes from moment to moment, so is the
stock of knowledge elaborated and reassembled into situation-relevant
typifications.

In each biographically determined situation, the actor constructs systems of relevance, and these in turn inform the way in which the stock of
knowledge is assembled and creatively used on that occasion:

It is our interest at hand that motivates all our thinking,
projecting, acting, and therewith establishes the problems
to be solved by our thought and the goals to be attained
by our action. In other words, it is our interest that breaks
asunder the unproblematic field of the preknown into various zones of various relevance with respect to such interest, each of them requiring a different degree of precision
of knowledge. [Schutz, 1970:111–12]

Relevance depends on interest. Having a certain purpose at hand, the
individual molds his/her experientially based or culturally transmitted stock
of knowledge to typify a situation or object, to render it meaningful, in-
terpretable, and providing the grounds for action. All the while, this typifying

work and the world-as-presented-through-typifying-work are taken for granted. That is, typifying includes the idea that objects and situations etc., have definite objective qualities. In taking typifying work for granted, referenced objects and situations are also taken for granted.

Far removed from a direct face-to-face relationship, typifications are totally anonymous. Another person is experienced as a certain type of person (not as a particular individual), who interacts in a typical way, having a typical pattern of motives and attitudes. So, for example, standing in line in a grocery store, I enact a typification of "grocery checkers," their typical motives and behaviors. In typifying the checker for my purposes, I typify myself reciprocally, e.g., as an instance of "customer." I further assume that the checker holds these same typifications. I take it for granted that my action as "customer" will induce the checker to perform his/her typical actions as a checker. Generally, I take it for granted that my construct of the other's action corresponds to his/her self-typification. Notice here that other "identities" of the checker and of me, the customer, are irrelevant for the purposes at hand. The anonymity of the typifications used operate well enough, and so we go no further in organizing our stock of knowledge.

A typifying scheme may also be derived from first-hand experience with another. Here, I gain direct knowledge of the other in a face-to-face "we-relation." In these cases, actors have a reciprocal thou-orientation, and typifications are both more personal and expansive. Zaner (1973:37) provides an example:

> I come home after work and learn that my wife has made plans to visit Peru; she has not told me of this before, nor have there been any signs indicating this was in her mind. I find such conduct "highly irregular," having known her for years; that part of my stock of knowledge at hand pertaining to her contains no constructs or interpretive schemes that would help me understand this, and consequently I think of the situation as "strange," "peculiar," "calling for discussion," "inquiry," and so on. Maybe she is ill, maybe "something has happened," as we sometimes say. That is, I call on my own prevailing stock of knowledge (including such items as "how to act when one is shocked," the asking of questions, the use of language and various gestures, perhaps also "what one does when one is upset, angry," etc.) in an effort to orient myself with respect to this atypical, unexpected conduct. It may turn out that she has received an urgent communication from a dear friend who I did not know is in Peru and who now needs her; *that*, I now understand, and I am then able to place it within those sets of typifications called "emergency situations concerning friends" and I set about doing other

equally typical things, such as planning with her and buy-
ing airline tickets. . . . The typical conduct becomes in-
terpretable within my prevailing typicality constructs.

Self as a Phenomenological Topic

Phenomenology places the intentionality of consciousness at the center of
inquiry, which includes the stream of conscious activity and any object as
it appears through consciousness. Therefore, in one sense phenomenology
takes the self-as-conscious-subject as its topic of study. Phenomenological
sociology is also about "self" as the originator of experience within a
biographically determined situation.

One could argue that there are many "selves"-as-originators-of-experi-
ence, corresponding to variations in intentionality, relevance, and interpretive schemes. In this regard, Schutz has written two excellent essays
depicting "the stranger" (1944) and "the homecomer" (1945). The stranger—
one who is about to join a group for the first time—finds him/herself in the
unaccustomed situation where everyday life cannot be taken for granted.
Indeed, the inability to use—or failed attempts at using—the acquired
stock of knowledge and typifying schemes is, in fact, what renders one
experientially a stranger. The homecomer, in contrast, expects to return
to a familiar world, shared in common. "Home" really means a place where
one can safely operate with recipe knowledge, relevance, and interpretive
schemes that are presumably shared. However, in the homecomer's absence, "home" has undergone change merely by people's having lived
through time. Such change is not problematic for those who experience
daily life together; in fact, they may not even recognize any transformation.
But the homecomer not only has missed this lived change but has changed
in her/himself; i.e., during an absence s/he has had a different set of
"heres" and "nows" than those at home. Alas, the homecomer faces a
radical discrepancy between anticipation and actual experience. To bring
this analysis "home," so to speak, the difficulty that Vietnam veterans have
had in attempting to reintegrate themselves into their previous daily lives
in the United States is a classic example of what Schutz was addressing.
Home appears strange to the homecomer, and the homecomer appears
strange to those who never left. Actual lived experience during the homecomer's absence created a painful breach in the ability to take the world
for granted; it may take years to repair, or the attempted repair may utterly
fail.

I have described self-as-subject to some extent. Self can also be an
object both in the ongoing stream of activity and in the retrospective construction of meaning.

The stock of knowledge provides the grounds for typifying others. But for that interaction to unfold, one must construct reciprocal self-typifications. That is, typification of others becomes the "in-order-to" motives for one's own self-typification and action. Schutz (1962:60) highlights this reflexive tie between typifying others and self-typifications:

> The world of everyday life is from the outset also a social and cultural world in which I am interrelated in manifold ways of interaction with fellow-men known to me in varying degrees of intimacy and anonymity. . . . I can, however, experience them in their typicality. In order to do so, I construct typical patterns of the actors' motives and ends, even of their attitudes and personalities, of which their actual conduct is just an instance or example. These typified patterns of the Others' behavior become in turn motives for my own action, and this leads to the phenomenon of self-typification.

Let me provide an example. At this particular moment, I use my stock of knowledge at hand to construct a typification of a "typical student" trying to grasp, in general, the essence of a phenomenological perspective. That typification includes my identification of the typical student's typical background in phenomenology (and theory in general), typical motives in reading this chapter, and typical attitudes, etc. This leads me to construct a self-typification. My "in-order-to" motive is to explicate this perspective. I assume the typical attitude, the typical style, and typical behavior of "one who explicates difficult material." I *am*, at this moment, Marilyn-the-explicator. Now, it could happen that my editor would tell me this book is not meant for a student audience but for an "expert" public. Then I would reorganize my stock of knowledge to construct a different typification of the "expert audience." My self-typification would be radically transformed from explicator to "critical analyst trying to produce unique insights." In so doing, I would take on a different set of typical (e.g., "critical") attitudes, motives, and behavior. In general, as systems of relevance and practical projects are transformed in the course of interaction or on different occasions, the stock of knowledge undergoes modification, and so do typifications of the Other and reciprocal Self-typifications. Jehenson (1973:219–47) further illustrates the changing nature of self-typifications in his phenomenological study of organizational behavior:

> . . . while asking the new director of the hospital for the authorization to do research in his institution, I had to conduct myself in the way the typical director expects the typical candidate-researcher to behave. My self-typification was naturally influenced by my own biographical situation (my age, my European culture, the feeling of being "legitimized" in the system where I had already conducted

research for nine months, etc.). The director, on his part, typified me as "a student who has to submit a detailed protocol of the research to him—the director—as if he were a supervisor." I could not accept his altercasting of me as a "dependent student" any more than he was ready to validate the type I had of him as "a newcomer who would do well to realize that I had already been doing research in the hospital." Actually, the types we were having of each other did not pass the test of our face-to-face confrontation, and we were soon in the process of negotiating our respective typifying schemes. . . .

Both Other- and Self-typifications may be modified in an actual face-to-face relation. However, while immersed in my working acts (e.g., interaction), I cannot simultaneously provide meaning for those acts or for myself as actor. Only by stepping outside my stream of activity in an act of reflection can I interpret "what's happening" or "who I really am." That is, meaning is always created in retrospect. In the retrospective glance, I can typify myself in a variety of ways, depending, of course, on the biographical situation. For example, stepping outside this project of communicating a sense of the phenomenological approach, I can typify myself as a scholar, teacher, member of a university community, etc. I am indeed an instance of each of these. At the same time, I go beyond being an exemplar of these "types," for what I share with others is specifically irrelevant at this moment. So, using a sense of the typical writer, typical scholar, and typical university member as a *background*, I can provide an account of the typical ways in which I am unique. What I share with others, then, may be specifically disregarded. Of course, far removed from this occasion, I will rely on my stock of knowledge in typifying myself as a woman, lover, friend, and so on. As my stock of knowledge is changed with my biographical process and as my relevances change, so do my self-typifications. However, I can also typify myself as "being consistently X, e.g., "I am a feminist." However, this "consistency" is the *result* of using the typification "I am X."

Phenomenological sociology takes us beneath questions concerning the content of self to explore the formations of people's experiences of anything.

ETHNOMETHODOLOGY

Beginning in the later 1950s and continuing for a decade, a few sociologists—independently of one another—began to discern fundamental theoretical and empirical weaknesses in traditional sociological wisdom. Questioned were traditional subject matters, methods, theories, levels of analysis, and the central place of norms in sociological conceptions. In this early phase of development, Harold Garfinkel's work (1959, 1960, 1962,

1967) and that of Aaron Cicourel (1964, 1968, 1974) stand out as crucial precursors for ethnomethodology and, later, as classic exemplars of it. Additionally, Egon Bittner (1963, 1965, 1967), Harvey Sacks (1963, 1972a, 1972b), John Kitsuse and Aaron Cicourel (1963), Peter McHugh (1968) and David Sudnow (1965, 1969) contributed to the early development of the perspective.

If they have accomplished nothing else, ethnomethodologists have provided important critiques of traditional sociology. However, they have gone beyond that. There is a growing body of theoretical and empirical works that share some important characteristics even if they are not all regarded as "ethnomethodology" (e.g., some are characterized as "cognitive sociology" and some as "conversational analysis"). There is also diversity among ethnomethodologists. Most important at this moment is the fact that some scholars trace the antecedents of their ideas to Alfred Schutz and the phenomenological view more generally (e.g., Harold Garfinkel, 1967; Melvin Pollner, 1974; D. Lawrence Wieder, 1974; and Don Zimmerman, 1970a, 1970b). However, Zimmerman (1979) cautions us not to confound the intellectual antecedents of a perspective with its content. That is, phenomenological ideas were greatly transformed from Schutz to Garfinkel and others (see Zimmerman, 1979:382). A different style of ethnomethodological work can be characterized as the study of natural-language use and, more specifically, as the study of conversation. Forerunners in doing this kind of work include Garfinkel but also linguists and linguistic anthropologists. Harvey Sacks's work (1963, 1972a, 1972b) is central to the development of conversational analysis. Other seminal researchers are Gail Jefferson (1972, 1973), Emanuel Schegloff (1968), Sacks and Schegloff (1973), and Candace West and Don Zimmerman's work on gender and conversation (1977).

The Perspective

Ethnomethodologists carefully differentiate the *topics* of sociological study from the *unexamined resources* used in research and theory development. They (e.g., Zimmerman and Pollner, 1970; Garfinkel, 1967; Cicourel, 1968) argue that conventional sociologists (like ordinary members of society) address the existence of social phenomena as independent of those phenomena "having been addressed by some method of investigation" (Zimmerman and Pollner, 1970:81), e.g., through "accounts," descriptions, and conversations. Concepts such as role, status, organization, and self are typically conceived and studied apart from people's practices for attending to, and providing accounts of, their existence. Zimmerman and Pollner emphasize this point:

> For both lay and professional investigation, the social world
> presents itself as an exterior field of events amenable to
> lawful investigation . . . ; the availability of social struc-
> tures to inquiry in the first place is masked over the course
> of inquiry by and through which features of such structures
> are made available. [Zimmerman and Pollner, 1970:86]

Essentially, people's "investigation" practices, courses of inquiry, descriptions and accounts, etc., are among the critical topics for ethnomethodology
because they provide for the appearances of social phenomena as such.
In somewhat different terms, the perspective is concerned with the ways
in which people use natural language to manage practical circumstances.
Natural language refers to a system of practices

> that permit speakers and auditors to hear, and in other
> ways to witness, the objective production and objective
> display of common-sense knowledge, and of practical cir-
> cumstances, practical actions, and practical sociological
> reasoning. [Garfinkel and Sacks, 1970:342]

I shall try to clarify this. Both lay persons and most professional sociologists
conceive the relationship between natural language and the world as follows:

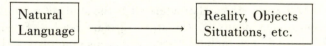

Objects (physical or social) exist in and of themselves. Natural language
or accounts *merely* describe this reality. Descriptions are viewed and assessed as more or less accurate. However, despite the assessment of accuracy, the world is seen to exist as totally independent of how people use
natural language to attend to the world, any object, etc. Ethnomethodologists rid sociology of this dualism. Zimmerman's (1974) illustrations and
comments below should help to elaborate this:

> The names appearing on or in each figure instruct the
> viewer to see each display in a particular structured way.
> They tell the viewer how to see the lines for what they are
> "this time." The names are embedded instructions. Their
> sense is fulfilled by their placement in juxtaposition with
> the figures. Although they are descriptive of the figures,
> they must "be there" as aspects of the figure for there to

be much likelihood that the figures will be seen in the
fashion that they are, in contrast to other possibilities that
the "lines on the page" offer, e.g., they could be seen as
merely lines on the page or as. . . .

The "objective" status of *each* aspect of the figure (e.g., "line") and its
relationship to others are derived from the embedded instructions to "read"
the "lines" as constituting a certain figure. So, with different embedded
instructions, what the figure "really is" and what each aspect "really is"
would undergo radical modification. Zimmerman's illustration is a simplified version of the *reflexive tie* between accounts and any social or physical
object. Accounts are part of any setting, situation, or object being attended
to through the accounts. The presence of each feature (of an object, event,
etc.) as a feature and its relationship to other features are outcomes of
people's use of natural language, e.g., in accounts. Writing earlier than
Zimmerman, Garfinkel (1967:8) states:

> . . . accounts, of every sort, in all their logical modes, with
> all of their uses, and for every method for their assembling
> are constituent features of the settings they make avail-
> able . . . ; members . . . take that reflexivity for granted.

Reflexivity is one crucial aspect of people's use of natural language to
render social reality. Another is the *documentary method of interpretation.*
This is the member-of-society's basic procedure for interpreting the relationship between observable appearances of objects and a presumed
underlying reality, order, and pattern. Garfinkel (1967), who transforms
Mannheim's (1962) original discussion of the documentary method, describes it thus:

> The method consists of treating an actual appearance as
> "the document of," as "pointing to," as "standing on be-
> half of" a presupposed underlying pattern. Not only is the
> underlying pattern derived from its individual documen-
> tary evidences, but the individual documentary evidences,
> in their turn, are interpreted on the basis of "what is
> known" about the underlying pattern. Each is used to
> elaborate the other. [P. 78]

A classic illustration of the documentary method comes from one of
Garfinkel's quasi-experiments (1967:chap. 3). He told individual subjects
that the department of psychiatry was exploring "alternative means to
psychotherapy as a way of giving persons advice about their personal
problems" (p. 79). Each subject was asked to describe a problem s/he was
having to a student "counselor"—in fact, the experimenter—located in
another room connected by a microphone. The subject was then instructed
to ask the counselor a question that could be answered by a "yes" or a

"no." Following the counselor's response, the subject "unplugged" the microphone and discussed the exchange. This procedure was repeated for at least ten questions. In fact, the "counselor" had a list of responses to give beforehand. "Objectively," the "counseling session" was nonsense. But it was not nonsense for the subject. S/he discovered the "real" intent (i.e., pattern) of the counselor's individual responses (documents) and used them for practical decision-making. The pattern of help received existed only in the subject's accounts of the counselor's responses. As an aside, several subjects said they felt better or learned something from the session. These subjects' use of the documentary method is unique only in its visibility.

One further example of the ethnomethodologist's treatment of natural-language use or accounts concerns the concepts of norm and rule. The traditional sociologist conceives of rules and norms as governing people's behavior and considers violation of norms or rules as deviant behavior. This sociologist thus uses people's *descriptions* of the causal ties between norms or rules and behavior as an unexamined resource. Such descriptions are therefore insignificant for traditional research and theory. In contrast, ethnomethodologists do not view rules as "things" that govern other "things," e.g., behavior. Rather, their interest is in how people *use* rules or norms in everyday situations to render their own and others' behavior (or situations or selves, etc.) as sensible, rational, and orderly, etc. To illustrate, Wieder (1974) describes how residents and staff of a halfway house for paroled addicts used a "convict code" to organize and manage practical circumstances. Rules of "the code," such as "Don't snitch" and "Don't mess with other residents' interests," were used in verbal interaction by both staff and residents to explain, organize, display, and otherwise manage circumstances in the house. The rules, however, are not "out there," prepackaged and merely applied to a situation. Rather, *in their use*, the meaning and applicability of the rules are actually established for the purposes at hand (see Garfinkel, 1967; Zimmerman, 1970a, 1970b). The meaning and applicability of rules are elaborated or reformulated on other occasions. As a general principle, the meaning and analytic status of accounts of rules (and accounts of everything else) are always situated. That is, rules, norms, roles, and other social prescriptions cannot be literally spelled out in advance of their actual use, nor can they constitute an objective template for measuring or assessing actual conduct. Since the "real" sense of the rule cannot be explicated in advance, rule-governed behavior is actually a logical impossibility (see Wilson, 1970).

In this section I have provided only some illustrations of how ethnomethodologists conceive and practice sociology. As in phenomenological sociology, ethnomethodological tenets are intertwined in many complex ways, and a complete exegesis here is thus impossible.

Self through Ethnomethodology

In regard to self, the normative, interactionist, and dramaturgical perspectives all take as an unexamined resource what an ethnomethodologist
would take as a topic: the practical methods (e.g., natural language) that
persons use to identify and display self or, in other terms, the ways that
self is made available as such. "Self" as a gestalt and the incidents, events,
and other bits and pieces of our lives that we use to identify and display
a pattern of who we are constitute *situated* accomplishments. Who one
"is," who one "was," and who one "might" or "will" be are made available
in the first place, are organized or structured, and are given meaning
through accounts, descriptions, assumptions, and common-sense knowledge. Even our biographies are not fixed objects but are assembled and
reassembled on different occasions. To put this another way: seeing and
displaying the self as "consistent" or fixed is itself a situated accomplishment, resulting from using the documentary method of interpretation.

An important idea glossed above is that the self is a *situated* accomplishment. Like accounts of everything else, presenting the self is done to
manage practical circumstances. On different occasions people assemble
and proffer "self" in various ways. Let me clarify this with some simple
illustrations. I create a sense of "Marilyn" or "Dr. Lester" for a large
introductory class on the first day of school. I may tell the class where I
got my degrees and talk about my orientation to students and my status
as a college academic advisor and I usually say that I, myself, do a "freaky"
kind of sociology, not the kind that they will encounter in this introductory
course. In roughly five minutes I assemble "who I am" for that occasion,
and it manages or suffices as an introduction (e.g., to give students a sense
of their instructor). The account I provide literally structures an identity
that will stand "until further notice" (e.g., until I briefly describe ethnomethodology and elaborate "freaky" sociology later in the course). In Advanced Social Psychology, a small seminar filled with talented sociology
and psychology majors, I assemble "Marilyn" the "social psychologist." I
may trace my commitment as an undergraduate to symbolic interaction,
to ethnomethodology at the Ph.D. level, later to a broader-based phenomenological sociology, and to my current resistance to labeling myself a
member of any one school of thought. Obviously, students who take several
of my classes witness alternative accounts of my self. After a couple of
these introductions, they say they are surprised each time because I'm
"so different" in each class, and a large part of that difference has to do
with how I proffer myself, with how I "frame" and display who I am.

Garfinkel (1967:chap. 5) has provided the most notable illustration of an
ethnomethodological perspective on self through his study of "Agnes," an
intersexed person. Garfinkel often relies on natural or manufactured

"breaches" of the taken-for-granted world to elucidate the seen but unnoticed work we do to sustain the world *as* taken for granted. Agnes is
one illustration. When the research took place, Agnes was "a nineteen-
year-old girl raised as a boy whose female measurements of 38–25–38 were
accompanied by a fully developed penis and scrotum" (p. 117). From the
age of sixteen, Agnes had lived as a woman and was, at the time of the
study, applying to the Medical Center of the University of California (Los
Angeles) for surgery to remove the penis and scrotum and create an artificial vagina.

Garfinkel translates the phenomenological analysis of the natural attitude
into a sociologically relevant set of ideas in order to conceptualize Agnes
as an unusually obvious instance of assembling or rendering "self." From
the standpoint of the natural attitude, the world is composed of two sexes:
"natural normal males" and "natural normal females." People are, always
have been, and always will be of one sex or the other. Like other components of the natural attitude, most of us take our sex status and sex-
related behaviors for granted. We do not notice the manifold ways in which
our accounts, common-sense knowledge, assumptions, and routine practical actions are used continuously to structure, frame and reframe, and
display who we are as men and women (or anything else). Agnes could not
take anything for granted, least of all her sex status. She had to do overt
work to achieve and make sense of herself as a natural normal female. A
few aspects of this achievement will illustrate.

Like other members of society, Agnes subscribed to the view that the
world is populated by natural normal males and natural normal females.
She defined herself as a natural normal female. She identified the sex-
change operation as merely a "correction" of an "original error," i.e., a
vagina "should have been there all the time." The penis and scrotum were
"accidents" of nature and "should be corrected." Agnes structures a particular "self" that would undoubtedly not exist in the absence of her account, and/or other accounts would organize different underlying patterns
to describe who she "really is." That one may dispute this particular account's veracity is irrelevant in terms of its analytic status as a "self-
structuring" mechanism. Disparate accounts would have the same "self-
structuring" status. Even when one account is adopted by people as the
"correct account of self," that is itself an account for managing practical
circumstances.

A second self-structuring strategy employed by Agnes was to carefully
monitor other females' accounts of their autobiographies (which they, but
not she, took for granted) so that she could fashion for herself and others
not just a typical but an "ideal" female history. Most important, Agnes
learned how to construct a female biography while simultaneously "doing"
one. That is, she had to manage herself as a "typical female" while simultaneously using others' accounts of self and their routine actions as

embedded instructions on what a female "is," "was," and "should be" in the first place. As Garfinkel describes this strategy:

> Agnes was required to live up to the standards of conduct, appearance, skills, feelings, motives, and aspirations while simultaneously learning what these standards were . . . ; they had to be learned in situations in which she was treated by others as knowing them in the first place as a matter of course. [P. 147]

Agnes used her autobiographical accounts to document her "original femininity" and so undergird her claim to "natural normal female-ness." In fact, her autobiographical accounts were so idealized that Garfinkel and other medical staff referred to her "presentation of the 120 per cent female" (p. 129).

The simultaneity of "learning" while "doing" was frequently used to manage practical circumstances. For example, Agnes learned the general principles of cooking while being instructed by her boyfriend's mother in how to prepare particular dishes he liked. Her boyfriend taught her how to be a "lady" when he criticized the behavior of some mutual female friends.

Agnes had to "do" her femininity while being constantly alert to possible detection of her anatomical differences. Virtually everything that the rest of us take for granted about the everyday world and our place within it as males or females had to be carefully managed by Agnes. Garfinkel (1967:181) provides a nice summary of what might be called "doing gender":

> Agnes' methodological practices are our sources of authority for the finding, and recommended study policy, that normally sexed persons are cultural events in societies whose character as visible orders of practical activities consist of members' recognition and production practices. We learned from Agnes, who treated sexed persons as cultural events that members make happen, that members' practices alone produce the observable-tellable-normal sexuality of persons, and do so only, entirely, exclusively in actual, singular, particular occasions through actual witnessed displays of common talk and conduct.

Agnes achieved her status as a natural normal female through displays of common talk and conduct. Because she could not take herself for granted as a natural normal female, her self-structuring practices are transparent. But in unnoticed ways we all make our sex status happen through the same types of practices as Agnes used.

Just as sex can be viewed as one's accomplishment, so can other aspects of self. Basically, our various statuses as professional, adult, mother or father, student, and so on are available as factual affairs through displays of common talk and conduct. Moreover, how often do we all "pass" as a case of "the real thing" while learning simultaneously what that is in the first place?

Hadden and Lester (1979) also studied self, relying on basic ethnomethodological tenets. Their focus—the *verbal* production of "self"—is, however, somewhat different from Garfinkel's. As they outline their study:

> Our topic of empirical and conceptual inquiry is the set of verbal practices through which persons assemble and display who they are while in the presence of, and in interaction with, others. We refer to this set of production practices as the *identifying process.* . . . Identifying is constituted by the practical activities through which people *produce verbal "markers" of who they are and the methods they use to assemble those markers into patterns while in interaction with others.* [P. 36; emphasis added]

Hadden and Lester are interested in the formal properties of accounts through which bits and pieces of "self" are identified and assembled into a pattern. How one identifies him/her "self" is partly dependent on the "interactional project." So, for example, "self" can be the explicit topic of conversation, or it can be secondary to other matters. The way in which self is identified and displayed varies accordingly. Moreover, identifications of self depend on *assumptions* about the Other. For example, an actor assembles his/her autobiography in different ways if s/he perceives the Other to value or devalue the Actor as an instance of a social type. Hadden and Lester elaborate many verbal practices people use in identifying and displaying self (a description of these is beyond the scope of this paper). The general analytic stance is reflected in part of their conclusion:

> Self-identifying consists of people proffering and patterning documents of who they are. As such, the "factual content" of such productions was not of specific interest. Instead, the work of "talking identities" creates the factual character of who one "really is" in any given situation. Such "realities" are elaborated or transformed as [identifying strategies] occur in the course of interaction. Thus, people do not merely add to previous identifying activity, but continually construct and reconstruct who they are, how they became what they are, and what they will be in the future. In slightly different terms, identity is an assembled corpus (Zimmerman and Pollner, 1970), which derives its sense of the factual from the particular creative work of the moment. [P. 38]

There are other ethnomethodological studies which have relevance for the concept of self. For example, Cicourel (1968) shows how probation officers assemble juveniles' identities. The ways in which bits and pieces of a juvenile's conduct are assembled into a pattern by the officer becomes the young person's identity, at least in terms of official consequences. The "pattern" receives its organization through the officer's verbal depictions, and the bits and pieces of conduct derive their sense from the constructed pattern. So, assembled differently, a particular behavior of a youth could be (1) merely seen but unnoticed, (2) a precursor to delinquency, or (3) part of an immediate and "serious" problem. Similarly, teachers actively construct identities for children-as-students through such commonplace events as conversing with other teachers over lunch; meanwhile, from the standpoint of the member of society, the teachers are merely describing reality (see Leiter, 1971, 1974). Thus, just as one's accounts assemble one's own self, so does one assemble others' selves.

Ethnomethodologists are fundamentally uninterested in the substantive content of self or identity. Their perspective rests at a different, perhaps more basic, level of analysis. They draw attention, instead, to the ways in which self, like everything else, is made available as such through natural language. Natural language—its structure (see Sacks, 1972; Sacks, Schegloff, and Jefferson, 1974) and the ways it is used in the everyday world to render the everyday world—is the focal point.

EXISTENTIAL SOCIOLOGY

Existential sociology's subject is human experience-in-the-world in all of its forms. A central orientation of this perspective is the fusion of rational thought, action, and feeling.

One major resource for existential sociology is, of course, existential philosophy. Key figures in this school of thought are Martin Heidegger (1962), Søren Kierkegaard (1946), Jean-Paul Sartre (1956), Albert Camus (1955), and Friedrich Nietzsche (1968). Other sources of insight come from phenomenology and ethnomethodology (see the preceding two sections of this chapter). Within sociology, important theorists and researchers are Peter Manning (1973), Edward Tiryakian (1962, 1965, 1968), Jack Douglas (1977), and the other authors appearing in this volume.

Existential Critiques of Society and Science

Edward Tiryakian (1968:75) refers to existentialists as "insurgents." There are two aspects to this insurgency, one dealing with the nature of social reality, the other with traditional science.

To a significant extent, existentialist ideas emerged as a reaction to social change in Western societies and what were perceived as its negative consequences. The issue is not social change in general but only particular types of change, as Tiryakian (1968:77) notes:

In our postwar world, characterized by significant changes
and upheavals in social structure both at home and abroad,
a philosophy which seriously addresses itself to the pre-
dicament of the human subject in a world no longer typified
by the stability of institutions and the permanence of things
around us is in consonance with the reality felt by many.

Not only are institutions deemed more unstable than in previous times;
they are also seen as more remote from people's daily lives. In other words,
they have become abstractions; they are difficult to concretize. And the
more remote and abstract institutions appear, the more people experience
them as coercive.

The existentialist critique of modern society is at odds with the traditional
sociological view. For example, writing in the late 1800s, Emile Durkheim
(1964) saw the interdependency of people in modern society as a positive
source of both cohesiveness and individuality. In contrast, existentialists
see the increased scale and "massification" of society as deindividuating
forces (Manning, 1973:216).

Existentialists also alert us to the *inauthentic* nature of many of our
associations in modern society: we reduce both ourselves and others to
objects. That is, many or even most of our associations with others take
the form of "it-it" communication (see Tiryakian, 1968:77–78). This form
of association prevents people from experiencing the responsibilities, pain,
intimacy, and ecstasy of subject-subject communication. Moreover, "inauthenticity in discourse implies that I am more motivated to hear myself
talk and to have others hear me talk than I am interested in sharing in-
tercourse with others" (Tiryakian, 1968:81). This remark is an example of
I-it association: others are but a vehicle for self-expression. But the inauthentic nature of the interaction renders the goal of self-expression a
dismal failure, and what began as an I-it association becomes an it-it one.
Along with objectification of self and others, manipulation is a key form
and property of inauthentic interaction. Finally, early existentialists abhorred
the conformity and complacence of human beings in modern society while
simultaneously recognizing that these individual and group characteristics
are the product of the abstract, remote, and coercive nature of institutions.

Existentialist thought joins phenomenology and ethnomethodology (and,
to a lesser extent, the dramaturgical perspective) in criticizing traditional
social science (see Manning, 1973). At base, existentialism is a reaction
against the traditional social sciences' overemphasis on the role of reason
in human existence and the consequent neglect of the nonrational components of thought, interpretation, and action. At the minimum, the cognitive and emotional aspects of experience are totally divorced by most
scholars. Even other nontraditional perspectives play to reason: "definitions of the situation" (symbolic interaction), "accounts" (ethnomethodology), and "presentation of self" (dramaturgical sociology) all imply the

primacy of cognition and rational constructions. This fragmentation does not correspond with actual lived experience. Existentialists therefore reject this stance, which they say results in an "image of the self as an isolated, bleak, negative, lifeless, past-determined, choiceless creature" (Tiryakian, 1968:76).

Existential sociologists have also taken traditional methods to task on other grounds. First, contributing to the fragmentation and destruction of people's experiential integrity is the traditional sociologist's inclination to study the social world in artificial environments (e.g., laboratory experiments, structured surveys). Second, as discussed above, traditional sociologists atomize their subject matter, e.g., fail to integrate intentions, interpretations, logical thought, actions, and feelings, and, third, they present purified and rationalized versions of the research process (see Johnson, 1977). Even in loosely structured field research, the investigator makes it appear that s/he sequentially entered the research site, gained rapport, gathered data, and exited the setting—all with a purely scientific stance. This is inauthentic communication and probably untrue. What is more important, the integrity of research-activity-as-human experience is lost. A final issue is that sociologists of all persuasions have sought universal laws about the social world before there is adequate description of lived experience.

> Sociology's emphasis now should be on exploring and understanding the contrasts and innovations in social life instead of prematurely reaching for universals. [Kotarba, 1979:349]

Self through Existentialism: Basic Tenets

Situations, experiences, human associations, and more generally, the total human being are all richly complex, multifaceted, and unique. At the same time, experiences and "selves" have a holistic integrity of their own. The existentialists seek to retain these qualities—to reflect these qualities—on both a theoretical level and in the research process (see Fontana, 1982; Manning, 1973).

This view of reality means that life is not a script that people simply learn and act out. Nor is consensual meaning the primary basis for human existence. Quite the opposite. Meaning can be fundamentally problematic, particularly the meaning of one's existence (see Fontana, 1982; Manning, 1973; Kotarba, 1979).

> . . . the existential image of the subject offers a challenging contrast [to traditional notions]: the human agent is seen as a volitional being who seeks to find meaning in his transactions with the reality to which he is intrinsically

> related by the nature of his existence; he is a being who
> fundamentally seeks meaning and a sense of life. [Tir-
> yakian, 1968:76]

Existentialists are committed to viewing social organization, associations, and meanings as constantly fluctuating, being destroyed, repaired,
and/or transformed.

> Man's existence is fundamentally problematic, both for
> man as actor and for anyone who would understand his
> existence. Man is varied, changeable, uncertain, conflict-
> ful, and partially free to choose what he will do and what
> he will become, because he must do so to exist in a world
> that is varied, changeable, uncertain, and conflictful.
> [Douglas, 1977:14]

It is not meaning, experiences, and selves, etc., in the abstract that concern
existentialists; what they are concerned with is *concrete* realities:

> Existential "analysis" is primarily a philosophizing en-
> deavor that aims at describing the concrete reality of the
> human subject; there is an implicit rejection of explaining
> human action in terms of abstract categories . . . which,
> in effect, reduce the vital whole to a lifeless part. [Tir-
> yakian, 1968:75]

More specifically, the *concrete situation* is an important concept for existentialism. It is not merely an environment or "context" within which
activity occurs, nor is it simply a stage to manipulate. In essence, a concrete
situation belongs to a concrete person; that is, situations are personal:

> [A situation] is an actualization of the locale as a result of
> the meaning the person finds in it. The situation thus is
> always to an important extent personal—it is *my* situation,
> *your* situation, *his* situation. . . . In an authentic engage-
> ment, the totality of the person is committed to his situ-
> ation. [Ibid., p. 84]

The existential sociologist's concern with reflecting the multifaceted nature of existence in concrete situations requires a particular methodological
stance. Wilhelm Dilthey (1961) argued that to understand human beings
one must empathize with their concrete realities. He used the term "Verstehen" to refer to this empathetic understanding. Dilthey, in turn, influenced Max Weber's (1947) conception of Verstehen: to comprehend social
action requires that one seek a deep understanding of people's interpretations of, and the meanings associated with, human activity and the social
world more generally. Dilthey and Weber were not existentialists. However, Tiryakian (1962) argues that there is an affinity between the concept
of Verstehen and the stance of existentialism: to understand concrete real-

ity requires one to be fully immersed in that reality. Therefore, only natural settings are studied by existential sociologists, and the researcher is not to regard him/herself as an outside observer or as a simple recorder of reality. S/he too is a human being immersed in a concrete situation. Moreover, the existential sociologist's own experiences of a situation are used overtly in interpretation, description, and the generation of conceptual insights.

It is important to note that the methodological tenets outlined are not unique to the existential perspective. Symbolic interactionists and phenomenological sociologists rely on similar procedures. What is unique is the combination of subject matter and methodological principles.

A cardinal tenet of all existential sociology is that feelings are as important in human life as reason, rationality, and rational codes of conduct. Feelings or emotions pervade all aspects of our lives and are an authentic way to relate to self and the world (see Manning, 1973:210).

> Love and hate, ecstasy and agony, pleasure and pain, lust
> and satiety, hope and despair, satisfaction and frustration,
> excitement and boredom, sympathy and spite, full and
> hungry, tasty and foul, comfort and discomfort. These and
> a vast number of other feelings, named and unnameable,
> are the core of our being, the stuff of our everyday lives.
> . . . They come before symbolic meaning and values, lead
> us continually to reinterpret, hide from, evade, overthrow,
> and recreate thoughts and values. [Douglas, 1977:51]

The self is a sentient self for existentialists (Manning, 1973:212), but not simply so. Rather, feelings and rationality are *fused*. Either one or both may dominate in any particular situation, as Douglas (1977:40) points out:

> The crucial thing to recognize is that there is a continuum
> of feeling independence and dominance over social rules,
> ranging from the situation in which either profound feel-
> ings or (perceived) profound situational threats (to feelings
> in the short run) sweep away considerations of social rules
> . . . to the situation in which the individual is a moral
> absolutist committed with profound feelings of fear (e.g.,
> pangs of conscience) to the social rules.

Moreover, situations that appear to be dominated by conformity to rules and norms may, in fact, be motivated by feelings. People may follow rules out of fear of reprisal or anticipated shame and guilt if they deviate. Feelings may totally dominate a situation, e.g., they may preside over externally imposed repressions, ideals, and norms, etc. Kotarba (1977) illustrates this in his study of the chronic-pain experience. It should be pointed out that Kotarba began this study with his own experience of pain.

> A person with chronic pain rarely conforms. . . . One's
> pain is first and foremost a private problem. When the
> pain is perceived as unbearable or a symptom of a more
> serious health problem, professional care is sought ac-
> cording to a person's practical knowledge of the healing
> arts. As pain persists, one feels little moral obligation to
> remain dependent on the definitions and treatments of
> scientific medicine. The desire for physical relief tran-
> scends any notion of how one ought to behave when sick.
> Thus, educated and sophisticated people—including many
> doctors of medicine—consult acupuncturists, chiroprac-
> tors, and other healers who offer hope of relief when sci-
> entific medicine fails. . . . The person with chronic pain
> adopts the definitions of others when they are meaningful
> to the management of the pain. But this is frontwork, not
> reality. The primary definitions of being sick come from
> the person's body. [P. 272]

Besides definitions and feelings, Kotarba also points to the importance of
the *physical self.* For existentialists, body images and sensations may be
fused with feelings and perhaps with rationality (Manning, 1973:211).

Just as rational codes of conduct may collide with feelings, so people
often find themselves having to manage conflicting emotions. Resolving
these conflicts may even be a life-long task for many people, and the ways
in which they deal with these conflicts in concrete situations are one source
of creativity, improvisation, and new self-feelings.

Existential sociologists reflexively turn the role of feelings inward. That
is, feelings rather than so-called objective observation can dominate research situations. At the minimum, the researcher is subject to all the
conflicts and quests for meaning that other people experience. An exem-
plary illustration is provided by John Johnson's (1977) study of welfare
agencies. While attending to the subject of study, his field notes simultaneously depict his experiences as a researcher, which included many
nonrational elements. Here is one segment:

> Not sure whether these comments have any relevance
> whatsoever, but I guess I'll add a couple of remarks to the
> notes to record some of my personal thoughts which I
> haven't noted before. I've been going down to [Metro] for
> nearly six weeks now. Even though I probably appear cu-
> cumber-cool to everybody down there, I am, for the most
> part, scared to death of some of these people, and in many
> cases I don't know any good reasons for this. Every morn-
> ing around seven forty-five, as I'm driving to the office, I
> begin to get this pain in the left side of my back, and the
> damn thing stays there usually until around eleven, when
> I've made my daily plans for accompanying one of the

> workers in the field. Since nearly all of the workers remain
> in the office until around eleven or twelve, and since there's
> only one extra chair in the two units and no extra desks
> yet, those first two or three hours are sheer agony for me
> every damn day. Trying to be busy without hassling any
> one worker too much is like playing chinese checkers hop-
> ping to and fro, from here to there, with no place to hide.
> [P. 211]

From several existentialist works, we can distill basic features of what
is referred to as the "existential self" or the "really me." (1) A person
accepts personal responsibility for self and associations with others. (2) The
self is always in the process of "becoming." (Regarding these two features,
Tiryakian [1968:81] notes: "The becoming-ness of the existential self, which
is inherent in the existential model, is constituted in part by the voluntary
acceptance of responsibility." (3) Authentic, i.e., subject-oriented, communication expresses the "real self"; "subject-oriented discourse is communion: it is meant for and it expresses the self's real consciousness of
the other as subject" (Tiryakian, 1968:81). However, most of our actions
fall somewhere between total authenticity and total inauthenticity. On the
surface, "performances" (in the dramaturgical sense) are fundamentally
an inauthentic mode of communication and interaction. However, wearing
"identity masks" may actually serve the existential self, for it

> protects the existential self from the gaze of others . . .
> until such time as the others are identified as being of the
> same *communitas* as the self. . . . Its protective function
> is to hide the true feelings of the self, for the true feelings
> of the self are what animates the person, what sustains
> and propels him in the fundamental existential process of
> becoming. Since such feelings, being at the core of the
> existential self, can only be expressed in intimacy and
> privacy, the mask enables the person to circulate freely
> in public life, particularly though not wholly in situations
> where the subject experiences a status of subordination
> vis-à-vis the other. [Tiryakian, 1968:82–83]

Additionally, performances may be used to arouse feelings in others or to
persuade, influence, and cajole them. Always beneath the performance
aspect of concrete situations are emotions, e.g., potential shame, hope, or
despair.

It is important to realize that, unlike other perspectives discussed, existentialism posits a "real self," one moved by a fusion of feelings and
thoughts. Moreover, this perspective (unlike others) makes clear value
judgments about self, associations with others, etc.; for example, it enables
one to speak of authentic vs. inauthentic communication.

REFLECTIONS

After reading this chapter, one might conclude simply that there are at least six different perspectives on self. Moreover, if each perspective has something to contribute, one might ask why no one has completed a synthesis of all the perspectives on self. It would seem logical that such a project would provide a comprehensive conception of self.

With slightly more reflection, one might conclude that six different perspectives on "self" have been presented but not six different perspectives on the *same* phenomenon, topic, and concept. It is that conclusion I want to address by probing the characteristics of a "theoretical perspective."

Many characteristics of theoretical perspectives resemble the properties of windows. For the moment, I wish to treat windows as a metaphor.

Windows vary in size. Peering through a small one may focus my attention on a small object or a narrow slice of a broad vista, a slice in which some particular objects dominate the scene. I will simultaneously lose the possibility of observing the relationship between the object or "slice" I can see and others that are not in view; yet, at that moment of gazing or peering, I am not likely to think about what I am not seeing. On the other hand, if I move from the tiny window to a large one, I may become so absorbed by the whole of the landscape that I do not see the particular objects within it.

A window also fronts in a particular direction. Suppose, for a moment, that you are in a strange city for the first time. As you gaze out a hotel window that faces north, you may recognize that the window provides only one view of the city and that another vantage point would present a different picture. However, the longer you stay in the city, the more likely it is that gazing out of the north window will become *the* routine viewpoint and the less likely you will be to recognize that you have only a selective view of the city.

Windows also vary in shape, texture, and thickness, among other things, all of which affect what one sees. More generally, the properties of windows selectively filter what one sees. At every moment that one spends gazing through a window, that activity forces one to *not* see as well. Each window provides both a vantage point for seeing and a limited array of objects.

The characteristics of windows themselves are only one source of variation in, and limitations placed upon, seeing and perceiving. A second set of factors involves the person who sees. For example, our person in the hotel room will bring to that setting a storehouse of memories of previous experiences of visiting strange cities and of peering through windows in general and hotel windows in particular. Such experiences will filter the form and content of looking through "this" window. Also, one's intention in gazing from windows and the time spent in doing so will affect how and what one perceives. Moreover, a person may vary his/her position at a window. Kneeling or standing on a chair, looking directly out versus turning one's head from something else to look out the window, taking eyeglasses off or putting them on will affect what one sees.

A third factor is also involved, namely, the condition of the window itself. For example, one's observations may differ if a thin film of smoke is left on the window, if it is cleaned, or if sprinklers splash mud on it. Here again, one is unlikely to notice that one's observations are other than a reflection of "what is."

What we know about windows and about gazing from them is a somewhat simplified version of the characteristics of a theoretical perspective and the consequences of adopting it.

First, the characteristics of a perspective affect both *how* the adopter of the perspective engages in observation and *what* the adopter sees. The scope or breadth of a perspective affects one's view of reality. For example, a conversational analyst "sees" overlapping speech and silences lasting a fraction of a second. S/he doesn't "see" institutions and legal orders. "Self" for the conversational analyst is "accomplished" in naturally occurring conversation. The normative theorist sees interlocking statuses and roles as major contributors to self—what one is—and would not be likely to perceive, much less notice, the structure of speaker turns in conversation. Between these, the symbolic interactionist sees and attends to definitions and interpretations of self as they arise through role-taking. It is also important to recognize that theoretical breadth and depth are likely to be negatively correlated. For example, Sacks, Schegloff, and Jefferson (1974) have taught us more about turn-taking practices in conversation than most of us need or want to know. In reverse, Parsons' theory of the social system never mentions conversation, let alone turn-taking. Similarly, Garfinkel (1967) details Agnes' methods for passing as a natural normal female while providing no indication that he recognizes the sexist bias in creating feminine and masculine roles in the first place. (In a different social structure Agnes would need neither to "pass" nor to undergo a sex-change operation.)

The texture of a perspective as well as its constituent concepts also filters the social world, the self, and interpretations of both. For example, compare the imagery connoted by the term "role-set" versus "internalized dialogue." In the former, the self is relatively static for normative sociology; in the latter, it is a dynamic process for symbolic interaction. Again, what is "self" if we use the concepts "presentation of self" versus the "really me" or "existential self"? For each perspective, the word "self" is a symbol. But it is not a significant symbol because each perspective has a different empirical referent for the term.

If we consider the characteristics of perspectives alone, we will see that they lead and direct the adopter in terms of the phenomena studied, the concepts used to theorize about phenomena, and the scope of the inquiry. In simpler terms, a perspective is a way of both seeing and not seeing.

Moreover, the characteristics of the adopter add to the variability just described. The degree to which one is committed to a perspective, one's previous scholarly work in using a perspective, one's previous education in and use of alternative perspectives, one's career and status goals and one's norms for scholarly productivity may all enter into the particular way one adopts a perspective and into what one takes as a subject of inquiry. That is, just as using the perspective filters perception, cognition, and interpretation, so do a scholar's biographical characteristics filter the use of a perspective. This double filtering, combined with the existence of many perspectives, renders consensus about the nature of the self almost impossible. Moreover, there is disagreement on a priori issues, such as the appropriate level of analysis and the relationship between observation and the empirical world. For example, symbolic interactionists are concerned with *definitions* of self, while the ethnomethodologists dive beneath that concept to address the formal properties of natural-language use, and the normative theorist generally takes definitional processes for granted in order to study social structure (from which the *individual* can be derived as a logical consequence).

Finally, as I have perhaps already implied, the adopter acts on the perspective, and this adds a third layer of selective filtering. For example, scholars interpret the meaning of classical works about a particular perspective in different ways, and they use these interpretations in their own work. They also develop favorite concepts within a perspective. Through time, then, some concepts may fade, while others come to dominate a perspective. Naturally, this affects theory construction. Alternatively, a favored research method may be combined with a perspective and affect the content of subsequent scholarly activity. In these and other ways, interaction between scholar and perspective can have a significant impact on theory. This has certainly been the case with most, if not all, the perspectives I have addressed in this chapter.

Thus, I am not convinced that the "self" is something that is simply defined differently according to each perspective or that each perspective simply presents different "aspects" of the self. I suspect, instead, that those using each perspective have observed different phenomena, and I therefore doubt that integration is possible by merely piecing together the different conceptions. One would have to seek integration of different phenomena. The open-ended method of inquiry in existential sociology appears to be a sound beginning for such a venture.

References

Bales, Robert. 1950. *Interaction Process Analysis: A Method for the Study of Small Groups*. Cambridge, Mass.: Addison-Wesley.

Becker, Ernest. 1962. "The Self as a Locus of Linguistic Causality." Pp. 101–15 in Ernest Becker, ed., *The Birth and Death of Meaning*. Glencoe, Ill.: Free Press.

Becker, Howard. 1953. "Becoming a Marijuana User." *American Journal of Sociology* 59:235–42.

———. 1963. *Outsiders: Studies in the Sociology of Deviance*. New York: Free Press of Glencoe.

Berger, Peter. 1963. *Invitation to Sociology*. New York: Doubleday.

Bittner, Egon. 1963. "Radicalism and the Organization of Social Movements." *American Sociological Review* 28:928–40.

———. 1965. "The Concept of Organization." *Social Research* 32:239–58.

———. 1967. "The Police on Skid Row." *American Sociological Review* 32:699–715.

Blumer, Herbert. 1956. "Sociological Analysis and the Variable." *American Sociological Review* 21:683–90.

———. 1962. "Society as Symbolic Interaction." Pp. 179–92 in Arnold Rose, ed., *Human Behavior and Social Process*. Boston: Houghton-Mifflin.

———. 1969. *Symbolic Interactionism*. Englewood Cliffs, N.J.: Prentice-Hall.

Brissett, Dennis, and Charles Edgeley, eds. 1975. *Life as Theater: A Dramaturgical Sourcebook*. Chicago: Aldine.

Burke, Kenneth. 1945. *A Grammar of Motives*. New York: Prentice-Hall.

———. 1965. *Permanence and Change*. New York: Bobbs-Merrill.

———. 1966. *Language as Symbolic Action*. Berkeley: University of California Press.

Camus, Albert. 1955. *The Myth of Sisyphus*. Translated by J. O'Brien. New York: Vintage Books.

Carr, David. 1974. *Phenomenology and the Problem of History*. Evanston, Ill.: Northwestern University Press.

Cicourel, Aaron. 1964. *Method and Measurement in Sociology*. New York: Free Press.

———. 1968. *The Social Organization of Juvenile Justice*. New York: Wiley.

———. 1974. *Cognitive Sociology*. London: Penguin.

Cooley, Charles Horton. 1902. *Human Nature and the Social Order*. New York: Scribner's.

Denzin, Norman. 1970. *The Research Art*. New York: McGraw-Hill.

Dewey, John. 1925. *Experience and Nature*. Chicago: Open Court.

Dickens, David. 1979. "Phenomenology." Pp. 325–47 in Scott McNall, ed., *Theoretical Perspectives in Sociology*. New York: St. Martin's Press.

Dilthey, William. 1961. *Patterns and Meaning in History*. Edited and translated by H. P. Rickman. New York: Harper & Row.

Douglas, Jack. 1977. "Existential Sociology." Pp. 3–73 in Jack Douglas and John M. Johnson, eds., *Existential Sociology*. Cambridge, Eng.: Cambridge University Press.

Douglas, Jack, and John M. Johnson, eds. 1977. *Existential Sociology*. Cambridge, Eng.: Cambridge University Press.

Durkheim, Emile. 1950. *The Rules of Sociological Method* (1895). Translated by Sarah A. Solovay and John H. Mueller. New York: Free Press.

———. 1964. *The Division of Labor in Society*. Translated by George Simpson. New York: Free Press.

Emerson, Joan. 1970a. "Nothing Unusual Is Happening." Pp. 208–22 in Tamotsu Shibutani, ed., *Human Nature and Collective Behavior: Papers in Honor of Herbert Blumer*. Englewood Cliffs, N.J.: Prentice-Hall.

———. 1970b. "Behavior in Private Places: Sustaining Definitions of Reality in Gynecological Examinations." Pp. 74–97 in Hans Dreitzel, ed., *Recent Sociology 2*. New York: Macmillan.

Fontana, Andrea. 1980. "Toward a Complex Universe: Existential Sociology." In Jack Douglas et al., *Introduction to the Sociologies of Everyday Life*. Boston: Allyn & Bacon.

Garfinkel, Harold. 1959. "Aspects of the Problem of Common Sense Knowledge of Social Structures." *Transactions of the World Congress of Sociology* 4:51–65. Milan: Stressa.

———. 1960. "The Rational Properties of Scientific and Common Sense Activities." *Behavioral Science* 5:72–83.

———. 1962. "Common Sense Knowledge of Social Structures: The Documentary Method of Interpretation." In Jordan Scher, ed., *Theories of the Mind*. New York: Free Press.

———. 1967. *Studies in Ethnomethodology*. Englewood Cliffs, N.J.: Prentice-Hall.

Garfinkel, Harold, and Harvey Sacks. 1970. "On Formal Structures of Practical Activities." Pp. 338–66 in Edward Tiryakian and John McKinney, eds., *Theoretical Sociology*. New York: Appleton-Century-Crofts.

Glaser, Barney, and Anselm Strauss. 1965. *Awareness of Dying*. Chicago: Aldine.

Goffman, Erving. 1952. "Cooling the Mark Out: Some Aspects of Adaptation to Failure." *Psychiatry* 25:451–63.

———. 1955. "On Face-Work: An Analysis of Ritual Elements in Social Interaction." *Psychiatry* 18:213–31.

———. 1959. *The Presentation of Self in Everyday Life*. New York: Doubleday.

———. 1961a. *Asylums: Essays on the Social Situation of Mental Patients and Other Inmates*. New York: Doubleday.

———. 1961b. *Encounters*. New York: Bobbs-Merrill.

———. 1963. *Behavior in Public Places*. New York: Free Press.

———. 1967. *Interaction Ritual: Essays in Face-to-Face Behavior*. Garden City, N.Y.: Doubleday.

———. 1968. *Stigma: Notes on the Management of Spoiled Identity*. Englewood Cliffs, N.J.: Prentice-Hall.

———. 1974. *Frame Analysis*. New York: Harper & Row.

Gurwitsch, Aron. 1964. *The Field of Consciousness*. Pittsburgh: Duquesne University Press.

———. 1966. *Studies in Phenomenology and Psychology*. Evanston, Ill.: Northwestern University Press.

Hadden, Stuart C., and Marilyn Lester. 1980. "Talking Identity: People's Practices for Producing 'Self' in Interaction." *Human Studies* 1:34–47.

Heap, James, and Phillip Roth. 1973. "On Phenomenological Sociology." *American Sociological Review* 78:354–67.

Heidegger, Martin. 1962. *Being and Time*. Translated by John Macquarrie and Edward Robinson. New York: Harper & Row.

Husserl, Edmund. 1962. *Ideas: General Introduction to Pure Phenomenology*. Translated by W. Boyce Gibson. New York: Macmillan.

———. 1969. *Formal and Transcendental Logic*. Translated by Dorion Cairns. The Hague: Nijhoff.

———. 1970. *The Crisis of European Sciences and Transcendental Phenomenology*. Translated by David Carr. Evanston, Ill.: Northwestern University Press.

———. 1973. *Cartesian Meditations*. Translated by Dorion Cairns. The Hague: Nijhoff.

James, William. 1892. "The Social Self." Pp. 189–226 in William James, *Psychology*. New York: Holt.

———. 1910. *Psychology: The Briefer Course*. New York: Holt.

Jefferson, Gail. 1972. "Side Sequences." Pp. 294–338 in David Sudnow, ed., *Studies in Ethnomethodology*. New York: Free Press.

———. 1973. "A Case of Precision Timing in Ordinary Conversation: Overlapped Tag-Positioned Address Terms in Closing Sequences." *Semiotica* 9:47–96.

Jehenson, Roger. 1973. "A Phenomenological Approach to the Study of the Formal Organization." Pp. 219–50 in George Psathas, ed., *Phenomenological Sociology: Issues and Applications*. New York: Wiley.

Johnson, John M. 1977. "Behind Rational Appearances: Fusion of Thinking and Feeling in Sociological Research." Pp. 201–28 in Jack Douglas and John M. Johnson, eds., *Existential Sociology*. Cambridge, Eng.: Cambridge University Press.

Kierkegaard, Søren. 1946. *The Concept of Dread*. Translated by Walter Lowrie. Princeton, N.J.: Princeton University Press.

Kitsuse, John, and Aaron Cicourel. 1963. "The Use of Official Statistics." *Social Problems* 11(2):131–39.

Kotarba, Joseph. 1977. "The Chronic Pain Experience." Pp. 257–72 in Jack Douglas and John M. Johnson, eds., *Existential Sociology*. Cambridge, Eng.: Cambridge University Press.

———. 1979. "Existential Sociology." Pp. 348–68 in Scott McNall, ed., *Theoretical Perspectives in Sociology*. New York: St. Martin's Press.

Kuhn, Manford. 1964. "Major Trends in Symbolic Interaction Theory in the Last Twenty-Five Years." *Sociological Quarterly* 5:61–84.

Leiter, Kenneth. 1971. "Telling It Like It Is: A Study of Teachers' Accounts." Ph.D. dissertation, University of California, Santa Barbara.

———. 1974. "Ad hocing in the Schools." In Aaron Cicourel, ed., *Language Use and School Performance*. New York: Academic Press.

Lindesmith, Alfred, Anselm Strauss, and Norman Denzin. 1975. *Social Psychology*. 4th ed. Hinsdale, Ill.: Dryden Press.

Linton, Ralph. 1936. *The Study of Man*. New York: Appleton-Century-Crofts.

Manis, Jerome, and Bernard Meltzer, eds. 1978. *Symbolic Interaction: A Reader in Social Psychology*. 3d ed. Boston: Allyn & Bacon.

Mannheim, Karl. 1962. "On the Interpretation of 'Weltanschauung.' " In P. Kecskemeti, ed., *Essays on the Sociology of Knowledge.* Oxford: Oxford University Press.

Manning, Peter. 1973. "Existential Sociology." *Sociological Quarterly* 14:200–225.

McHugh, Peter. 1968. *Defining the Situation.* Indianapolis: Bobbs-Merrill.

Mead, George Herbert. 1925. "The Genesis of the Self and Social Control." *International Journal of Ethics* 35(3):251–73.

————. 1932. *The Philosophy of the Present.* Chicago: Open Court.

————. 1934. *Mind, Self, and Society.* Edited by Charles W. Morris. Chicago: University of Chicago Press.

————. 1936. *Movements of Thought in the Nineteenth Century.* Edited by M. H. Moore. Chicago: University of Chicago Press.

————. 1938. *The Philosophy of the Act.* Edited by Charles W. Morris. Chicago: University of Chicago Press.

————. 1964. *On Social Psychology.* Edited by Anselm Strauss. Chicago: University of Chicago Press.

Meltzer, Bernard. 1978. "Mead's Social Psychology." Pp. 15–26 in Jerome Manis and Bernard Meltzer, eds., *Symbolic Interaction: A Reader in Social Psychology.* 3d ed. Boston: Allyn & Bacon.

Merleau-Ponty, Maurice. 1962. *Phenomenology of Perception.* Translated by Colin Smith. London: Routledge & Kegan Paul.

————. 1964. *Sense and Non-Sense.* Translated by Herbert L. Dreyfus and Patricia A. Dreyfus. Evanston, Ill.: Northwestern University Press.

Merton, Robert. 1957. *Social Theory and Social Structure.* New York: Free Press.

Messinger, Sheldon, Harold Sampson, and Robert Towne. 1962. "Life as Theatre: Some Reality." *Sociometry* 25:98–110.

Natanson, Maurice. 1970. "Phenomenology and Typification: A Study in the Philosophy of Alfred Schutz." *Social Research* 37:1–27.

Nietzsche, Friedrich. 1968. *The Portable Nietzsche.* Edited by Walter Kaufmann. New York: Viking.

Parsons, Talcott, and Edward Shils. 1951. *Toward a General Theory of Action.* Cambridge, Mass.: Harvard University Press.

Pollner, Melvin. 1974. "Mundane Reasoning." *Philosophy of Social Sciences* 4(1):35–54.

Psathas, George, ed. 1973. *Phenomenological Sociology: Issues and Applications.* New York: Wiley.

Sacks, Harvey. 1963. "Sociological Description." *Berkeley Journal of Sociology* 8:1–17.

————. 1972a. "An Initial Investigation of the Usability of Conversational Data for Doing Sociology." Pp. 31–73 in David Sudnow, ed., *Studies in Social Interaction.* Englewood Cliffs, N.J.: Prentice-Hall.

————. 1972b. "On the Analyzability of Stories by Children." In John Gumperz and Dell Hymes, eds., *Directions in Sociolinguistics.* New York: Holt, Rinehart & Winston.

Sacks, Harvey, Emmanuel Schegloff, and Gail Jefferson. 1974. "A Simplest Systematics for the Analysis of Turn-Taking in Conversation." *Language* 50:696–735.

Sartre, Jean-Paul. 1956. *Being and Nothingness.* Translated by Hazel E. Barnes. New York: Philosophical Library.

Schegloff, Emmanuel. 1968. "Sequencing in Conversational Openings." *American Anthropologist* 70:1075–95.

Schutz, Alfred. 1944. "The Stranger: An Essay in Social Psychology.' *American Journal of Sociology* 49(6):499–507.

———. 1945. "The Homecomer." *American Journal of Sociology* 50(5):369–76.

———. 1962. *Collected Papers I: The Problem of Social Reality.* Edited by Maurice Natanson. The Hague: Nijhoff.

———. 1964. *Collected Papers II: Studies in Social Theory.* Edited by Arvid Brodersen. The Hague: Nijhoff.

———. 1966. *Collected Papers III: Studies in Phenomenological Philosophy.* Edited by Aron Gurwitsch. The Hague: Nijhoff.

———. 1967. *The Phenomenology of the Social World.* Translated by George Walsh and Frederick Lehnert. Evanston, Ill.: Northwestern University Press.

———. 1970. *On Phenomenology and Social Relations.* Edited by Helmut R. Wagner. Chicago: University of Chicago Press.

Shibutani, Tamotsu. 1955. "Reference Groups as Perspectives." *American Journal of Sociology* 60:562–69.

———, ed. 1970. *Human Nature and Collective Behavior.* Englewood Cliffs, N.J.: Prentice-Hall.

Simmel, Georg. 1950. *The Sociology of Georg Simmel.* Edited and translated by Kurt Wolff. New York: Free Press.

Spiegelberg, Herbert. 1960. *The Phenomenological Movement.* The Hague: Nijhoff.

Stone, Gregory. 1962. "Appearance and the Self." Pp. 86–118 in Arnold Rose, ed., *Human Behavior and Social Processes.* Boston: Houghton-Mifflin.

Stone, Gregory, and Harvey Farberman, eds. 1981. *Social Psychology through Symbolic Interaction.* 2d ed. New York: Wiley.

Sudnow, David. 1965. "Normal Crimes." *Social Problems* 12:255–76.

———. 1969. *Passing On: The Social Organization of Dying.* Englewood Cliffs, N.J.: Prentice-Hall.

Thomas, W. I. 1931. *The Unadjusted Girl.* Boston: Little, Brown.

Thomas, W. I., and D. S. Thomas. 1928. *The Child in America.* New York: Knopf.

Tiryakian, Edward. 1962. *Existentialism and Sociologism.* Englewood Cliffs, N.J.: Prentice-Hall.

———. 1965. "Existential Phenomenology and the Sociological Tradition." *American Sociological Review* 30:674–88.

———. 1968. "The Existential Self and the Person." Pp. 75–86 in Chad Gordon and Kenneth Gergen, eds., *The Self in Social Interaction.* New York: Wiley.

Truzzi, Marcello. 1968. "Lilliputians in Gulliver's Land: The Social Role of the Dwarf." Pp. 197–211 in Marcello Truzzi, ed., *The Sociology of Everyday Life.* Englewood Cliffs, N.J.: Prentice-Hall.

Turner, Ralph. 1962. "Role-Taking: Process versus Conformity." Pp. 20–40 in Arnold Rose, ed., *Human Behavior and Social Processes.* Boston: Houghton-Mifflin.

———. 1968. "The Self in Social Interaction." Pp. 93–106 in Chad Gordon and Kenneth Gergen, eds., *The Self in Social Interaction.* New York: Wiley.

———. 1976. "The Real Self: From Institution to Impulse." *American Journal of Sociology* 81(5):989–1016.

Warriner, Charles. 1962. "Groups Are Real: A Reaffirmation." *American Sociological Review* 21:549–54.
Weber, Max. 1946. *From Max Weber: Essays in Sociology.* Translated by Hans Gerth and C. Wright Mills. Oxford: Oxford University Press.
———. 1947. *The Theory of Social and Economic Organization.* Edited and translated by Talcott Parsons. London: Collier-Macmillan.
West, Candace, and Don Zimmerman. 1977. "Women's Place in Everyday Talk: Reflections on Parent-Child Interaction." *Social Problems* 24:521–29.
Wieder, D. Lawrence. 1974. *Language and Social Reality.* The Hague: Mouton.
———. 1977. "Sociology and the Problem of Intersubjectivity." Paper presented at the annual meetings of the American Sociological Association.
Wilson, Thomas P. 1970. "Conceptions of Interaction and Forms of Sociological Explanation." *American Sociological Review* 35:697–709.
Zaner, Richard. 1970. *The Way of Phenomenology.* New York: Pegasus.
———. 1973. "Solitude and Sociality: The Critical Foundations of the Social Sciences." Pp. 25–43 in George Psathas, ed., *Phenomenological Sociology: Issues and Applications.* New York: Wiley.
Zimmerman, Don. 1970a. "The Practicalities of Rule Use." Pp. 221–38 in Jack Douglas, ed., *Understanding Everyday Life.* Chicago: Aldine.
———. 1970b. "Record-Keeping and the Intake Process in a Public Welfare Agency." In Stanton Wheeler, ed., *On Record.* New York: Basic Books.
———. 1974. Preface to D. Lawrence Wieder, ed., *Language and Social Reality.* The Hague: Mouton.
———. 1979. "Ethnomethodology." Pp. 381–96 in Scott McNall, ed., *Theoretical Perspectives in Sociology.* Chicago: University of Chicago Press.
Zimmerman, Don, and Melvin Pollner. 1970. "The Everyday World as a Phenomenon." Pp. 80–103 in Jack Douglas, ed., *Understanding Everyday Life.* Chicago: Aldine.

_____**three**

The Emergence, Security, and Growth of the Sense of Self

Jack D. Douglas

No human being can live for long, except in a state of total dependency, without a reasonably stable but slowly evolving sense of inner self. The sense of inner self, as I shall try to show, is the highest-order centrally integrating sense that our mind has of our overall being-in-the-world. It is this sense of inner self that partially orders the vastly complex subsystems of our mind and orients us continually toward acting in the vastly complex and changing situations we face in everyday life.

Our need for a sense of inner self seems to spring directly from our sense of time, from our immense memories, from the vast complexity and pluralism of our human mind (with its immensely complex interrelations among subsystems), from our awareness of the many potentially conflicting basic emotions and values that might push us in different directions in life at any given time, and from the necessity we face of choosing plans of action to satisfy (optimally) these conflicting emotions and values over relatively long periods of time.

It is our sense of inner self that gives a partially unifying, but changing, form (a general, meaningful gestalt) and an overall sense of slowly shifting direction, of evolving intentionality, to our lives. Without a basically secure sense of self, however taken for granted it is, we are continually threatened by a sense of being formless, meaningless, lost, disintegrated, confused, and shattered, and life becomes constricted, tyrannized by anxiety, dread, and panic. With a basically secure sense of self, one that is largely taken for granted in everyday life, we are free to grow, to expand joyfully in meaningful conquest and creation.

Just as the sense of inner self is the cornerstone of any healthy life, so is it the cornerstone of any basic model of human nature in the social world and, thus, of any theory of social life. All major thinkers concerned with the mind and action (meaningful behavior) have seen the "self" as crucial to understanding mind and action. (Behaviorists and other mechanists, as long as they are consistent, have nothing to say about the "self" because they have nothing to say—except emotional denials—about the mind or

about meaningful social action.) Given the vast complexities and the inherent uncertainties in understanding the human mind and human action,
it is not surprising that they have proposed a very large array of different
ideas and theories about the "self." Since the major alternative ideas and
theories have been well reviewed in other sources (especially in Sherif and
Cantril, 1947; Sherif, 1968; Zurcher, 1977; and Rosenberg, 1979), there is
no need to do so here. Instead, I shall concentrate on what seem to be the
dimensions of "self" that are generally seen as vitally important in understanding the human animal and on my own proposals for improving that
understanding.

It is almost universally recognized by social thinkers that deeply embedded in our common-sense conceptions of our "selves" is some recognition
that each individual has a *conglomerate of selves* along with a more general
sense of self that somehow orders this conglomerate. For example, almost
all social thinkers today distinguish between the self as "I-experience"
and the self as "me-experience." This distinction is normally considered
by social scientists to have been first clearly stated by the pragmatists and
their successors, Charles H. Cooley and George Herbert Mead (see Adler
and Adler, 1980). But Adam Smith (1967) obviously had such distinctions
in mind when he discussed the "looking-glass self." Many psychologists
and therapists have made the distinction independently, and I have no
doubt that it would be easy to find numerous philosophers and other hu-
manists around the world making the same distinction, since it is basic to
our human experience in the world.

All human beings recognized by their fellows as socially competent ("sane"
and "adult") realize, with widely varying degrees of implicitness, that they
are both distinctive, separate, individuated beings and socially defined
beings. As we shall see shortly, the degree varies widely from one culture,
subculture, and individual to another, but sane human adults always know
in some way that they conceptualize themselves and feel about themselves
at the most basic level as both *different from* (individuated from) all other
human beings and as what significant others see us as, that is, as social
beings, beings who are in some way the *same as*, interdependent with, and
even, at times, partially fused by love with the selves of those others. The
part of us that is different from the others is the "subjective I," the willing,
intending person. The part of us that is socially defined, that anchors us
to the social world, that embeds our beings in the way significant others
react to us, is the "social me," what others see in the "I."

The socially defined aspect of the self-conglomerate is the easy part to
get at because it is the more public, more symbolized, more verbalized,
more presented, and thus more visible and easily grasped aspect of the
whole self system. Who am I? What is my self or identity as a social being?
I am the son of *x*, the husband and father of *y* and *z*, the citizen of this
country, and so on and on. These social identifications, which are normally

communicated by names or labels that embody typifications of emotion-laden, rule-governed, and expected behaviors ("roles"), become self-identifications or parts of the self-conglomerate to the degree that we accept them or identify our "self" with them and commit ourselves to them emotionally.

But here exactly is the sticking point in theories of the self. The most widely accepted sociological theory of the self, the interactionist theory of Cooley and Mead, as well as most theories in social psychology and psychology, see both the social selves and the individuated self, the "I," as in some way the product, the effect, of social reactions to the individual. In oversimplified terms, they see even the "I" as either determined by or almost totally constrained by the reactions of others to the individual. The "me's" of an individual are clearly "looking-glass selves," reflections of ourselves that we see in other's reactions to our selves. But what happens to the "I," the individuated self? In most sociological theories the "I" becomes little more than the "stream of consciousness" taking awareness of or reflecting upon these reflections of our social actions. (Some theorists even define the self as the sum total of an individual's experiences.) The individuated self becomes a composite of—that is, a summed-up reflection of—the many social reflections of the individual.

Only the most extreme structural or behavioristic theories see the individuated self as some simple additive reflection of all the external social reflections. As Rosenberg (1979), Zurcher (1977), and others have argued, our world, and probably any social world, is far too complex, changing, and conflictful for any individual to develop a unifying, integrating conception of himself simply by summing up in some way the social reactions to him. Consider, for example, the implications of "adolescent rebellion" for any extreme form of the looking-glass-self theory.

While overt adolescent rebellion is not universal in human societies, it is extremely widespread. (It is even found quite frequently in other social animals. This, combined with its widespread appearance in human societies, has led Edward Wilson [1975] to suggest that there is a genetic basis for conflicts between parents and adolescent offspring.) The essence of adolescent rebellion is the adolescent's partial rejection of or outright rebellion against the parents' attempts to determine his patterns of actions and his self-image. Instead of meekly seeing himself in the mirror of his parents' ideas and values for his self, the adolescent shatters (or at least cracks) the mirror and belligerently insists on their seeing him as a new person, as a self of his own choosing that is in conflict with their values and desires.

A relatively simple, unconflictful, and unchanging society might well serve an individual as a largely acceptable looking-glass for creating his self. This may well be one reason why anthropologists have reported at times that they have found primitive societies with little sense of self;

either the self is largely undifferentiated from society, or, at the least, the two tend to merge, even partially fuse, in individuals' everyday experience. But few human societies are like that today, and certainly no civilization has ever approximated the condition of totally static equilibrium and social harmony.

Colin Turnbull (1972), for example, has argued that most primitives are so completely enmeshed in a matrix of kin and other social relationships that they conceive of their personalities and, presumably, their selves as social. Such conclusions are no doubt overdrawn, largely as a result of the great difficulties anthropologists have in grasping inner experience from the standpoint of the "natives" and their structural preconceptions. All competent higher animals have some minimal sense of individuation, that is, of the differences between themselves and their intraspecific fellows. If they did not, they would not have conflicts within their societies; but, of course, conflict is universal in higher-animal societies. Higher animals show some degree of recognition of their individual existences in the idle and sometimes slightly perplexed curiosity they show about their reflections in mirrors. Cats and dogs will often go repeatedly to mirrors to look at themselves before losing interest. Chimpanzees will manipulate mirrors to get a better look at their backsides, which are not otherwise clearly visible to them. But animals never seem to show the shock, fear, and even dread that are so common when primitive adult human beings first see their reflections in mirrors and their pictures in photographs. I suggest that the reason for this shock and fear is that the high degree of abstractness in the adult human being's conception of himself allows him to fear that the image he sees might be his self separated from his body. Animals know in some way that they are distinct individual bodies, but they are not able to abstract their "thinking" from their images of their own bodies. All adult human beings, except primitive behaviorists, are able to take an abstract view of their own thinking, so that they are always, to varying degrees, mind-body dualists. That is, they always distinguish in some way between themselves as bodies and themselves as minds, commonly called "spirits" or equivalent names. The human being always sees himself to some degree as both a distinct, individuated body and as a distinct, individuated mind that is in some way, to some degree, independent of the body, able to reflect upon *and* control the body by willing. (Though it is vitally important to constantly keep in mind the significance to human beings of their body-selves, including their body-images, and to see the way that this is interdependent with their mind-selves, it is the mind-selves that we have in mind when we speak of the sense of self.)

In what is probably the best-known work on the relation between the individual self and society, Dorothy Lee (1959) originally reached conclusions that led many theorists of the self to conclude that she believed the Wintu Indians made no distinction between the individual self and the social world. (This conclusion was possibly prompted by such statements of Lee's as "With the Wintu, the self has no strict bounds, is not named, and is not, I believe, recognized as a separate reality" [Lee, 1959:34].) Later, surveying all of her experience and knowledge of simpler societies, Lee concluded,

> To say that the self is open is not to say that the self is fused with or submerged in the other. In all the cultures which I have studied, reference is made to a differentiated self. In the Wintu language for example, in addition to the personal pronouns, we have at least two suffixes whose function is to differentiate and emphasize the self. . . . The Wintu did not use an *and* when they spoke of two or more individuals. In our terms, they would say: not John *and* Mary have arrived but: John Mary they have arrived. This may imply that the coming of John and the coming of Mary are not separate, to be joined by an *and;* yet John and Mary were clearly differentiated. [Lee, 1976:11]

THE NATURE OF SELF-AWARENESS

While some primitive societies may approximate a state of simplicity, static equilibrium, and harmony that will allow individuals to have only a minimal sense of self, distinct from themselves as mere social objects, it is obvious that no civilization has remotely approximated such a state. The great majority of individuals in civilized societies experience a relatively high degree of complexity, change, and conflict. Civilized societies always show some unmistakable signs of a highly developed sense of self-awareness (however taken for granted it may be), which may be especially evident precisely in the anguished attempts to transcend individual selfhood and "return" to some state of Cosmic Selflessness (a state of totally dependent and fused consciousness that does not involve a sense of individual self-ness) that we see in Hindu and Buddhist civilizations. The degrees of self-awareness have varied greatly from one civilization to another and, within civilizations, from one era to another. Eras with the least *internal* complexity, change, and conflict over beliefs and values show the least explicit awareness of self. In such eras individuals can *open* themselves to, and *identify* themselves to a maximum degree with, their communities. As internal social complexity, change, and conflict grow, openness and identification erode and concern with the individual grows. In an age of simple faith, the faithful may be content to submerge their selves for the most part in the community of the faithful, seeking the glory and salvation of the self through that of the community. In this situation the individual's sense of self and thus his life become highly dependent on the society or on God (or on the loved one—see below). Though it is obvious that Medieval

Europe had far more individualists—including extreme ones, such as Abe-
lard—than dared to reveal themselves publicly, it is still true that their
concern with self and self-assertiveness was pale compared to that expressed in the ideal of *virtù* in the rapidly changing and conflictful era of
the Renaissance. When we look at a society like the ante-bellum American
South, we find intense suppression of public expressions by women of their
concerns with self. Publicly, they had to be highly submissive and self-
sacrificing. Privately, in their diaries, they generally accepted this in the
abstract, but even those who did had doubts about such self-sacrifices and
often indulged in soul-searching to determine why they were still so concerned with themselves. But even the few femininists of that era of relative
social consensus revealed no private identity crises remotely comparable
in intensity or frequency to those of our more conflictful era.

The basic processes leading to increased self-awareness are most obvious
when we observe individuals intensively over time. Most developmental
psychologists who have studied infants (see, especially, Bowlby, 1969) have
concluded that the human being begins life with no sense of separateness.
In the earliest days (which psychoanalysts designate as the period of "primary narcissism") the child seems to experience the world as part of the
self. As consciousness develops, the child seems to identify the self increasingly with the parents—above all, with the all-gratifying mother, who
is "magically" controlled by the child's expressions of pleasure and pain
so that she feeds, cleans, rocks, and so on on cue. (This period of magical
omnipotence involves at its height a sense of fusion or oneness with the
all-giving parent. It is a period of such intensely joyful loving that human
beings seem always to crave a return to it by fusing the self with a lover
and, at the extreme, by fusing the self with an omnipotent and all-loving,
hence all-giving, God.) As the child's ability to understand develops, parents begin the long processes of cultural training necessary to develop the
human animal into the most highly developed cultural animal. This training
necessarily involves some degree of constraint and purposeful punishment,
as well as increasing independence, which allows the individual to suffer
the consequences of his very faulty understanding of the world. Some of
these experiences are experienced as threats by the child. These threats
arouse anxiety and at times even dread. It is this anxiety and dread, aroused
by threats, that triggers the emergence of the sense of self (a point I shall
shortly elaborate upon). The initial sense of self seems to consist of little
more than a sense of separateness from others, of individuation, which
slowly grows over the years. Self-reflecting awareness comes only later.

Social psychologists who compare children with adolescents are struck
by the great differences between them in self-awareness. Children *on the
average* show extremely little self-reflection, rarely even referring to internal states, such as their own feelings. (When they do refer to feelings,

such as "being mad," they tend strongly to be concerned with why they are mad, at whom they are mad, and what they can do about it.) Adolescents (who in American society achieve this status between the ages of twelve and fourteen, with the beginning of junior high school) suddenly become extremely concerned with themselves, with their inner experience of thought and feeling, and spend a great deal of time thinking about themselves and often writing their thoughts about themselves in their diaries. (Before adolescence children rarely keep diaries. Diaries are very self-reflective and are rarely kept by boys, a fact indicating that girls experience greater insecurity.) They talk and write about how they feel, and they often examine these feelings minutely (Rosenberg, 1979). As R. D. Laing has said, "The heightening or intensifying of the awareness of one's own being, both as an object of one's own awareness and of the awareness of others, is practically universal in adolescents, and is associated with the well-known accompaniments of shyness, blushing, and general embarrassment" (Laing, 1965:106). Part of this great heightening of self-awareness is no doubt due to the greater ability of the neurally and intellectually more developed adolescents to abstract from their immediate situations, to look at themselves as abstracted from the situation, rather than to think of themselves only as part of the concrete whole of their experience. But that this is only part of the process is obvious when we note that some children, specifically those who feel very threatened by their worldly situation, do become quite self-conscious, even morbidly ruminating on their feelings and other internal states and on what has distinguished them from the other children (What's wrong with me?), and when we also note that the typical "identity crisis" of adolescence may be put off or maintained at a chronic level by "identity moratoria" long after full development of the ability to abstract has been achieved (Erickson, 1959); this postponement may be the result of a prolonged college education, paid for by parents or government. Psychoanalysts have often tried to explain the intensity of adolescent self-awareness in terms of guilt (such as guilt over masturbation), but Laing (1965) has rightly pointed out that individuals who feel intensely guilty often do not have heightened self-awareness. Nonpsychoanalysts have usually explained the heightened self-awareness in more common-sense terms, as due to the sudden changes in adolescents' lives resulting not only from the sudden upsurge of urgent sexual feelings and cravings to be in love—feelings that demand many problematic changes—but also from the many new social demands made on them to prepare for adulthood and to be self-supporting—demands that are especially problematic in a society like ours, which provides immense freedom to choose from an immensely complex set of possible paths that adolescents (and most adults) know little about. As usual, the common-sense explanation is much closer to the mark and provides the crucial beginnings of an explanation.

THREATS TO THE INNER SENSE OF SELF

The *average* child in our society, at least after the initial harsh encounters with the "no-saying" parents, which most analysts see as the early mirror-image progenitors of the childhood sense of self, lives a relatively secure, slowly changing, and unconflictful and undemanding life. As long as this world continues, the child shows little sense of self-awareness. Certainly, a secure child in a secure world has a sense of self, but it is restricted to a barely reflective sense of separateness and is taken for granted, largely unexamined, and certainly not a matter of anxious, tortured reflection and reexamination. If something happens that threatens the child's sense of security in a fundamental way, such as being rejected (hated) by the parents or losing a loved parent through death or divorce, then the child becomes highly self-conscious, turning the thoughts and emotions (such as self-hatred or, more commonly, self-pity) back upon the self, largely in an attempt to discover "What's wrong with me?" or "What have I done to make them do this to me?" One of my life-studies, Laura, developed a high degree of self-reflectiveness at a very young age precisely because her early experiences were so painful and threatening. Her mother seems to have been either a "borderline" psychotic or a full-blown psychotic from Laura's infancy, and Laura's earliest memories include the feeling of being rejected by her mother. She felt that her father was always favorable toward her and possibly loving, but he was always distant and reserved. Her older brother had beaten her up and called her "ugly" from as early as she could remember. By the time she was in the fifth grade, she was heavily involved in day-dreaming, was keeping a diary of her thoughts and feelings, and was writing "love letters" to boys in her classes. (I first became aware of her when she wrote such a love letter to my son, who was in her class. I kept the letter because it showed such acute loneliness and yearning for love. It also showed Laura's acute awareness of how my son and others would react to such a letter and, thus, of embarrassment.) At nineteen Laura still showed an acute sense of self-awareness, of searching painfully for self-understanding, and of basic insecurity. She was deeply convinced that she was ugly and that no one could ever love her (though she was in fact quite attractive). (In her desperate search for love, she had become an amateur detective and secretly followed young men for long periods of time, photographing them with telephoto lenses, and so on.)

It is very important to note that the "self-crises" of adolescents in our society are not simply the result of the rapidity or extent of the changes they undergo at that time. It is quite common for human beings to undergo sudden self-transformations without experiencing self-crises. Though sudden self-transformations probably always involve a heightened sense of self-awareness, they are not experienced as "crises," which can produce the greatest possible self-awareness and self-searching (soul-searching), provided they are not experienced as a *threat to the inner sense of self*, as a change in the human self that might not be coped with or accommodated by the present inner self. Strokes of luck, such as sudden wealth or transformation from being a lonely waif to being a person in love or from being a vice-president of the United States to being president, increase self-awareness (even to the point of looking at oneself with incredulity: "Is this really me?!"), but they need not be experienced as a crisis and arouse anxiety or dread, as crises normally do. Unless persons suffer from a fear of success, or feel threatened by a lack of self-confidence to fit the role or think themselves unworthy of it, they bound with joy into the sudden possibilities of the new position. Even persons undergoing sudden painful, perhaps even dangerous, transformations of the self may do so without experiencing a crisis *if* they receive enough support from outside (especially social confirmation of the worthiness of the transformation process and of the new self) and *if* they have prepared for the transformation (through "anticipatory socialization," for example, by watching others do it—others with whom they can identify—or by playing at being the new self, i.e., by rehearsing) and thus feel confident that they can do it. "Rites of passage" normally involve the full panoply of anticipatory socialization and social support, so sudden transformations from childhood to adulthood (and so on) may be accomplished without a sense of threat to the past self or to the new one, thus without a self-crisis and the accompanying anxiety or dread, even if the transformations involve painful rites like circumcision or clitoridectomy. Sudden conversion experiences are normally preceded by a long period of self-crisis, but the sudden transformation to a new self is the solution to the crisis, not the source of it. As long as the individual feels that his self, with or without external support, is capable of coping with the external or internal changes, however great they may be, he experiences the changes as *challenges*, not as threats.

It is only when the sense of self is threatened that the individual experiences a self-crisis (or identity crisis) and the intense anxiety, dread, and self-awareness associated with it. When the individual feels that the very existence of his sense of self is threatened, he feels *self-insecurity*, or what Laing (1965) and other existential analysts (e.g., Yalom, 1980) have called "ontological insecurity," that is, insecurity with regard to one's very being. The dread of death is one of man's most powerful and overriding emotions. It is almost always a deep-background assumption of our lives, very systematically evaded (and sometimes denied in the conscious experience of everyday life in all the ways that Ernest Becker [1937] and many others have analyzed) because it is so painful and because the conscious experience of this dread of death, this dread of the destruction of the self, would override and sweep away all of our everyday concerns and programs, producing a panicky disorientation and disruption—a paralysis—of everyday life so severe that life would soon be impossible. It is little wonder that man has evolved an inborn (largely genetically pro-grammed) *ontological hope*, which inspires the nearly universal conviction that the inner sense of self (commonly called the soul or spirit—and named the "core self" by Lifton [1976:71]) is immortal. This hope and conviction almost always come into play when the individual must face death, and they prevent his experiencing dread in its catastrophically disorienting proportions. But any degree of dread of death, of the threat of ontological insecurity, is enough to produce an extreme degree of self-awareness and self-examination, and these commonly lead to attempts to escape, to es-capism, or to mourning for the self and to some effort to reconstruct the self, which decreases the dread.

The *threat of self-degradation* is a lesser form of threat to the self, but it has somewhat similar effects. The self is threatened with degradation when the individual believes he may have to do or endure things that produce severe embarrassment, shame, or guilt. In their most extreme forms these three powerful emotions actually arouse some dread of onto-logical insecurity, of nonexistence. This is seen in the way the body may be temporarily paralyzed and cave inward. (The experience is expressed by such statements as "I was so shamed, I felt like I would die.") Deg-radation commonly threatens one's social existence by threatening one's sense of competence (if one experiences embarrassment) or one's worthi-ness and lovability (if one experiences shame and guilt). All forms of ex-treme stigmatization threaten the individual with self-degradation and commonly lead, just as the stigmatizers intend it to, to anguished soul-searching (reexamining the core self) and to reconstructions, and possibly transformations, of the self.

The threat to *self-integrity* is a threat to the *integrated functioning* of the self in the world. (Lesser forms, such as minor conflicts within the self and inconsistencies between the self and its actions, may be experienced as challenges rather than threats.) Threats to the integrated functioning of the inner sense of self in the world may be due to basic conflicts within the self or to conflicts between the sense of self and the perceived external situation. Threats from within the self are predominantly the result of conflicts between powerful emotions, such as are found in the classic psychoanalytic cases between the desire for love or sexual fulfillment and the dread of love or sex generally produced by traumatic rejection of love or by punishment for sexual behavior. When these emotional conflicts are severe, the individual may come to *feel* that even such basic feelings as love or sex are not part of the self; that is, they are ego-alien, not ego-syntonic—they do not feel "natural" or "do not feel like me." Depending on his basic cognitive processes, the individual may, in extreme conflicts, reject and "project" his desires outside his body, so that he is haunted by paranoid interpretations that lead him to see others as responsible for them, trying to force upon him what he himself secretly desires. Alternatively, and again in extreme cases, the threat may be dealt with by *dividing the conscious self* into separate selves, which, by expressing and fulfilling the conflicting desires in partitioned situations, prevent the conflict from threatening the core (dominant) self. This seems to be what happens in the great majority (and I suspect *all*) of the truthfully documented cases of *divided personality.* (Hilgard [1977] has analyzed the available physiological and psychological evidence for divided states of consciousness.)

Less extreme conflicts of basic emotions often produce a less extreme form of divided consciousness, one in which both selves are potentially conscious of each other (though the rigid values of rationalism today often lead individuals to suppress their recognition of the division); and, just as with divided personalities, the conscious core-self of everyday life, the rational self, in accord not only with the socially respectable self but generally with the ideal self as well, is overriden by the actions willed by an *inner self* (called the "daimon" or "daimonic self" through most of Western history [see May, 1969], or the "inner voice" or "guardian self" [see Hilgard, 1977], and so on). If the conflicting emotion is still great enough to threaten the sense of self, this inner self, which is dominated by the repressed emotion, may secretly (predominantly out of consciousness) override the outer, socially oriented self by leading the person to put himself in situations where his desire will be fulfilled in a way that absolves him of responsibility. As Matza (1964) and others have said, "deviants" often *drift* into deviance. That is, they never *choose* to violate the rules—to which they are committed by the powerful feelings of pride invested in conformity and by the embarrassment, shame, and guilt that result from nonconformity; instead, they manage somehow, by *little choices that add up,* to put themselves in situations in which they are seduced, overwhelmed, or swept away by emotion. Individuals in the grip of these powerful emotions commonly go through long and complex processes of self-deception, sometimes convincing themselves that the earnest convictions they had before the emotion overrode their conscious self were untrue (see Douglas, forthcoming). They often come to recognize that they are "impulsive" and even recognize, on the edge of consciousness, that they are impulsive precisely because impulsiveness alone allows them to fulfill their secret desire without suffering paralyzing guilt. One of the beautiful women we studied dealt with her repressed sexual desires in this way and found that guilt could not be avoided when she was confronted with the explanation of her impulsiveness. Yet another woman we studied was quite conscious that she avoided guilt by "allowing" her sexual desire to grow until it "swept her off her feet." She knew that she "went along with" actions and situations that allowed her desire to grow until she could no longer resist it or, as seemed more common, until she could resist it only verbally while her clothes were being taken off by her "seducer"; but this recognition of her stratagem for outwitting her guilt feelings did not trigger guilt, perhaps because she was simply more able to accept inconsistency than most people are.

Individuals who are highly introspective, such as those skilled in ethnomethodology or in the ancient arts of contemplation and meditation, often become aware of this division between an upper, outer (socially conforming) self and a lower or inner self that can override the outer one because it is fulfilling a basic emotion that has been suppressed or repressed. They sometimes even report experiencing a more "shadowy" (hardly conscious) self that might be able to override the inner self.

Hilgard (1977) found that most people who become aware of an inner self see it as a guardian, but some reject it with resentment. The inner daimon can be seen either as benign, as Socrates saw his daimon and as most religious seekers view the "cosmic consciousness" within, or as an evil demon that must be exorcised.

When the inner self, ruled by a powerful emotion, is successfully repressed for a long time because of deep fears, the individual's *will*, which is at the very center of the inner sense of self, may be so *blocked* that he is unable to will—to intend—anything effectively. He may "wish" for many things, but his wishes cannot produce actions. Individuals who repress basic emotions find their will blocked until they are able to get in touch with and recognize the blocked emotion. Once they recognize the emotion, their will eventually becomes unblocked: they "exorcise" their demon, just as ancient exorcists did, by facing it, "naming" it, and willing it to "come out." The crucial step in this self-exorcism is commonly *getting outside oneself* by writing to oneself, talking to others, etc.—all ways of partially "objectifying" the self, a process that often allows one to "get perspective on the self" in the same way that getting outside one's everyday (habituated) patterns of life often allows one to recognize what one really wills rather than what one does by habit. (Carl Rogers, [1972] describes a case in which a woman who had repressed her love out of fear got "in touch" with her love feelings by talking to her image in a window. Her will was immediately unblocked, and she was able to move toward marriage.)

The integrity of the inner sense of self, functioning in the world, may also be challenged or threatened by conflicts or inconsistencies between the biographical inner self (the memories of one's inner self from the past), the present inner self, the (future) ideal inner self, and one's present actions. The inner self must, at any given moment, choose its commitments in the world, and thus its willed actions, in such a way as to balance (or "center"; see Lifton, 1976) its present against both its past and its hoped-for future inner selves. While individuals differ widely in their emotional commitments to past, present, and future selves, and while this balance shifts throughout life, the temporal dimension is inherent in human existence: what we *have been, are becoming,* and *will become* are always important aspects of any major commitments and actions that we make—

commitments or actions that involve our inner selves. Our past inner self is commonly called the *roots* of our being. When the past is consistent with the present inner self, we feel that our roots have created our present inner self and now support and *nourish*. Individuals who have a firm *sense of rootedness*—a strong feeling that their present inner self is consistent with and grows out of their historical roots—can find ever-renewed strength by *returning to their roots*. Such individuals generally cannot be understood until their roots are understood, because their roots are generally an ever-present ground for their core selves, often consciously so. Robert Bork, a United States solicitor general from 1973 to 1977, has given an excellent example of the sudden grasp he got on Justice William Douglas's whole life (self) when he discovered Douglas's sense of historical rootedness in his autobiography:

> One reads William O. Douglas's account of his thirty-six years on the Supreme Court with growing discomfort and frustration. Discomfort because of the careless writing and organization. This is less a book than a mélange of anecdotes about, and evaluations of, presidents, justices, politicians, lawyers, friends and enemies, with cursory summaries of Mr. Douglas's thoughts about particular fields of law. Discomfort, again and to a greater degree, because Mr. Douglas's swift evaluations of people and events are often savage, frequently wildly unfair, and in some instances, obviously untrue.
>
> It must be said in fairness that Mr. Douglas's reactions are not entirely partisan. He is often remarkably generous to those with whom he disagreed most profoundly, men such as Felix Frankfurter and Stanley Reed. I know this admirable quality of the man first-hand, for during a particularly stressful time in government, Justice Douglas, with whom I had never exchanged a word except across the bench and who knew my unfavorable estimate of his judicial performance, went well out of his way to express personal support.
>
> The man behind the book seemed an enigma, therefore, until, at the very end, there came a sudden illumination. Mr. Douglas writes that from his earliest days his mother drummed into his ears Sir Walter Scott's lines: "And darest thou, then / To beard the lion in his den, / The Douglas in his hall."
>
> She was convinced that through the Douglas blood "we had acquired an indomitable will and capacity for achievement." This sudden vision of William O. Douglas as a turbulent, implacable Scottish chieftain makes somehow more comprehensible his embattled life, the anger and ferocity apparent in the book, the strong loyalties he gave

and received and his bursts of warmth even toward those whom he regarded as philosophical and political enemies. These personal characteristics are important to an understanding of his judicial career. Those strands of intuition about the limits of judicial capacities and the requirements of democratic theory, which add up to the "philosophy" of "judicial restraint," are likely to prove too tenuous a web to constrain a man of such passion and energy for long. His sympathies went straight and undiluted into his view of politics and society, and that view, in turn, went, with precious little dilution, into his reading of the Constitution and laws. [Bork, 1980]

Home-grounding is such a vital and common strand of *self-grounding* that it seems likely that it springs originally from a genetically determined sense of and craving for territoriality and nesting. It is seen in its starkest form in peasant societies, in which the individual and the "good earth" (with its house) are inalienably bound to each other. Grounding is, for most people, vital to a well-developed sense of ontological security. Home-grounding is often of intense emotional importance to individuals precisely when they feel most insecure ontologically, as we see in the craving we all have to "die at home" rather than in a distant, unknown, impersonal environment. The intense craving for home known as "homesickness" (which feels the same as "lovesickness") is often precipitated by one's first bout of physical sickness after leaving home. Insecurity resulting from identity crises, such as those resulting from soul-wrenching divorces or from other failures and losses, often lead individuals to reground themselves by looking homeward and returning home. The feeling of homelessness and the conviction that "you can't go home again," so poignantly evoked in Thomas Wolfe's novels, involves a feeling of being lost (uncentered) and, indeed, of losing a vital part of the self. Those who are ostracized, and émigrés forced to flee their homelands by repressive governments, almost universally suffer homesickness and a feeling of a loss of creativity; the roots of home that nourish the new life of creations have been torn up, and the self must be replanted, rerooted, regrounded before the *sense of vitality*, the *feeling of life*, will again flow freely.

In the same way that our sense of self centers us temporally, it also centers us spatially and socially. Just as with temporal centering, individuals differ widely in the form and degree of their spatial centering or orienting, but it is a necessity of all life-processes. Where do I come from? Where am I? Where am I going? must be answered, at least in some implicit way, to *give physical direction to our life-processes*. It is common for members of a culture to share a cosmology (theory of the physical universe) that potentially orients them toward all things in existence. Cosmology in the Western world has always been of vital importance, and our cosmological revolutions (the Copernican revolution and the revolution in our galactic and intergalactic self-conceptions in the twentieth century) caused violent disorientations until they were assimilated and became our new taken-for-granted physical orientation. The individual who "loses his way" in life or "feels lost" for any reason normally feels severely threatened and may suffer acute self-awareness (because of ontological dread) and panic. Less extreme forms of physical disorientation may be risky enough to constitute an exciting challenge, like that felt on entering and exploring a maze. Changes in the world that threaten our sense of relation to the world produce a sense of disorder, chaos, and dissolution that threatens our sense of self and thus arouses a dread of death.

VALUES AND EMOTIONS

Basic values, supported by strong feelings of pride when we live in accord with them and by shame and guilt when we do not, orient us toward our social world. *These basic values are a necessary and vital part of human life.* Without these basic values, shared with other members of our social groups, we would be unable to act successfully as the cultural animals we are genetically determined to be (Dawkins, 1976; Bonner, 1980; Douglas, 1981). Socially we would be continually *lost.* An individual who violates his own basic rules or those of the groups in which he is emotionally grounded feels that he has betrayed his self, and he experiences the pain of severe guilt or shame; this pain in turn reinforces the rules, making it more likely that he will not betray his self the next time. This does not mean that we are doomed to meek cultural conformity. As Durkheim said, we do not feel that living by our basic values is an external constraint, because these values *are* part of us. We take pride and joy in living by our basic values, in constructing our social lives in accord with the blueprint they provide. But, as Durkheim did not see, everyone finds that in some situations his basic values are in severe conflict with his basic emotions, and in our highly pluralistic civilizations we find this to be very common; moreover, we find that our own basic values very frequently come into conflict with some of the values that are important to other members of our society. While the details need not concern us here (see Douglas, forthcoming), there are ways in which we can manage, over considerable time and with some pain, to "get around" a basic value to which we are committed; we do this by reinforcing a new value with the emotionally gratifying new behavior that it produces. (Of course, it is easier to "get around" a group value when we do not share the group's commitments to it.) We do have some power to progressively free our selves from conformity to a basic value we feel is in conflict with more important aspects of our selves, but we must have basic values to guide our interactions with other human beings.

When we do "get around," and change, a basic value, it is almost always because we believe that that value has come into conflict with a basic emotion in our life-situation. Our basic values guide us in choosing the social form of actions that fulfill and enhance our basic emotions, *but it is our basic emotions that orient or guide our will in choosing to act at all and then in choosing what kinds of actions to perform.* Some powerful feelings are consistently experienced as something external to the self, though not external to the body image. Shame, guilt, depression, and physical pain, for example, are not felt to be part of the sense of self; rather, they are experienced as things or emotions that *happen to* the self, and, when they are severe, they can seem to seize, override, or even "break" (annihilate) the sense of self. This is seen, for example, in the letter a friend wrote to me about a severe tooth "ache":

> Sorry I've been so much out of touch. These past three weeks have been perhaps the worst of my life. It's a long story, and I'll spare you all the gory details. It began with a cracked tooth, with five days of severe pain between the temporary cap and the subsequent root canal, where they discovered the abcessed tooth had infection, which spread up into the bone area above the jaw. Then followed two "misadventures" in the dentist's office, where they put a temporary filling in the canal area, which sent me into so much pain they had to go in and grind it out before I left the office! Well, all these dental details are secondary— what has been so distinctive about it has been my experience of the pain as a subjective/existential experience. It has been the most extraordinary, unique experience; I have nothing to compare it to. Here's an analogy which seems to make sense to me: I feel like I've been thrown into a concentration camp, threatened with torture unless I betrayed my friends/family, then finally, following some initial attempts at resistance, I was broken, and betrayed my friends. That may sound very silly, but I have this overwhelming sense of having been broken, of being less than human because of all this, of being weak, cowardly. I haven't had any pain for two days now, but I'm overwhelmed with this feeling of having been broken. Wow! And it isn't even over yet! I have to go in for another root canal on Monday, and then, if all goes well, perhaps 2 visits after that. Really has shown me how close we are to physical breakdown, how frail we are, even when we think quite otherwise. Quite extraordinary!

As Silvan Tomkins (1980) has pointed out, physical (afferrent) pain is so vitally linked to basic life-processes that, when intense, its demands override all other emotional demands on the self and its willpower (see also

Kotarba, 1983). Being less intense, frustration and depression can normally be endured and do not override the self and its willpower. Yet it is clear that in their extreme forms, like those associated with extreme "lovesickness" and other forms of extreme depression, they have the same effect and can, when associated with hopes and convictions of afterlife (and reunion), lead to suicide, the destruction of the body-self (Douglas, 1967). As we saw earlier, when the pain or threat of pain is very great, especially when the threat to the entire self is great, the most effective defense becomes a division of the self into a detached, observing, inner self and a partially experiencing, outer (object) self. In his work *On Pain*, Ernst Jünger argued that this "detachment of life from itself, the objectification of self," is the only way to avoid destruction in the face of continual threats to vital aspects of the self (see Kahler, 1957:85–90). In an absurd world, one that is unpredictable and continually threatens the self, the individual must learn through practice not to invest his positive emotions in the world but to become, instead, detached, coldly aloof (like Sartre's "heroes" in *Nausea* and *The Age of Reason*). In *The Myth of Sisyphus* Camus called for the threatened self in the absurd world to have "perpetual consciousness" (a hyper-self-consciousness, to guard against the threats to the self) and at the same time to practice "lucid indifference." The individual who practices "lucid indifference" becomes the complete "stranger," an infantile narcissist, whose positive, vital emotions are saved from destruction by turning them inward on the self, detaching them from the world. Such an individual becomes a primitive narcissist who "saves" his self by petrifying it. This petrified living becomes a living death for the self because it involves a blocking of all the thrusting of life's vital, positive emotions into the world. For the narcissistic counterphobe and counterdependent and the narcissistic beautiful woman, for whom beautification has become a counterphobic strategy—a warding-off of terrifying threats by objective petrifaction of the self—life becomes a near death (Douglas, 1980). Suicide becomes an ever present temptation, perhaps the only hope for release from this death-in-life.

Most of our basic, positive emotions are felt by most people to be the *vital* aspects of our sense of self. Each of these basic emotions constitutes a dynamic core of feeling, which, when aroused and willed (not successfully repressed), orients our self toward the world by orienting our perceptions and thoughts toward acting in the world to fulfill and enhance itself. The more powerful the emotion, the more the self is oriented, until, at the extreme, the entire sense of self is pervaded by, overridden by, completely in the grip of, the emotion. These powerful emotions of love, sex, joy, excitement, exultation, curiosity, and so on fill us with life. When they pervade our being, we feel totally alive; when they are lacking, we feel deadened (and, at the psychotic extreme of feelinglessness, may even believe we are dead; see Arieti, 1975). Our "peak experiences" in life are those dominated by these powerful emotions of vitality, those in which the emotion becomes the focal point of our whole life, the aspect of our self about which all else turns and toward which all else is directed. The self is then identified with the consuming emotion, as when we feel that "My love *is* my life!"

Love, intimacy, sex, and the feelings that are aroused by these, especially joy and excitement, are the most powerful of our vital emotions. (As one of our life-studies put it, "Love is the highest high possible.") They are equaled only by the exultation of triumph, the glory of victory in the struggle for dominance, which involves a powerful love of self—soaring pride— and, of course, excitement and joy. As long as our needs for physical security seem to be met, our inner selves are oriented overwhelmingly toward enhancing and fulfilling these two sets of powerful emotions—the emotions associated with bonding and dominating. We are in harmony with our selves, that is, our self is at peace with itself, only when the two sets are equally fulfilled and enhanced. If one set is blocked, either by failure in our strivings or by repression, it will generally be partially expressed ("sublimated" or "vented") by a total, rigid orientation to the other set. Thus, those who cannot find love, intimacy, and sex commonly become "power hungry" and "aggressive"; those who cannot successfully dominate become submissive and are commonly very dependent in their loving, intimate, and sexual relations. (Baechler, 1979, has developed a similar theory of self-security.)

Love, intimacy, and sex are the foundation on which human vitality is built. While exultation in triumph is as powerful an emotion, and the feelings of security given by lasting dominance may pervade our lives and support love, intimacy, and sex, even the most triumphant life eventually becomes empty, a lifeless shell, without love, intimacy, and sex. The genetic function and emotional purpose of dominance in life is to provide security for love, intimacy, and sex and for the children they produce. Lacking these, dominance loses its biological function and its emotional purpose and eventually becomes undirected bloodlust or a meaningless, temporarily exciting, "game."

Love, intimacy, and sex begin with our earliest human contact. The newborn infant is genetically primed to receive warm, sensual pleasure from its mother's body and to give it by sucking her nipples; it learns very soon to receive her love and intimacy and then, in a matter of months, to return that love and intimacy. The loving mother, nursing her child, smiles the universal smile of adoration. At first the child responds only with silent contentment, but later it smiles the universal smile of happy contentment. Then, before long, it *returns* the look of adoring love, exactly the same smile of adoration that the grown child will show when gazing into the eyes of a romantic lover. If this genetically primed schedule of receiving and giving love, intimacy, and sensual pleasure is not fully met, the foundation, the basic security, of the innermost self will always be weak and shaky. As Erikson (1959) has argued, the individual will lack "basic trust," a sense of ultimate security that he is facing the dangers of life *together* with other human beings. Instead, the basically insecure individual, the individual whose life-giving emotions are starved by neglect, will face life with an anxious ambivalence, swinging between the poles of clinging, undifferentiated dependency and rejecting, domineering independence. The basic trust born of love inspires the sense of basic confidence, worthiness, and lovability necessary to facing the world independently enough and with enough trust in human beings so that one can later unite in love without losing the self. Without trust, we use other human beings rather than love them, and we feel the need to lose our self through "love"—often love of an all-powerful God. If, instead of warm love, intimacy, and pleasure, the child receives cold rejection, aloofness, and painful frustration, his full humanness will probably remain stunted throughout his life, because his innermost self will not sense completely how to receive and give love, intimacy, and sex. The love-bereft baby will become an incomplete adult self. he will feel forever a sense of being "lost,' ungrounded; and though he will crave and search desperately, sometimes with frantic violence, for love, intimacy, and sex, he will probably never "find" them to any satisfying degree because he does not grasp them completely even when they are given completely. Such individuals are very likely to develop sexual behavior that lacks emotional depth and to launch out on a desperate career of "casual" sex—of seeking and seeking and—depending on how severe the deprivation has been—possibly never finding. At the extreme, the love-bereft child becomes the "schizoid personality" or the "stormy pre-psychotic" (Arieti, 1975), in whom the vital, life-giving emotions do not "connect correctly" with the sense of self and social interaction. (These syndromes, and the crucial part played in them by parental rejections, are described by Day and Semrad, 1978; see esp. pp. 220–21.)

The individual who has not been loved unconditionally (securely), and who thus has not learned to love himself and others, cannot develop a clear and secure sense of self. While he may *act* "as-if"—may pretend—he is self-confident, loving, and all the other things a competent adult is supposed to be, he is aware in some sense that this is a fiction. He develops complex strategies for defending his insecure self from a threatening world—strategies that in their extreme form issue in "borderline," schizoid reactions, hysteria, and narcissism. (We have observed such reactions in some beautiful women [see Douglas and Weinstein, forthcoming] and in others.)

PESSIMISM AND OPTIMISM

Having devoted so much attention to basically insecure selves, I must hasten to balance my analysis of the self. The intellectuals who developed the original ideas of the existential analysis of human life were inspired in their creative searches largely by their own dread of death, isolation, and meaninglessness. (These three horsemen of the existential apocalypse are presented most vividly in the works of Nietzsche, Kierkegaard, Kafka, Heidegger, Sartre, and Camus. All of them, and other existentialist writers to a lesser degree, were obviously haunted by basic distrust. I would suspect from their works, which dwell so much on the problems of relatedness, that their basic distrust was born of a lack of secure love as infants or children, but that does not matter for our purposes here.) Their form of *grim existentialism* was later reinforced by the equally grim perspective of therapists who dealt exclusively with neurosis, "borderline" cases, and psychosis, especially by those who, like Bettelheim (1943), Frankl (1978), and Kahler (1957), dealt with the victims of death camps. The grim existentialists see life as necessarily pervaded by a sense of these grim realities or by neurotic or psychotic defenses against facing them. They believe that only by facing and accepting the grim realities can individuals free themselves from the defenses that inhibit the vital, positive emotions and the growth of the self they inspire. (Yalom [1980] probably presents the best systematic exposition of this point of view.)

I believe that this argument is true in general for those who suffer from basic insecurity in life. I also believe that it has some relevance for understanding the way all of us feel in extreme situations—situations that arouse grave threats to our sense of self, especially those that arouse ontological insecurity, the dread of death. This is true partly because almost no one escapes infancy and childhood with feelings of basic trust unbalanced by feelings of basic mistrust. Parents and others necessarily do things that are intended to challenge the child but that at times are experienced by him as threats to his self. The basic trust that even total nurturing first inspires in the baby will later be partially counterbalanced by the anxieties inspired by these experiences of threat. Without these, the child would be so Panglossian that he would likely not last very long. The typical life, even in a society such as ours, is a mixture of basic security (trust) and basic insecurity (distrust), a mixture of the sense that life is ultimately good and the sense that it is ultimately bad. The crucial question is whether the individual is more secure or insecure (trustful or distrustful). Does he typically orient himself to life's problems with more hope or more despair? If he has more hope, he will be basically secure and experience problems as challenges, except in situations that are overwhelmingly threatening. If not, he will be basically insecure and will develop defenses to ward off the dread of the threats he would otherwise see looming in all directions.

Our in-depth life-studies have been done with all kinds of individuals. Most have seen themselves, and have been seen by others, as "psychologically healthy"; some of those most committed to the search for self-understanding have been "neurotic"; and a few, especially in our study of beautiful women, have been "borderline" cases (primarily of narcissism). Our goal has been to determine the full gamut of human experience and to infer from this what is common to human life (that is, what is human nature); we have also sought to discover the variable importance of situations and individual genetic differences. This has generally been the implicit goal of most philosophers and psychotherapists, but they have looked at all of human life from the narrow perspective of extreme situations and extreme individual reactions to more common situations. Their justification has been that they can supposedly see what is more common ("healthy") by seeing human reactions writ large through the distorting lens of extreme situations and extreme ("ill") individual reactions. I believe on the basis of our life-studies of nonextremes that their focus on extremes has distorted their general understanding of life by selecting precisely those individuals who are "unbalanced" in one direction or another. Human life is not normally "unbalanced" or "uncentered," though all human lives contain extreme experiences (such as life-threatening ones) at some time or another. Rather, human life normally involves a balancing of conflicting basic emotions and other ways of orienting toward the world, but the balance is skewed to the side of the life-giving emotions and other perceptual and cognitive orientations. All individuals experience at some level, in some situations, a dread of death (though in our society this often does not occur until the individual is in his twenties or even his thirties). When this occurs, most individuals do indeed have to wrestle in anguish with, come to terms with, this dread. Moreover, it seems obvious that the dread of death is a constant background emotion in life; it is always there, and it can be triggered at any time a life-threatening situation is perceived. But this does not mean that individuals live with the dread of death as a constant, subconscious dread that must be either repressed or else acknowledged and dealt with. Most individuals in our society today do not appear to repress a dread of death in their everyday lives. Instead, they consciously *suppress* (avoid) encountering death precisely so that they can avoid feeling dread and thus go on living more hopefully and creatively. A very high percentage very consciously hope that they will die suddenly in their sleep, so that they do not have to suffer, do not have to come to terms with, the dread of death and the meaning of death to life. Instead of repressing death from their consciousness and thus developing neurotic symptoms, they have consciously, purposefully, dismissed it from consciousness in order to live more fully. Some of them consciously recognize that they do not know how to deal with the dread of death and believe that they will have to wait for the situation to arise, with all of its unique emotions, before they can adequately come to terms with it.

The case against the grim existentialist view of the human self and its becoming is even stronger when we look at the relatedness of the self to other selves. The grim perspective sees the human self as necessarily alone, necessarily isolated from other human selves by the gulf of individual differences and physical separateness. They believe that the individual necessarily suffers from "existential isolation," either consciously or (after repressing it) unconsciously. The extreme form of this grim existential view of human isolation is found in such works as Camus' *The Stranger*, the icy picture of a man who is always walled off from other human beings, untouched by mother love, by romantic love, by friendly intimacy, or by altruistic caring. It is unlikely that anyone would mistake this extreme for the common human experience (anyone other, that is, than a French intellectual who has spent all of his childhood and youth immured in a lycée world of bureaucratized words). The less extreme, but still grim, picture of human isolation and love presented by Erich Fromm (1956) in the *The Art of Loving* is far more representative of existential theory.

Fromm argues that the human being necessarily begins life with an awareness of isolation. This awareness of isolation is the ultimate source of all anxiety, and the human being's primary psychological task in all ages has been to overcome this anxiety. Creative activity, orgiastic activity (mystical union, drugged highs, sexual abandon), and submersion in the community have been three major forms of attempted but abortive escape from this initial separateness. "Symbiotic love" has been the fourth and probably most common form of the pseudo-unions intended to provide escape from the anxiety of separateness. These symbiotic love relations involve sadistic partners who dominate masochistic partners. All of them fail because they are only temporary escapes and do not produce a real and complete union of the individual self with another self. The individual remains ultimately separate. The answer to the initial separateness is to find another self with whom the individual can "fuse," so that the "two beings become one and yet remain two." "The full answer lies in the achievement of interpersonal union, of fusion with another person, in love" (Fromm, 1956:37). Yalom (1980) has carefully compared Fromm's (minimally) grim existential theory of separateness and love with the more hopeful theories of Martin Buber (1970) and Abraham Maslow (1968) and has concluded that Fromm's theory fits his own experience in psychotherapy with neurotic individuals, which is exactly what we might expect and exactly what Buber and Maslow would expect.

Buber's theory of the isolation and relatedness of the human self is the most thoroughly hopeful of any well-known theory (and probably springs both from his childhood and his religious convictions). He distinguishes between two fundamentally different types of relatedness. The "I-It" relationship involves the relation of a self to an object, including other selves, who are treated as objects to be manipulated by self-presentations, ploys, games, force, and so on. The "I-Thou" relationship is the relationship between two selves, a relationship of mutuality, of communion. Buber sees relatedness, especially of the "I-Thou" type, as the foundation of human life. Relatedness, not isolation, is the necessary beginning of the human self: 'In the beginning is the relation." The ultimate goal of the "I-Thou" relation is a loving fusion with the other in which each self realizes itself by being itself with and through the other: "The basic word I-You can be spoken only with one's whole being. The concentration and fusion into a whole being can never be accomplished by me, can never be accomplished without me. I require a You to become; becoming I, I say You" (Buber, 1970:11). *Loving-and-fusing with the other self is a precondition of the vitality, the growth, and the wholeness of the individual self.* This loving-and-fusing is the "natural" and normal orientation of the human self. When the individual cannot relate to other human beings in this way, presumably because of some feeling of threat that is so overwhelming that it forces him to build defenses and so relate to other humans as inhuman "Its," he does not live to the full, does not grow to the full, and is indeed neurotic; instead, he "plays roles," "presents himself," and, in general, acts out his inner problem inauthentically by building defenses against the perceived threats of other selves.

Maslow (1968), more concerned than Buber with neurosis and therapy, makes clearer the connections between threats and relating to others as objects. He argued that individuals who early in life do not experience a feeling of basic security—whose needs for physical safety, love, worthiness, and confidence are unfulfilled—become "deficiency"-oriented. That is, they remain permanently fixated on (neurotically) finding and building "love" relations that give them a semblance, however transitory, of the basic security they lack. "Deficiency love" makes the individual highly dependent on the other. The dependent lover demands support and unconditional "love" from the loved one because the inner void, the basic insecurity, demands continual external reassurance that the individual is lovable, worthy, and competent. The dependent lover is a clinging lover, unable to face life without the confidence the loved one's immediate presence and love gives, except with a dread that must be escaped by the constant use of defense mechanisms. The personally deficient, dependent lover is commonly a damned lover. Most of the time his basic insecurities, and the resulting clinging dependency, make him interpret the slightest independence on the part of the loved one as a dreaded rejection. He tends to develop paranoid jealousy and guilt and to demand more attention and love than anyone can give—anyone, that is, except an equally dependent lover or a parent figure. The most dependent lovers are often the most com-

pulsively independent in their social presentations. Individuals who act
independently in a compulsive manner (counterdependents) do so because
they are counteracting feelings of extreme insecurity, which make them
secretly wish to remain dependent. Such individuals can love only rarely
and with great difficulty, generally in a situation and with a person that
make them feel *safe*. But when they do find that situation and that person,
they love deeply and profoundly, with almost total dependency. This kind
of love is seen, for example, in narcissistic beautiful women whose narcissism is a counteraction against the most extreme forms of insecurity
and for whom being beautiful is a way of feeling lovable, worthy, and
confident (secure). The characteristics of the extremely dependent lover
are most obvious when the loved one is lost, either through death or desertion. Almost any leaving, including death, is experienced by the dependent lover as a desertion. (One of our most insecure narcissistic beautiful
women became profoundly depressed, anorexic, and suicidal when her
"ultimate love" chose to "desert" her for his wife and children.) This
reaction is most common in widows and widowers, who must face sudden
ontological insecurity in addition to all the other basic insecurities they
suddenly face when their dependency bond is severed by death. One of
the compulsively independent and successful women I studied, described
by her intimates as "a cold block of a woman," had been profoundly in
love with her immensely successful husband. As far as I could determine,
he was the one person she had loved, since even her relations with her
children were generally distant. (Her relations with her daughters were
extremely cold, sometimes hostile. One son, whom she appeared to identify
with her husband, was often treated warmly.) Her husband had died ten
years before the study. She appears to have gone into a state of psychic
shock at his death, warding off the deep mourning that alone could free
her from her profound love-dependency but that might also have caused
such deep depression that it would have killed her. In the ten years she
had built a tight cocoon of defenses, which, when temporarily fractured
by such intrusions as "failures" by her children, would lead to hysterical
outbursts of anger, including, at times, anger at her husband, who had
"left" her to face all the problems alone—had "deserted" her, though she
would never use that term. She gave every indication of *feeling* that she
was still married to her dead husband. She knew rationally that she had
suffered immensely from her loneliness. She could talk perfectly rationally
about her loneliness, sexual starvation, and her need to free herself from
the memory of her husband so that she could rebuild her life. She could
even plan to find a new love or, at least, a male companion. She could
even take initial steps to do so, such as going to dinner (after eight years)
with a few men sent her way by friends. But she could not free herself
emotionally from the dependency bond. This continued bonding was dramatically symbolized by her wedding ring. She was able to discuss quite

rationally the need to take off the ring. She seemed to wish sincerely to do so, but some dread held her back. (Her dread even infected me. I cautiously urged her to take the ring off to free herself to live again. I believed that she had to do it herself to have the emotional effect desired. But I was very cautious in my urging, both because I could feel her dread, and thus recognize how profound the consequences might be, and because I myself feel fear.) I believe that she was waiting, even tentatively searching, for a new "rescuer" to come along to fill her dependency void, to still the dread aroused by her basic insecurity. Once she had successfully clung to a new rescuer, she could take off the symbol of her earlier dependency without even going through much grief.

It is easy enough to find dependency-love, including these extreme forms, which fit the most dreadful images of the grim existentialists. I believe, on the basis of my studies thus far, that it is impossible to find the extreme opposite, that of the totally unselfish, unneeding, growth-oriented, self-transcendent love that Maslow describes. Nathaniel Branden (1980) has described this kind of love as an ideal that some few people can attain later in life (possibly as early as their forties), presumably after most of the insecurities of youth have been overcome. There is little doubt that loves developed later in life by individuals who no longer feel very insecure involve very little dependency and are far more directed toward the growth of both selves involved. These (partially) self-transcendent loves add a new dimension to the self. They become the way to a new, expanded orientation toward the world by the self through the other self. The other self, as experienced, becomes a partial general mode of orientation for each of the two selves. Each grows beyond itself by partially fusing with the other. Buber himself saw that even the most extreme forms of the "I-Thou" relation could not be continuously sustained in everyday life. Most of the time the self must act even toward the "Thou" as an "It"—matter-of-factly, without full consideration of the nature of the other self. All such relations that I have studied also retain some of the dependency needs (and thus jealousy) that lingering insecurity arouses in some situations. (There are some individuals who sincerely think they are in love with someone yet show no signs of dependency on the other, such as jealousy. These individuals tend to be very insecure. They commonly counteract insecurity with compulsive displays of self-confidence and independence, including casualness in their love and sex lives. If the other leaves them or they leave the other, they experience little sense of loss, simply because the other was never very important to them emotionally.)

But this mixture of dependent love and transcendent love does not mean that the grim existentialists are right and that we human beings are always, inevitably, haunted by feelings of basic insecurity unless we develop defenses against them or work them out in therapy by facing and conquering them. What it means is that most human beings experience feelings of basic insecurity in some situations and feelings of basic security in others. In most adults the balance is tipped toward security, largely *by situating the self in the world in such a way as to avoid basic threats to the self*. The most secure individual can experience a fit of insecurity if he is forcefully thrown into a situation that is new and demands something he cannot do or give. An individual might feel quite secure in his everyday life, needing few or no defenses, until he is strapped to a hang-glider and pushed off a 1,000-foot cliff or thrown out of a plane at 30,000 feet. He might also be quite secure in his sex life until he finds himself at a sex party, where strangers are watching him and expecting him to have sex repeatedly with strangers. Almost everyone will experience such situations as threats, and they will be very insecure in them. But they are *situationally* insecure, not *basically* insecure. Once the situation is overcome *by escaping it*, the average individual will once again feel secure, though often he may retain a sense of having been temporarily "shaken," that is, of having had to face the fact that his feeling of basic security is dependent on the situations of his everyday life. Anyone can be situationally threatened. It is only the neurotic selves (and the psychotics) studied by the grim existentialists who carry their insecurity around with them, either relatively unalloyed (not counterbalanced by feelings of security, though they must have some) or as a basic ambivalence between the two orientations which can swing wildly from one situation to another or even within the same situation as their moods shift.

As long as the individual does not feel situationally threatened, the more basically secure an individual's sense of self is, the more he expands his sense of self to open himself to new experiences and to create new experiences. The less threatened his sense of self, the more the individual seeks challenges that engage his basic emotions and lead him to thrust himself into the world in new ways. This is what Victor Frankl (1978) means when he says that the individual seeks meaningful challenges in life rather than a tension-free state of equilibrium. The greater meaning orients the self to the broader world, to the world beyond the everyday-life situations to which the individual has become accustomed (and which become boring when they are repeated over and over again and are not needed to fend off emotional threats). The basically secure self seeks to transcend the past and present self by striving to become the future ideal self, which will fulfill and enhance the basic values, and thus the basic emotions, of the whole self. In this sense the self rebuilds, recreates, and expands (enhances) itself into the future. (It is only the basically insecure, neurotic self that compulsively strives to live up to an ideal self that is imposed from outside. Karen Horney [1950] was right when she said that striving for an ideal self is the source of neurosis, but she was wrong in not emphasizing the creative striving for the ideal self that the basically secure self makes possible and desirable.)

The True Sense of Self

We have now seen the basic properties and the fundamental workings of the self. What, then, is the sense of self? It should be clear by now that the self is not what it is normally portrayed to be in structural ("role") theories or even in interactionist theories. These traditional theories have described the self as a "self-concept" or a "self-image" or a "self-definition." All of these conceptualizations portray the self as a clear and distinct, consciously symbolized, even rationalized, set of ideas that guide the individual's will in deciding how to act in the world. I believe that those who developed these theories were basically right in their intuition about what, in general, the self does—it does "guide" our actions. But they were wrong in thinking that the average individual has some clear and distinct, consciously symbolized and rationalized, set of self-guidelines. (I should note that probably the basic reason I have never before written about my own basic ideas about the self was that I did not have any that went beyond these earlier conceptions, and I was acutely aware that something was wrong with them. I was aware, above all, that I myself, as symbolic and rational as I am, do not have a symbolic and rational idea that I could call "myself." When I asked the traditional question, Who am I?, I could find only social roles; yet I have a strong sense of selfhood, almost certainly an overly distinct sense of myself as separate from and distinct from everyone else. I sensed that the whole traditional way of conceptualizing the self missed the crucial aspects of the self, the basic properties of the inner self, the basic or ultimate guidelines to action. But, until I set about systematically trying to assess in this paper what the self does, how it works, I had no clear idea of what we should be talking about when we speak of the "self.") The highly symbolized and rationalized accounts of selfhood, the kind that can be elicited by the verbal measuring devices that so delight positivistic social psychologists, are generally either irrelevant to understanding the most basic aspects of the self, since they tap little more than social definitions of selves, or are actually very misleading, because they tap neurotic definitions of "ideal selves" (of the Horney sort). (If the outer selves, the socially trained selves, were an expression of, and thus in harmony with, our inner selves, then tapping them with such indexes would partially reveal the inner self. But in our highly conflictful society, in which individuals are trained by bureaucratic educational organizations to believe all kinds of things that are in conflict with their inner selves, this is rarely the case.)

The inner self is a vastly complex, open-ended, slowly evolving set of intuitive senses that our mind has about our entire being-in-the-world. This idea about the self is obviously not simple to understand, so let me try to make it clearer by comparing it with some well-known phenomena. We all have experiences that we refer to as "I have a sense of . . ." (or "My grasp of the situation is . . ."). (I have previously examined the way in which we grasp or sense what is going on in a group or an individual relationship long before we can say specifically in words what it means. See Douglas, 1976.) A common example is the "*déjà-vu*" experience. When we have the *déjà-vu* feeling, we feel or sense that we have had this experience before, have seen this person somewhere before, and so on. This is an instantaneous awareness of a meaningful relationship, such as a past association, which we cannot explain and commonly cannot remember in any detail. We know immediately that something in our vast memories is relevant to what we now see or feel, but we can only sense what the relation is, not define it clearly and distinctly. We have a haunting feeling of the relationship, not a clear definition of it. Sometimes we can spend days thinking about it, searching our memories, before we realize consciously what, exactly, the relationship in the past was. But there is some part of the mind that is able to scan our vast memories and compare them to our immediate perceptions or thoughts almost instantaneously and give us a sense of relationship long before we can become consciously aware, in symbolic terms, of what that relationship is. (One of the most fascinating aspects of daimonic love relations, which are normally experienced today as "love at first sight," is the way in which something in the past experience of the individual seems to be responding to a new person. Wilder Penfield [1975] was able to show that there is, indeed, a specific part of the brain, the interpretive cortex of the temporal lobe, that produces this sense of *déjà-vu* when it is electrically stimulated in specific ways. This part of the brain is in fact connected directly with the midbrain centers, which Penfield thinks are the center of self-consciousness and the willing mind, and diffusely with the whole neocortex. It seems to be a vital part of the centrally integrating function of the brain.)

This seemingly simple experience, which probably involves a vastly complex though rapid screening of the immense human memory, must certainly be simple in its operation compared to the form of presymbolic sensing known as "creative insight" or "intuition," but the general form is the same. The clearest, most reliable finding of all the work on creative thought is that creative thoughts come as sudden insights after long experience with a particular realm of phenomena. In some vastly complex way the mind seems to analyze, sort out, and integrate complex experience and then present us with a sudden insight or sense of the whole meaning, a new gestalt (general form), of the experience, long before we can figure out symbolically and rationally why the insight is right. (In fact, our minds tell us that certain experiences of reality feel right or true, regardless of what reason tells us.)

The self seems to be a very similar high-order sense (scan) of our inner being in relation to the world and to itself (since the self is reflective). The self is our general sense of how our basic emotions and values are related to our past, present, and future situations, and this sense is vital in giving us an immediate sense or creative insight into how we should orient ourselves toward the world, how we should thrust ourselves into the world, in order to fulfill and enhance (build and or expand) our basic emotions and values. It is our sense of self that gives us the feeling that "That is not like me," "But I'm not like that," "But I'm not the sort of person who would do such a thing," "But I could never," "But I feel violated," "I would not feel right," "I just sense that it's wrong for me," and so on, all the time. We cannot generally say exactly why "it is not like me." We do not know in words, but we know immediately.

Our sense of self is a set of general guidelines, not a set of specific instructions, for orienting ourselves in the world and for acting. It is up to our rational minds to use this sense of self, these general guidelines, as crucial information in planning a specific path of action that will best suit our entire life. Our sense of self is, then, our set of guidelines for integrating any specific actions into our whole life-situation (past, present, and future) so as to fulfill and enhance our selves. This sense of self is both closed and open. It involves an irreducible closed set of survival or *security guidelines*, which must be followed to insure the continued existence of the self-in-the-world. But the sense of self is also open to the changing world, and, in a very important way, once the basic security guidelines are met ("satisfied"), the sense of self orients us toward building, expanding, and enhancing the self-in-the-world. The inner self is a searching, growing, creating self, both in the inner realm of thought and feeling, and outwardly, in the physical universe. The basic survival or security guidelines operate on the principle of feedback, so that such action is self-limiting (hunger, when satisfied, is replaced by satiation, and we stop eating; the hypothalamic centers associated with such behavior work on very simple feedback programs). But once these security needs are met, the "higher" guidelines operate on a principle of "feedforward" (as a once-positivistic neurophysiologist now calls it). That is, our higher guidelines lead us to crave newness, to reach out, to thrust ourselves into the world, to strive to grow, to create, to expand. Man first seeks security physically and socially; this is most obvious in the case of the child, who is overwhelmingly concerned with survival values, love values, and competency values. But then he becomes the seeker after the new, the great risk-taker, seeking excitement, the explorer, the creator of new selves and of new worlds.

References

Adler, Peter, and Patricia A. Adler. 1980. "Symbolic Interactionism." In Jack D. Douglas et al., *Introduction to the Sociologies of Everyday Life*. Boston: Allyn & Bacon.

Arieti, S. 1972. *The Will to Be Human*. New York: Dell.

————. 1975. *Interpretation of Schizophrenia*. New York: Basic Books.

Baechler, Jean. 1979. *Suicides*. New York: Basic Books.

Becker, Ernest. 1973. *The Denial of Death*. New York: Free Press.

Bettelheim, Bruno. 1943. "Individual and Group Behavior in Extreme Situations." *Journal of Abnormal and Social Psychology* 38(4):417–52.

Bonner, John Tyler. 1980. *The Evolution of Culture in Animals*. Princeton, N.J.: Princeton University Press.

Bork, Robert. 1980. "Justice Douglas." *Wall Street Journal*, October 3.

Bowlby, John. 1969. *Attachment and Loss*. 3 vols. Especially vol. 1, *Attachment*. New York: Basic Books.

Branden, Nathaniel. 1980. *The Psychology of Romantic Love*. Los Angeles: Tarcher.

Buber, Martin. 1970. *I and Thou*. New York: Scribner's.

Dawkins, Richard. 1976. *The Selfish Gene*. New York: Oxford University Press.

Day, Max, and Elvin V. Semrad. 1978. "Schizophrenic Reactions." In Armand M. Nicholi, ed., *The Harvard Guide to Modern Psychiatry*. Cambridge, Mass.: Belknap Press of Harvard University Press.

Douglas, Jack D. 1967. *The Social Meanings of Suicide*. Princeton, N.J.: Princeton University Press.

————. 1976. *Investigative Social Research*. Beverly Hills, Calif.: Sage.

————. 1981. "The Myth of Rationalism versus Human Nature." Unpublished manuscript.

————. Forthcoming. *Creative Deviance and Social Change*.

Douglas, Jack D., Patricia A. Adler, Peter Adler, Andrea Fontana, C. Robert Freeman, and Joseph A. Kotarba. 1980. *Introduction to the Sociologies of Everyday Life*. Boston: Allyn & Bacon.

Douglas, Jack D., and Stephen Weinstein. Forthcoming. *Beautiful Women*. Beverly Hills, Calif.: Sage.

Erikson, Erik H. 1959. "Identity and the Life Cycle." In G. S. Klein, ed., *Psychological Issues*. New York: International Universities Press.

Frankl, Victor. 1978. *The Unheard Cry for Meaning*. New York: Simon & Schuster.

Fromm, Erich. 1956. *The Art of Loving*. New York: Harper & Row.

Hilgard, Ernest R. 1977. *Divided Consciousness*. New York: Wiley.

Horney, Karen. 1950. *Neurosis and Human Growth*. New York: Norton.

Kahler, Erich. 1957. *The Tower and the Abyss*. New York: Braziller.

Kotarba, Joseph A. 1983. *Chronic Pain: Its Social Dimensions*. Beverly Hills, Calif.: Sage.

Laing, R. D. 1965. *The Divided Self*. New York: Pantheon.

Lee, Dorothy. 1959. *Freedom and Culture*. Englewood Cliffs, N.J.: Prentice-Hall.

————. 1976. *Valuing the Self*. Englewood Cliffs, N.J.: Prentice-Hall.

Lifton, Robert Jan. 1976. *The Life of the Self*. New York: Simon & Schuster / Touchstone.

Maslow, Abraham. 1968. *Toward a Psychology of Being*. New York: Van Nostrand.

Matza, David. 1964. *Delinquency and Drift*. New York: Wiley.

May, Rollo. 1969. *Love and Will*. New York: Norton.

Penfield, Wilder. 1975. *The Mystery of the Mind: A Critical Study of Consciousness and the Human Brain*. Princeton, N.J.: Princeton University Press.

Rogers, Carl R. 1972. *Becoming Partners*. New York: Dell.

Rosenberg, Morris. 1979. *Conceiving the Self*. New York: Basic Books.

Sherif, Muzafer. 1968. "Self-Concept." In *International Encyclopedia of the Social Sciences*, vol. 14. New York: Macmillan.

Sherif, Muzafer, and Hadley Cantril. 1947. *The Psychology of Ego-Involvements*. New York: Wiley.

Smith, Adam. 1967. "Self-Approbation, Self-Disapprobation and the Man within the Breast." In Louis Schneider, ed., *The Scottish Moralists*. Chicago: University of Chicago Press.

Tomkins, Silvan S. 1980. "Affect as Amplification: Some Modifications in Theory." In Robert Plutchik and Henry Kellerman, eds., *Emotion: Theory, Research, and Experience*. New York: Academic Press.

Turnbull, Colin. 1972. *The Mountain People*. New York: Simon & Schuster.

Wilson, Edward. 1975. *Sociobiology*. Cambridge, Mass.: Belknap Press of Harvard University Press.

Yalom, Irvin D. 1980. *Existential Psychotherapy*. New York: Basic Books.

Zurcher, Louis A. 1977. *The Mutable Self*. Beverly Hills, Calif.: Sage.

An Existential View of Organizations: Is the Member Condemned to Be Free?

Ronald W. Smith

Sociologists have formulated numerous rational and functional theories and positivistic methodologies for studying complex organizations (Benson, 1977). A growing number of theorists, however, have rejected these conceptions on the grounds that organizations are too narrowly conceived when approached in such a manner. They argue instead that we need to know more about how the feelings, interests, goals, and creativity of members of organizations come to bear on organizational life. These theorists hold in common the idea that attention should be given to what Schutz (1953) called the attitudes of everyday life and socially sanctioned typifications.

In this paper I too will assert that we need to look at the person in the organization, and I will draw on several notable efforts that have been made in this direction. Bittner (1965) viewed organizations as consisting of a stable association of individuals engaged in concerted activities to accomplish some objective(s), and he maintained that formal structures remain undetermined until the organization's members, as actors, give meaning to them through their actual use. Similarly, Goffman (1959) conceived of organizations "as congeries of overlapping moral orders created and re-created in the course of social interactions that are constructed in order to facilitate the work of making a self" (Blankenship, 1977:30). He showed the innovativeness of members as they "worked" the organizations, i.e., gave meaning to the formal structures of their organizations and simultaneously shaped their own personal careers (Goffman, 1961).

Manning, also, has contended that a study of an organization must focus on the use of it by actors. "Features of organizational settings," he says, "are not exhausted by structural characteristics. To subscribe to this view is analogous to believing that language behavior can be understood by a close study of a dictionary" (Manning, 1970:246). In his examination of member socialization he maintained that this is not a process whereby members simply learn formal rules and "slots" into which one is to fit. People also create their own organizational roles, and they apply rules to specific areas on the ground of their situated activity. "Rules," he says, "take on an indexical quality, that is, they can be understood only contextually, as practical problems that themselves arise out of the association of those people facing those periods of time" (1970:241). Silverman (1971) agrees that member conduct is far from routine and is, in fact, socially accomplished, i.e., dependent on specific problems that arise and on unstated assumptions. He utilized the "action frame of reference" in his analysis and accordingly viewed organizations as expressions, or artifacts, of participants' orientations, commitments, and meanings for their own acts, the acts of others, and life in general. Thus, an organization must be examined through the "eyes of its members," and the actions of an organization should be seen as the result of the individuals who participate in the group. Weick (1979:chap. 1) has argued that the interdependencies among members, not official plans and procedures, are the substance of organizations, and these interdependencies are always fluid and shifting. Members spend much of their time negotiating meanings among themselves, principally to decide on acceptable versions of what is going on in the organization. Denhardt, in his recent philosophical discourse about individual freedom in an age of organization, likewise views organizations as settings for human action. A reconstituted sociology would approach organizations as "historically constituted, humanly derived institutions, always subject to analysis and reformulation; individuals would be seen as active participants in the process of constructing and modifying these institutions" (Denhardt 1981:73). Finally, Arams (1976) and Drabek and Haas (1974) have pointed out that organizational members are considerably freer in terms of their thinking and conduct than they have been depicted in both popular literature and organizational theories.

My effort here is to add to the growing body of literature that focuses on the organizational member and on the way that individual feelings impinge on organizational life. Appropriately, much of my analysis is based on the basic tenets of existential sociology. It is unnecessary to provide a detailed discussion here of the perspective's historical origins, assumptions, varying definitions, and overlap with other approaches, since this information is contained in the introductory chapters of this book. (But see also Tiryakian, 1962, Manning, 1973, Craib, 1976, Douglas and Johnson, 1977, and Kotarba, 1979.) It will suffice to say that existential sociology puts forth the following basic principles: first, it is concerned with the study of human experience in the world in all its forms. Second, its focus is on how people live, think, and act, but special attention is given to feelings and emotions, a part of human existence that has been dismissed or treated superficially by other perspectives. Third, the human is seen as situated in action, yet free to create his or her own life-ways. The human capacity to innovate, change, and emerge is especially witnessed when problematic features in our lives develop. Fourth, existential sociology

enables the user to see how problematic most of life's meanings and understandings are for us all. It shows us how the person uses personal
interests and feelings in the formulation of public conduct, sometimes
hiding and at other times disclosing these personal considerations. And,
fifth, as for method of discovery, human experience is best understood via
direct personal experience. The study of human conduct should be grounded
in concrete socially situated experience, including events in the researcher's own daily life. As Douglas and Johnson argue, "Any study of the world
ultimately depends upon the mind knowing itself: upon some form of systematic introspection and rational analysis" (Douglas and Johnson, 1977:xi).
As with any theoretical approach, the ultimate worth of existential sociology
lies in how well it helps us understand human conduct. In this paper,
existential sociology will be seen as a valuable tool for describing the day-
to-day realities of member conduct in organizational settings.

I shall use a tripartite scheme for examining organizations: (1) the nature
and importance of individual members' interests, feelings, and goals; (2)
the organizational identity that the member is expected to perform; and
(3) some of the particular existential selves that members choose relative
to the organization. Many of my examples are drawn from university life.
Most universities appear to be what Weick (1976) calls "loosely coupled"
systems. In such systems, organizational elements and events are linked,
yet each possesses its own identity; also, goals are often inconsistent and
ill-defined, and participants vary in the time and effort they devote to the
organization. Thus, any complexities and confusions that may characterize
the following analysis simply reflect the nature of the organization studied.
The description also reflects my own observations as a faculty member,
department chairman, and assistant dean, for I contend that understanding
human behavior begins with an examination of one's own conscious awareness and self-observations. A common theme throughout my analysis is
that existential choice is an inherent and necessary part of all organizational
roles.

MULTIPLE INTERESTS AND FEELINGS OF MEMBERS AS INDIVIDUALS

Some of the early literature concerned with organizations alluded to the
idea that members' feelings and thoughts did, indeed, affect the organization. In the now classic *The Functions of the Executive* (1938), Chester
Barnard maintained that both logical and nonlogical mental processes are
important to organizational work. He described nonlogical processes in
terms of intuition, inspiration, and enthusiasm. In their discussion of decision-making theory, March and Simon (1958) viewed organizational members as creative problem-solvers searching for alternatives, choosing either
optimal or satisfying solutions, and establishing programs based on both
organizational mandates and members' interests and emotions. A recent

discussion by Denhardt gives even more importance to the role of individual feelings in organizations:

> The sterile words which comprise the organization—rationality, efficiency, objectivity—appear foreign to our actual experience. Those surges of emotion and meanings, those "special moments" which occur from time to time in our lives and work, simply cannot be comprehended in instrumental terms. Yet these are important, vital experiences, deserving of our attention, for they represent our efforts to break free from the restrictive categories of a rationalized existence. They should not be defiled by imposing on them standards or concepts which do damage to their essential meaning. [1981:44–45]

Examples of how feelings relate to the preplanned purpose of an organization are numerous. A business employee may be personally committed to reaching the formal goals of his company, actively work to subvert them, remain indifferent to them, or attempt to establish an entirely new set of goals for members to achieve. It is also the case that organizational members' interests and feelings toward each other, such as dislike, mistrust, envy, competition, sexual desire, overconfidence, pity, respect, admiration, and altruism, impinge not only on the members' interpersonal relationships but ultimately on the output of the organization. College deans might question each other's competence and so refuse to work together; faculty might be intimidated by deans and so offer suggestions reluctantly, if at all; and coworkers might simply enjoy each other's company and, as a result, eagerly form work teams. It is often difficult for some administrators to accept the notion that a purely personal consideration—for example, the fact that two coworkers have children who play on the same basketball team—may well affect the relationship between coworkers and thereby influence their daily work in the organization. Members also interact with a variety of extraorganizational people, including their family, neighbors, and club members, and this interaction frequently comes to influence their behavior *within* the organization. A prime example is the person who brings his or her personal life—his marriage problems, for instance—to the office and is, as a result, distracted or less efficient in his or her work. The essential point is that the personal characteristics, mannerisms, problems, and temperaments (i.e., idiosyncrasies) of individual members penetrate the organization. As Kotarba (1979:350) has stated, "The goal of all human behavior is the accommodation of satisfaction of feelings. This does not mean that people are simply pleasure-seeking creatures. Our point is that social decisions and actions are made primarily in accord with related feelings." And, as Benson (1977:4) has stated, "Social arrangements [in organizations] are created from the basically concrete, mundane tasks confronting people in their everyday life." Thus, nonrational features of organizations form much of the basis of organizational reality. I am not arguing here that organizational structure never has impact on member conduct. The essential point I am making is that this impact has received most of the attention by professionals, to the neglect of examining the impact that individual members have on the organization.

That feelings and thoughts are prime movers of organizational life is especially apparent if we look at role occupants who have been granted formal power to make decisions, solve problems, and initiate new ideas. Presidents, vice-presidents, deans, and other administrative officials can change the course of a university, sometimes quickly, sometimes only with time and careful manipulation. No doubt, some organizations define members' roles more closely or do not allow for such free latitude of conduct. That is, the formal structure of some organizations sets forth detailed and specific regulations that govern members' actions; managers may employ coercive power and have great surveillance over members, and participants may be morally committed to the organization's purposes and the formal structure that they allow to govern them. Even in these situations, however, the control of members' thoughts and deeds may be more apparent than real. For example, even under monocratic authority structures, like those employed in prisons and mental institutions, we find that prisoners and patients "work" the organization to meet their own individual needs. It is sometimes thought, too, that other types of "lower" participants in an organization have insignificant impact. However, hospital nurses, secretaries in universities, assembly-line workers in factories, and other such participants bring to their work roles their personal fears, moral obligations, personal pride, revenge, political beliefs, joys, dislikes, and so forth. As a result, they may slow or speed up their daily work, define features of jobs as problematic, so that management must direct its attention to the issue, decide on what work requires priority and special quality, choose work rules to violate, and create speedier methods of getting jobs done.

The importance presently being given to personal thoughts and feelings in organizational life must be measured against two arguments that have been used to justify organizational reality. One argument is referred to as "exteriority," the other as "constraints." By "exteriority" Durkheim (1933) meant that patterns continue over time, that order remains despite changing membership; by "constraints" he meant the limits imposed on organizational members' thoughts and conduct. His most fundamental contention was that patterns of social order exist independently of constituent members. Few observers of complex organizations would disagree that organizations have a remarkable stability in the face of members entering and exiting, yet here again the role of the person in the organization has been grossly underestimated. Exteriority is true to some extent, but, as members come and go, especially those who have power to influence both goals and other members, the organization does change. New values and rules may be introduced, and new actions may be taken. The texture of the organization is altered, sometimes drastically, as in the case of a new college president who decides to abandon old priorities and emphasize, instead, intercollegiate athletics. As for constraints: the rules and limits that prescribe roles do, indeed, guide members' action, but members can create and reinterpret constraints. A new graduate dean may inspire a collective push for academic standards over enrollment considerations, or a department chairperson may plead for more emphasis on applied vs. pure academic research by faculty (see Olsen, 1968:40–44). Thus, Durkheim's social-order perspective, which is still assumed in most organizational theories, is too absolutist. A perspective that gives us a broader and clearer look at organizational reality is one in which social order and individual interests and feelings are seen to interpenetrate each other's existence and functioning (Olsen, 1968:44).

In contrast to the multiple interests and feelings on which organizational participants base their actions, members are also confronted with organizational identities they are expected to assume. These identities now become our focus of concern.

Multiple Organizational Identities

Sociologists have often thought of organizations as providing well-planned scripts for their members to follow. And, of course, these scripts are learned via socialization, an ongoing learning process that generally begins when any new member enters an organization. This socialization, however, can be initiated before actual entry into the organization, by schools and training programs. As Denhardt (1981:106) has observed, "the organization takes shape as a result of the interaction of the individual's store of knowledge (those norms, values, and standards of behavior which individuals bring with them to organization)." The image that members of an organization are expected to present is referred to here as the organizational identity. Some of the typical components of the organizational identity are the specific work duties and rights associated with a particular organizational role. For example, a university faculty member may be required to teach several classes and serve on departmental committees, and he or she may also be expected to engage in research and publication. Some work duties and rights may be formalized requirements, and Manning (1970) informs us that many others are unwritten and simply known among members. Further, some duties and rights may also be considered of greater importance than others.

Another usual and important component of organizational identity is the notion that members are representatives of the organization and should, as such, project its positive attributes in all of their activities. This presentation consists of putting forth the merits, ideologies, and goals of the larger organization. For example, a university professor is to show dedication to students, illustrate intellectual curiosity, and give evidence of concern about the university's goals and problems. Of interest is the fact that this portrayal of the organization is expected to occur not only "on the job" but frequently when one is beyond the usual organizational boundaries. A professor, for instance, is expected to present the positive features of the university not only when he or she is teaching a class or conducting a research project but also in "nonschool" settings, including the home or neighborhood, the local club or cocktail party; and if a relative, neighbor, friend, stranger, or any other outsider calls into question some feature of the university, the professor must speak in its defense. Of course, there are nonorganizational situations in which others may be unaware of one's organizational status; the organizational identity may then have little or no influence on the subsequent interaction. Still, there are many non-organizational situations where others are keenly aware of the individual's organizational status. And, even when others may be unaware of one's organizational status, the member "is" conscious of his or her participation and may then choose to act in reference to that status (for example, a faculty member may ask himself/herself, "Should I act as a professor and/or sociologist?").

As Scott and Lyman (1968), Seider (1974), Kamens (1977), and Smith and Asher (1980) have indicated, organizations may provide members with linguistic accounts that defend the university in the face of adversity. These accounts may be further components of one's organizational identity. A university administrator, for example, is expected to relay accounts that justify declining enrollments—that the problem is the end of the "baby boom" enrollments, for example, and not the effectiveness of the university, or that the university is now becoming more conscious of quality over quantity. He or she is to defend notions of faculty sabbatical leaves or released time, including the account that professors need this time to engage in research and develop new knowledge. Manning (1970:256) has also given much importance to the role of language in organizational settings. He suggests that if sociologists are to understand members' socialization they must learn the natural language of the organization, giving special attention to terms that designate roles and functions of members.

The organizational identity will often reflect aspects of the larger culture. By reflecting what is highly valued in the culture, the organizational identity is linked with the virtues and ideals of life; the organization is thought to be further protected in this way. Professors, for example, are to echo the importance of education in producing an informed electorate, in promoting individual fulfillment and job mobility, and accomplishing numerous national goals. Organizational identity thus comprises many features.

There are several reasons why the organization's identity is seen as important by the participants who devise it. By presenting a favorable image of the organization, the member is said to help the organization express its mission and protect it from environmental challenges. Adherence to the organizational identity is then said to contribute to organizational survival. In management theory and principles, managers and other functionaries are told to encourage a shared perspective, a common reference for all to follow, so that members will comply with the collective will and cooperate in mutual goal-seeking and daily work routines. The prevailing thought is that when members reflect the organizational identity, conflicts and other "disruptive" conduct are reduced. Thus, in keeping with the purposive-rational features of organizations, adherence to the organization's identity is, in general, thought to bring about reason, technical rationality, stability, efficiency, and the accomplishment of formal goals. The contrary is also believed; that is, organizational identity can "help eliminate those bothersome, inefficient human qualities, such as feelings, that interfere with rational endeavor" (Denhardt, 1981:28). A significant point has been forgotten or glossed over by those organizational theorists, such as Weber, who stressed organizational rationality, the desirability of the collective self, and the socialization that has produced this self. The point is that what is most desired in organizations is that members' activities "appear" rational, not that they necessarily are rational in day-to-day experience or that rationality is always necessary to the fulfillment of the organization's purposes.

On closer examination of the organizational self, we find that the so-called organizational view is always "someone's" view. This someone will claim that this is the appropriate view for all members to follow. Selznick (1948) stressed this very point when he examined the importance of informal forces in organizations. The person who puts forth a version of the organizational identity is frequently an official representative or member with power, such as a president, vice-president, or dean. As might be expected, we generally find that not one but several organizational identities may be put forth for individual members to portray. Organizations are seldom unitary in purpose and may contain different factions, each representing different interests and goals. As Silverman (1971:194) tells us, "There is thus not one rationality (residing in the work organization or the official goals of the system) but a 'multitude' of rationalities each of which generates the 'in-order-to' motives of participants." Within a university, for example, one group may want the faculty to show concern for increased enrollment, another may lobby for a return to classical education, still another may call for more professional programs, and, finally, someone's preoccupation may be with educating the masses. Each subgroup desires, and often actively pressures, members to put forth its version of the organizational identity, with all its particular priorities, values, procedures, and modes of conduct. Moreover, constituencies need not always be found "within" the organization; powerful sources "outside" the immediate organization, such as university regents, state legislators, and publics, may each want the university's faculty to reflect a particular image consistent with its expectations. It is also true that his or her profession provides the faculty member with perspectives that are to be expressed in performing his or her organizational role. Sociologists are to reflect the profession's values of academic freedom, desirability of theory and systematic research, and concern with social problems and with improving the human condition. It may well be that these versions of how the member is to act, these organizational identities, will conflict with each other. For instance, while the organization often expects the member to profess institutional loyalty, the academic profession teaches its members to pay allegiance to the values of the profession and to be responsive to fellow professionals. This classic conflict has been discussed in the literature as the "professional-bureaucratic dilemma" (see Blau and Scott, 1962:245–46).

Selznick (1948) argued that formal structures within organizations (as stated earlier, organizational identities often incorporate such formal elements) are ideal representations and hence seldom attainable, and that attention should rather be given to many of the adaptive and cooperative manipulations of organizational members. Similarly, Katz and Kahn (1966:453) have stressed that human organizations are totally dependent on members to enact organizational "performances." Thus, the fact that an organization (actually certain participants) puts forth an organizational identity for members to follow does not necessarily mean that members take this script and enact it automatically and without reformulation. Meanings that are provided by the larger collective certainly influence members' thoughts and actions, yet role-making on the part of members also results (Blumer, 1962). Over the years, for instance, successive chairmen of the same university department will profess different values, portray different images of the collective, and use wide-ranging strategies to solve crises. A more accurate portrayal of organizational life is that the organizational identity(ies) is present for role occupants to utilize—to a greater or lesser degree and depending on the situation, audience, constituency, and problem confronted. It is often the case that some organizational identities are contradictory; some offer incomplete guides for action; the socialization regarding a particular organizational identity is never perfect; some aspects of an organizational identity have been internalized, while some are external to the individual; or a discrepancy may exist between what others think is being performed and the reality of how things are done in day-to-day work tasks. Thus, while the organizational identity(ies) influences members' thoughts and actions, this representation of the collective does not determine member conduct. Considerable freedom is left to the individual member, and, accordingly, these individual participants fill roles, official purposes, and established procedures with unique content (Benson, 1977:6).

Manning (1970:243–44) supports this view when he says that "The construction of organized social action remains in the hands of the actor."

My contention here is that to know an organization requires knowledge of its formal structures, especially the organizational identity(ies) the member is expected to present to others, but this knowledge provides a far from total picture unless one also knows how the formal structures are actually used by members and under what circumstances. And, as my discussion has already indicated, personal interests and feelings are quite frequently forces behind the actual implementation of formal structures. I now turn to those existential selves that the participant chooses to perform relative to the organization.

EXISTENTIAL SELVES RELATIVE TO THE ORGANIZATION

I will begin my discussion of existential selves within organizational life by quoting Denhardt:

> We act. And through our actions we give expression to the personal and social commitments we have made. At best, this expression is incomplete in the sense that neither our actions nor the language we use to embody the idea of action can fully represent the complete psychic circumstance upon which our actions are based; yet we are inevitably forced to act and to be judged by our actions. Here we encounter the problem of choice—the independent comprehension of reality permits authentic and informed choices about the way in which we carry out the tasks of life. Choice, then, provides the connecting link between meaning and action; to seek the clearest expression of our passions, we must constantly seek to expand the possibilities for choice. [Denhardt, 1981:7]

In the day-to-day activities of organizational life individual members face problems of choice—crucial ones being that of weighing personal interests and feelings against the organizational identity(ies) one is to perform. The eventual behavioral outcome of this choice is viewed here as constituting much of the individual's existential self relative to the organization. Thus, as a beginning definition, the existential self may be seen as consisting largely of the conduct created and performed by the individual member and as based on his/her interests and feelings and perception of the organizational identity(ies) that he/she is expected to portray. This conception is consistent with that provided by Manning in that it emphasizes the interaction between feelings and environmental expectancies in the creation of conduct. Manning (1973:212–13) has stated that "The self exists in situations where it is intertwined with sentiments and feelings—the existential self is a sentient self. It is further an intentional self, tested in interpersonal acts, and having a degree of significance derived from types of relationality to others. The self in a situation is open physically and symbolically to new possibilities; it is a congeries of unfolding, open possibilities."

In some situations personal interests and feelings may be the prime components of the existential self relative to the organization. For example, an administrator who has an intense commitment to some religion may choose to bring this personal belief into his/her performance as an organizational member; he/she may then actively support the promotion of a colleague who shares the same religious ideology. In contrast to this, a member may allow the organizational identity to dominate; he/she may then appear to meet the widespread image in modern society of the complete official, the soulless bureaucrat who reflects the organization to the point of having no personal feelings or commitments. In this context, Riesman's (1950) discussion of the "other-directed" man indicates someone who overresponds to the organizational identity. Similarly, Whyte's (1956) notion of the "organization man" illustrates how the individual may elect to portray the corporation's model of behavior to the exclusion of his/her own personal characteristics. As Simon, et al. (1950:82) have also observed,

> Administrative man accepts the organizational goals as the value premises of his decisions, is particularly sensitive and reactive to the influences upon him of the other members of his organization. . . . What is perhaps most remarkable and unique about administrative man is that the organizational influences do not merely cause him to do certain specific things . . . but induce in him a pattern of doing "whatever" things are appropriate to carry out in cooperation with others the organization goals.

It is of interest to note that complaints of bias, lack of dignity, and lack of personal control are often leveled at the organizational member who is perceived as allowing personal interests and feelings to dominate his/her behavior. Ironically, there also seems to be considerable disdain for the person who chooses to portray the organizational identity exclusively (Bensman and Lilienfeld, 1979:2–4). A dramatic example, often cited, concerns World War II German officials who justified their actions of destroying millions of Jews and other minorities by saying that they were simply carrying out orders from above.

I have so far mentioned two major choices for the organizational member (the choice to allow personal interests and feelings dominate and the choice to let the organizational identity prevail), but a third major choice is also available. One may so completely reject the organizational identity that is to be performed that one chooses to cease to participate in the organization. In other words, one may quit one's job, church, community group, etc., in the belief that continued involvement restricts personal growth. Such a choice is often difficult to make, since the member's livelihood, contacts with others, etc., may be at stake. Further, one organizational identity may be merely replaced by another when the person enters a new organization.

The creation of the existential self is unproblematic when the member's personal interests and feelings and the organizational identity coincide, but when conflict exists the member must decide which of the two domains should take priority. For example, a college dean who is personally committed to academic quality is likely to experience little difficulty in formulating and presenting his existential self when other administrators and faculty support the same image. The formulation of the existential self becomes troublesome for this dean, however, when others are solely concerned with increased enrollments at the cost of lowered academic standards. It would seem that considerable introspection and anxiety may occur when the member faces conflict between his/her innermost being and the organizational identity on which his/her physical and social survival may depend. In fact, it may well be that the most frequent and personally troublesome conflicts within organizations are not those between individual rivals or conflicting departments, between staff and line personnel, or between workers and managers, all of which are frequently mentioned in the literature, but those that are internal to the person and often kept private, i.e., those between the organizational identity to be presented and one's personal interests and feelings (Bensman and Lilienfeld, 1979:3).

The formation of existential selves is always going on, but certain situations seem to call forth this creative process more than others do. New, unexpected situations arise, for example, and the member must weigh personal as well as organizational considerations. For example, if a state law requiring budgetary restraint is passed, such as California's Proposition 13 in the late 1970s, a university administrator may consider how the law affects his/her own property taxes, but as an administrator he will be forced to look beyond his personal feelings to consider the law's effect on taxpayers and other state programs, and, most of all, its effect on his/her own university. The administrator may not believe all the information that comes in; he/she may define the problem as serious or trivial. Ultimately, the administrator will try to present a meaningful interpretation of the problem as it pertains to the members and aims of his/her organization.

Other situations that especially call forth existential selves may involve problems of worker morale, decreased productivity, loss of capital, unfavorable public opinion, and other forces that threaten organizational survival. It is also the case that the formal structures of organizations never provide complete guidelines for every situation, and the guides that do exist may be unclear. These incomplete or vague organizational patterns will also call forth the expression of the existential self. For example, a faculty advisor may well be called on for help by a student with a graduation problem, where the catalogue provides no rule at all on whether some course may be counted or where the rule is vaguely stated and its interpretation is therefore left to the advisor's discretion. Finally, some conflicts occur as a matter of course in organizations, and their resolution may necessitate the formation of an existential self by members. Aram (1976), for example, points out five conflicts found in organizations that allow managers existential choice: self versus collective interests; control versus initiative; personal versus group norms; status quo versus change; and rational efficiency versus humane considerations.

Why do situations of uncertainty, challenge, and conflict seem especially to call forth the creation of the existential self? It is because these situations call into question the social order of everyday interaction. More specifically, the organizational identity and/or the individual member's own personal sense of harmony are disrupted. Consequently, the organization's members are moved to reestablish order, for the sake of the organization and/or for themselves.

The existential selves that are presented to organizational members, the public, or other constituencies take on many shapes and forms. Someone may account for a deviation by indicating that it is absurd, crazy, or bizarre; for example, a faculty member may explain a regent's policy by indicating that the rule resulted from irrationality or ignorance. Or someone may be unable to explain a situation and so resort to remarks like "I don't know what to say!" or "I just don't know what to tell you!" A seemingly rational presentation of self may be given forth by members, yet nonrational motives were the sole consideration that led to the performance. In an annual evaluation a department chairperson may describe the secretary as a fast and accurate typist, an efficient supervisor of the office, and other descriptions that are linguistically acceptable within the organization, but the actual basis for the evaluation could have been the secretary's charm, wit, and undying loyalty to the boss. Douglas (1977:58) has noted that in organizations there is often a gap between "true" situations and the rational accounts offered to explain behavior. It is easy to think of other instances in which the existential self presented serves to screen actual thoughts and feelings. For example, deans may reify the organization, give it a reality, when they say, "The university just will not allow that," when answering a faculty request that it is really being defined by the administrator him/herself as nonsensical, trivial, or impossible to solve. Or members may utilize organizational rules, principles, and policies in a manipulative fashion when expressing their existential selves. For example, an overly cautious dean, who wishes not to make a decision on a controversial faculty tenure case, may claim that the academic department in question is an autonomous unit, with expertise and the power of decision; thus the decision is passed down the administrative ladder. In contrast, the dean who personally disagrees with some departmental decision may claim that departments are merely advisory and that authority rests in his/her administrative purview.

Do those within the organization come to believe their own rational accounts? Surely some do, but others know that the existential self presented is sometimes a "front," nothing but a fabrication of "reality," and then ridicule these accounts to other trusted insiders. It seems apparent that the enactment of existential selves may ultimately either reinforce, undermine, or create altogether new parts of the organizational self. In the last instance, members sometimes devise new solutions when omissions, conflicts, and other problems of organizational life arise. A dean may form a liaison group to resolve conflicts among several academic departments. This innovation may bring about a shared perspective by members of the two units, mutual respect for problems, and greater coordination of effort. Thus, the member has created meaning for the organization. On the other hand, parts of the organizational identity may be undermined. For example, if several academic deans fail to echo the regents' and higher administrators' policies and accounts regarding the need for higher enrollments at any cost, then this particular feature of the organizational identity is partially destroyed.

In the process of formulating an existential self to present to other organizational members, the individual will mentally test it for acceptability, a process that many symbolic interactionists have examined. Of course, the assumption here is that members hope others will accept this existential self as believable and reflective of reality. Sometimes the test for acceptability will take the form of one member's talking to another in a private setting so as to see the other's reaction. For example, one dean will "bounce an idea off" another dean before presenting an existential self on some issue to faculty members, students, a group of higher administrators, or even family members. If the performance is not accepted—if there is negative feedback—the member's presentation may be reformulated so as to achieve approval, although it should not be concluded that a presentation will always be adjusted for purposes of acceptance. For example, a professor may continue his presentation of being obstinate in the eyes of his peers, all the while knowing others' reaction but choosing this existential self to present. Sometimes the actions of those who present unacceptable selves will be defined by others as "odd," be attributed solely to the individual, and be regarded as in no way representative of the larger organization. Those judged unsuccessful in their presentations may be thought to have been improperly socialized into the ways of the organization or the profession. One might conjecture that organizational members who have been granted formal authority usually reflect some of the organizational identity and, in fact, have likely internalized some of it as part of their personal feelings and interests. It would also seem that successful managers also possess both knowledge of the other members' existential selves and insight into the forces that have led to their creation.

Early in my analysis I argued that all organizational members have their existential moments. Michel Crozier, in *The Bureaucratic Phenomenon*, also found that while the lowest subordinate groups in French bureaucracies do not participate much in their organizations, they insist on personal autonomy and still have some leeway in their conduct. He maintained that the French bureaucratic system allows the person "to retain something of the independence of another time within the framework of modern organization. One always obeys rules, but need not submit to another man's whims" (1964:223). However, some organizations, organizational roles, and situations allow for greater expression of the member's existential self than others. For example, armies, prisons, asylums, and other organizations with rigid, monocratic control structures provide much less freedom for members to express themselves than do collegial organizations, such as universities, hospitals, social service agencies, and law firms. In the former types of organizations the organizational identity is well structured, and those charged with enforcing compliance with official rules and policies, usually selected administrators, have been granted the authority and means to enforce conformity. Still the literature is filled with examples of how even in these so-called coercive organizations soldiers, prisoners, mental patients, and other members "work" their organizations for personal gain and thereby express their existential selves. Greater expression is allowed—in fact, is sometimes expected—among organizational members who are assigned the task of dealing with people rather than objects in the course of their work; such persons tend to be professionals as compared to other workers, individuals assigned specifically to problem-solving tasks (so called "trouble shooters"), and organizational administrators. Members occupying these positions are expected to be innovative and problem-solvers or "thinkers," and they are usually given the resources and authority to implement changes.

Finally, it should be noted that the existential selves ultimately forged and enacted may influence numerous organizational features, including members' cohesiveness, worker morale, efficiency, and accomplishment of formal goals. The fact is that virtually every conceivable part of an organization is affected by the existential selves generated by its members.

CONCLUSION

There is considerable value in approaching organizations from the perspective of existential sociology. As I noted at the outset, the perspective draws attention to the ignored topic of the individual in organizations, especially giving importance to the individual's interests and feelings. This scheme for viewing organizational life, however, is also useful for generating theory. For example, instead of assuming that order in organizations is a given, as some sociologists have done, it provides some insight into how this order takes form. It indicates that order is created in organizations largely by two interacting forces. Order is first of all imposed by the formal structure of an organization, which is in fact the result, or artifact, of "someone's" earlier-created existential self. Individual members have invented this mechanism, which is a major component of the organization's identity, to represent the collective and to perpetuate further stability and control in daily behavior. Weick (1979:12) reflected that organizational identity is "viewed as the inventions of people, inventions superimposed on flows of experience and momentarily imposing some order on these streams." Second, order within the organization is formulated by its members in the course of their day-to-day interactions. Participants interpret and reinterpret the formal structure, sometimes confirming and at other times recasting formal patterns. When members are faced with new, ambiguous, and conflicting situations, they must formulate new forms of order to deal with them. Existential sociology indicates that this ongoing interaction from which order derives is often based on personal considerations. Related to this notion, that personal interests and feelings are a prime factor in organizational life, is the idea that individuals generally seek to cooperate with each other and try to achieve harmony for the larger good in daily matters pertaining to the organization. As George Mead and other symbolic interactionists have argued, the basis of society and all group life rests on agreement as to common meanings in life and cooperation with others. This observation would seemingly apply to the actions of members of organizations.

The idea that social order results from the interacting forces of meaning given to formal guidelines by members and the desire of members to create order in their own lives is supported by Strauss and his colleagues (Strauss et al., 1964). In a study of mental hospitals these researchers maintained that

> order is the product of negotiations between members—negotiations conditioned by ideology, power, and situational considerations, but only slightly limited by rules or formal guidelines. While some agreements were of long standing, others were called into question or ignored after only a short time; although some negotiation was deliberate and produced explicit contracts, other understandings emerged from apparently insignificant interactions. [Blankenship, 1977:36]

Existential sociology is also valuable in helping us to distinguish and to show relations between key variables in organizational behavior. Some of these relationships are as follows: existential selves are the initial creators of the organizational identity(ies) put forth for members to portray; organizational identity(ies) and personal interests and feelings are primary influences on the formation of a member's existential self relative to his/her organization; the existential selves of members potentially influence all aspects of the organization, such as morale, efficiency, goal accomplishment, and organizational survival; and the type of organization, situations, and assigned work roles influence the degree of freedom one has in expressing the existential self. An implicit assumption that should be made in studying all of these relationships is that the organizational member is both situated and free, that he/she is an actor who draws on personal interests and feelings as problematic issues arise. Finally, the perspective has practical value for the operation of organizations. Managers who utilize the insights of existential sociology should have genuine concern for the interests and feelings of members of their organizations, because these variables have such great impact on the organization's success in its day-to-day operations.

There are, of course, limits to the knowledge that existential sociology can provide. One could argue that its method, i.e., direct personal experience, neither assures objectivity in observation nor allows for generalization beyond the few cases studied. It should be remembered, however, that the greatest strength of this tool is that it gives an in-depth, comprehensive picture of conduct. Regarding generalizability of findings, the information reported here about universities may apply to other organizations or, minimally, provide a comparative basis on which researchers can examine behavior in other organizations. Whether participants behave differently in other organizations, such as businesses or voluntary associations, remains to be seen in subsequent research. As for another problematic feature of the perspective, existential sociology presently cannot give us much specificity about the creation of the existential self. We do not yet know what conditions will cause the member of an organization to choose the organizational identity or what exact conditions will, on the contrary, cause a member to choose personal interests and feelings. Like most of our theories, existential sociology is too undeveloped to allow us to make such specific predictions. As the new perspective is applied to different groups and situations, we will be able to see its worth. On the basis of my observations here, the perspective seems best suited to help us understand organizational behavior in a post hoc fashion rather than to predict future organizational events. However, this problem of predictive ability no doubt applies equally to most other existing organizational theories.

A final note should be made about how existential sociology offers a promise to organizational members who are seeking innovation and change. If this scheme of interpretation is used, the importance of the individual member cannot be underestimated. Bittner, Goffman, Manning, Silverman, Weick, Denhardt, and others were correct when they defined the organization chiefly in terms of the members who compose it. Sartre once noted that "men are condemned to be free." Contrary to Weber's "iron cages" image of the restraining effect of bureaucracies, it would seem that Sartre's comment could be appropriately modified to read, "Organizational members are condemned to be free."

References

Aram, John D. 1976. *Dilemmas of Administrative Behavior.* Englewood Cliffs, N.J.: Prentice-Hall.

Bensman, Joseph, and Robert Lilienfeld. 1979. *Between Public and Private: The Lost Boundaries of the Self.* New York: Free Press.

Benson, J. Kenneth. 1977. "Organizations: A Dialectic View." *Administrative Science Quarterly* 22(3):1–21.

Barnard, Chester. 1938. *The Functions of the Executive.* Cambridge, Mass.: Harvard University Press.

Bittner, Egon. 1965. "The Concept of Organization." *Social Research* 32 (3):239–55.

Blankenship, Ralph L. 1977. *Colleagues in Organization: The Social Construction of Professional Work.* New York: Wiley.

Blau, Peter M., and Richard Scott. 1962. *Formal Organizations: A Comparative Approach.* San Francisco: Chandler.

Blumer, Herbert. 1962. "Society as Symbolic Interaction." In A. M. Rose, ed., *Human Behavior and Social Processes: An Interactionist Approach.* New York: Houghton Mifflin.

Craib, Ian. 1976. *Existentialism and Sociology: A Study of Jean-Paul Sartre.* New York: Cambridge University Press.

Crozier, Michel. 1964. *The Bureaucratic Phenomenon.* Chicago: University of Chicago Press, 1964.

Denhardt, Robert B. 1981. *In the Shadow of Organization.* Lawrence: The Regents Press of Kansas.

Douglas, Jack D., and John M. Johnson, eds. 1977. *Existential Sociology.* Cambridge, Eng.: Cambridge University Press.

Drabek, Thomas E., and J. Eugene Haas. 1974. *Understanding Complex Organizations.* Dubuque, Ia.: Brown.

Durkheim, Emile. 1933. *The Rules of Sociological Method.* Translated by Sarah A. Solovay and John H. Mueller. New York: Free Press.

Goffman, Erving. 1959. *The Presentation of Self in Everyday Life.* Garden City, N.Y.: Doubleday/Anchor.

———. 1961. *Asylums: Essays on the Social Situation of Mental Patients.* Garden City, N.Y.: Doubleday/Anchor.

Kamens, David H. 1977. "Legitimating Myths and Educational Organization: The Relationship between Organizational Ideology and Formal Structure." *American Sociological Review* 42:208–19.

Katz, Daniel, and Robert L. Kahn. 1966. *The Social Psychology of Organizations.* New York: Wiley.

Kotarba, Joseph A. 1979. "Existential Sociology." In Scott McNall, ed., *Theoretical Perspectives in Sociology*. New York: St. Martin's Press.
Manning, Peter K. 1970. "Talking and Becoming: A View of Organizational Socialization." Pp. 239–56 in Jack D. Douglas, ed., *Understanding Everyday Life*. Chicago: Aldine.
———. 1973. "Existential Sociology." *Sociological Quarterly*. 14:200–225.
March, James G., and Herbert A. Simon. 1958. *Organizations*. New York: Wiley.
Olsen, Marvin E. 1968. *The Process of Social Organization*. New York: Holt, Rinehart & Winston.
Riesman, David. 1950. *The Lonely Crowd*. New Haven: Yale University Press.
Schutz, Alfred. 1953. "Common Sense and Scientific Interpretation of Action." *Philosophy and Phenomenological Research* 14:1–38.
Scott, Marvin B., and Stanford M. Lyman. 1968. "Accounts." *American Sociological Review* 33:46–62.
Seider, Maynard S. 1974. "American Business Ideology: A Content Analysis of Executive Speeches." *American Sociological Review* 39:802–15.
Selznick, Philip. 1948. "Foundations of the Theory of Organization." *American Sociological Review* 13:25–35.
Silverman, David. 1971. *The Theory of Organization*. New York: Basic Books.
Simon, Herbert A., Donald W. Smithburg, and Victor A. Thompson. 1950. *Public Administration*. New York: Knopf.
Smith, Ronald W., and Bruce Asher. 1980. "Organizational Accounts." *Free Inquiry* 8(2):121–25.
Strauss, Anselm, Leonard Schatzman, Danuta Ehrlich, Rue Bucher, and Melvin Sabshin. 1964. *Psychiatric Ideologies and Institutions*. New York: Free Press.
Tiryakian, Edward A. 1962. *Sociologism and Existentialism*. Englewood Cliffs, N.J.: Prentice-Hall.
Weick, Karl E. 1976. "Educational Organizations as Loosely Coupled Systems." *Administrative Science Quarterly* 21:1–19.
———. 1979. *The Social Psychology of Organizing*. Reading, Mass.: Addison-Wesley.
Whyte, William H., Jr. 1956. *The Organization Man*. New York: Simon & Schuster.

The Victimized Self: The Case of Battered Women

John M. Johnson and

Kathleen J. Ferraro

INTRODUCTION

In existential sociology the self is not fixed but continually changes and adapts to new situations. The self is essentially open to the world of experience, both positive and negative. When the existential self is confronted with challenging or taxing circumstances, it does not usually recoil or shatter. Instead, it struggles to incorporate new experiences into its evolving reality. Battered women provide an excellent example of this. The victimization experienced by battered women illustrates how the existential self moves from one identity to another under varying conditions.[1] Contrary to much of the research and mass-media reporting about battered women, they do not become victims simply by being the recipients of physical violence. In fact, many women live their entire lives experiencing episodic outbursts of violence from their mates without developing the feelings and identity of a victimized self.[2]

The victimized self is a complex mixture of feelings and thoughts based on the individual's overriding feeling of having been violated, exploited, or wronged by another person or persons. It develops when an individual feels a fundamental threat to his or her very being or existence. The actions or situations people interpret as fundamental threats are varied. Some women feel deeply threatened by verbal assaults, while others may come close to death regularly without feeling themselves to be victims (Ferraro, 1979).

THE VICTIMIZATION PROCESS

Women who experience repeated violence or abuse without feeling victimized make use of rationalizations and belief systems that allow them to maintain a feeling of being in a good, normal, or at least acceptable marriage. For example, some women play the role of a "caring wife" and view situations of violence as occasions for taking responsibility to "save" their husbands. Others deny the injuries done to them, even relatively serious ones, and act as if the violence had not occurred. Some will acknowledge the existence of the abuse but reject the husband's responsibility, blaming instead external factors, such as unemployment, alcoholism, or mental illness. Others may feel they "had it coming," an attitude commonly based on feelings of submission to the husband's traditionally defined absolute dominance in the home. And some appeal to higher or institutional loyalties, such as religion, the church, or the sanctity of family life. All of these rationalizations are used by individuals to make sense of their feelings, to make rational what might otherwise be seen as irrational. For some women, these rationalizations can sustain a marriage through a lifetime of violence or abuse. Some may go to their graves believing in them, as did over 3,600 victims of family homicides in 1980 (Ferraro, 1982).

Some battered women experience a turning point when the violence or abuse done to them comes to be felt as a basic threat, whether to their physical or social self or to both. Such turning points may stem from dramatic events or crises. They may additionally originate from progressive, gradual realizations by women. In all cases, however, the experience of the turning point produces retrospective interpretations of past events, where individuals creatively seek out new understandings of "what went wrong." What had been rationalized as acceptable is recast as dangerous, malicious, perhaps life-threatening. Before this point, many women may have felt guilt concerning their own complicity in their family situations and perhaps hopefulness that things would improve over time. But these feelings commonly change to feelings of fear and despair. The experience of the turning point produces changes in feelings and interpretations. A new sense of self emerges to meet these emergent conditions. While the development of a victimized self is commonly temporary for individuals, at this juncture the self becomes organized around the perceived facts of victimization. Once women develop a victimized self—a new feeling of being exploited and a new interpretation of the causes and consequences of this exploitation—they may become sufficiently motivated to leave violent situations.

An individual's adoption of a victimized self is all-consuming. For the immediate present it tends to override (but not necessarily destroy) other aspects of the self. It becomes an organizing perspective by which all other aspects of life are interpreted or reinterpreted. It has some similarities to what Everett C. Hughes termed "master status," and indeed, for some rare individuals, the victimized self may assume such importance for long periods of time, perhaps even for the remainder of the person's life. But for most, the victimized self is temporary. After leaving a violent relationship a woman soon begins to take practical steps toward recovery and the rebuilding of her life. She must either set up a new, independent household, arrange for marriage counseling, or return to the marriage with renewed optimism that things will be different. These actions militate against continuance of the individual's sense of victimization. Thus, the victimized self tends to be temporary, certainly for those who mobilize their personal and social resources for change.

The victimized self emerges during moments of existential threat, and it dissolves when one takes actions to construct new, safer living conditions. The victimized self emerges when the rationalizations of violence and abuse begin to lose their power; it becomes the all-consuming basis for however long it takes to transcend this period of crisis and threat. It tends to dissolve, over time, for those who change their lives in new, creative ways, although the sense of victimization never disappears altogether. For all who experience it, it becomes incorporated into an individual's biography as lived experience.

CATALYSTS IN THE VICTIMIZATION PROCESS

When the process of victimization begins, events that previously had been defined as acceptable, although unpleasant, aspects of the relationship begin to take on new meanings. Violence, which had been rationalized as either insignificant in its consequences, beyond the abuser's control, or necessary to the relationship or some other value, is now redefined as abuse or battering.

Changing the definition of events is not an isolated process. It is linked to other aspects of the relationship, and, when these aspects change, specific events within the relationship undergo retrospective reinterpretation. As in cases of nonviolent divorce, what was previously accepted as part of the marriage becomes a focus for discontent (see Rasmussen and Ferraro, 1979).

There are a number of catalysts that can trigger this redefinition process. Some authors have noted that degree of severity is related to a woman's decision to leave a violent situation (Gelles, 1976). However, it is known that women can suffer extremely severe violence for many years without leaving (Pagelow, 1981). What does seem significant is a sudden change in the *level of severity*. Women who suddenly realize that their lives are literally in danger may begin the victimization process. At the point where death is imminent, rationalizations to protect the relationship often lose their validity. Life itself is more important to maintain than the relationship. A woman beaten by an alcoholic husband severely over many years explained her decision to leave on the basis of a direct threat to her life:

> It was like a pendulum. He'd swing to the extremes both ways. He'd get drunk and beat me up, then he'd get sober and treat me like a queen. One day he put a gun to my head and pulled the trigger. It wasn't loaded. But that's when I decided I'd had it. I sued for separation of property.

> I knew what was coming again, so I got out. I didn't want
> to. I still loved the guy, but I knew I had to for my own
> sanity.

Of course, many homicides do occur, and in such cases the wife has
obviously not correctly interpreted increases in severity as a threat to her
life. Increases in severity do not guarantee a reinterpretation of the situation, but they may play a part in the process.

Another catalyst for changing one's definition of violence may be a *change
in its visibility.* Creating a web of rationalizations in order to overlook
violence is accomplished more easily if no outsiders are are present to
question their validity. Since most violence between couples occurs in
privacy, victims do not have to cope with conflicting interpretations from
outsiders. In fact, they may have difficulty in convincing others that they
have a problem (Martin, 1976; Davidson, 1979). However, if the violence
does break through the bounds of privacy and occur in the presence of
others, it may trigger a reinterpretation process. Having others witness the
degradation of violence is humiliating, for it is a public statement of sub-
ordination and powerlessness. It may also happen that an objective observer will apply a different definition to the event than what is consistent
with the victim's prior rationalizations, and the mere existence of this new
definition will call into question the victim's ideas.

The effect of external definitions on a battered woman's beliefs about
her situation varies with the source and form of external definitions. The
opinions of those who are highly regarded by the victim, either by virtue
of a personal relationship or an occupational role, will be the most influential. Disbelief or an unsympathetic response from others tends to suppress a woman's belief that she has been victimized and to encourage her
to accept what has happened as normal. However, when outsiders respond
with unqualified support and condemnation of the abuser, their definitions
can be a potent catalyst toward victimization. Friends and relatives who
show genuine concern for the woman's well-being may initiate an awareness of danger that contradicts previous rationalizations. As one woman
reported:

> My mother-in-law knew what was going on, but she wouldn't
> admit it....I said, "Mom, what do you think these bruises
> are?" and she said, "Well, some people just bruise easy.
> I do it all the time, bumping into things."...and he just
> denied it, pretended like nothing happened...but this
> time, my neighbor *knew* what happened, she saw it, and
> when he denied it, she said, "I can't believe it! You know
> that's not true!"...and I was so happy that finally some-
> body else saw what was goin' on, and I just told him that
> this time I wasn't gonna come home!

Shelters for battered women are one source of external definitions that contribute to the victimization process. They offer refuge from a violent situation, a place where a woman may contemplate her circumstances and what she wants to do about them. Within a shelter she will come into contact with counselors and other battered women, who are familiar with the rationalization process and with the reluctance to give up the image of a good marriage. In counseling sessions, rap groups, and informal conversations with other residents, women will hear horror stories from others who have already defined themselves as victims. They will be encouraged to express anger over their abuse and to reject responsibility for the violence. A major goal of many shelters is to help women overcome feelings of guilt and inadequacy so that they will make choices in their own best interests. In this atmosphere, violent incidents are reexamined and defined as assaults in which the woman was *victimized* (Ferraro, 1981).

The emergence of shelters as a place to escape from violent marriages has also established a catalyst for the victimization process simply by providing a *change in resources*. When there is no practical alternative to remaining married, there is no advantage in defining oneself as a victim. When resources become available, however, it may be beneficial to reassess the value of remaining in the marriage. Roy (1979) found that the most commonly stated reason for remaining in a violent marriage was having no place else to go. Certainly, a change in resources, then, would alter one's response to violence. Not only shelters, but a change in personal circumstances, such as having the last child leave home, getting a grant for school, or finding a job, can be the catalyst for beginning to think differently about violence.

Apart from external influences, there may be *changes in the relationship itself* that initiate the victimization process. Walker (1979), in her discussion of the stages of a battering relationship, has noted that violent incidents are usually followed by periods of remorse and solicitude. Such phases can be very romantic and thus bind the woman to her husband. But as the battering progresses, this phase may shorten or disappear altogether, eliminating the basis for maintaining a positive outlook on the marriage. When the man realizes that he can get away with violence, he may view it as his prerogative and no longer feel and express remorse. Extended periods devoid of any show of kindness or love may alter the woman's feelings toward her attacker so that she eventually begins to define herself as a victim. One shelter resident described her disenchantment with her marriage this way:

> At first, you know, we used to have so much fun together.
> He has kind've, you know, a magnetic personality, he can
> be really charming. But it isn't fun anymore. Since the
> baby came, it's changed completely. He just wants me to

> stay at home, while he goes out with his friends. He doesn't
> even talk to me, most of the time. . . . No, I don't think
> I really love him anymore, not like I did.

Changes in the nature of the relationship may result in a loss of hope
that things will get better and lead to feelings of despair. As long as a
woman can cling to a hope that the violence will stop, she can delude
herself about it. But when these hopes are finally destroyed and she feels
only despair, she may begin to interpret violence as victimization. The Al-
Anon philosophy, which is designed for spouses of alcoholics, who are
often also victims of abuse, emphasizes the importance of "hitting bottom"
before a person can make real changes in his or her life. The director of
an Al-Anon-organized shelter explained hitting bottom to me:

> Before the Al-Anon program can really be of benefit, a
> woman has to hit bottom. When you hit bottom, you realize
> that all of your own efforts to control the situation have
> failed; you feel helpless and lost and worthless and com-
> pletely disenchanted with the world. Women can't really
> be helped unless they're ready for it and want it. Some
> women come here when things get bad, but they aren't
> really ready to be committed to Al-Anon yet. Things hav-
> en't gotten bad enough for them, and they go right back.
> We see this all the time.

She stressed that it is not the objective level of violence that determined
hitting bottom but, rather, the woman's feelings of despair. Before one can
develop a real, effective sense of victimization, it is necessary to feel that
the very foundations of the self have been threatened or attacked, that
one's very life or social being is endangered. It isn't until that primordial
threat has been experienced that it is likely that the individual will be
mobilized for effective action, the kind sufficient to break love-bonds or
to change external circumstances. Many do not reach this point. In 1980
over 3,600 persons were killed in family homicides. This figure alone indicates that the interpretive processes discussed here are problematic ones
for individuals. Violence may never be interpreted as life-threatening even
if it eventually has mortal consequences.

THE TURNING POINT

The victimization process involves redefining past events, their meanings,
and one's role in them. Violent incidents must be interpreted as violations
of one's rights, as unjustified attacks on one's self, and as the responsibility
of the attacker in order for a victimized self to emerge. Whatever the
original context of the violence, it is now viewed as the most explicit
expression of a generalized pattern of abuse. The positive aspects of the

relationship fade into the past, the interactional subtleties and nuances become blurred, and the self becomes organized around victimization.

For some, the awareness of the victimized self may begin with a relatively dramatic event, a "turning point," perhaps similar to what anthropologists have termed "culture shock," that heightened existential awareness associated with meeting persons from foreign cultures, when attempts at communication lay bare the artificiality of social conventions. For others, the process may be more gradual. In either case, the result is similar: for the individual, an awareness of the social reality previously taken for granted. For all individuals, almost all of the time, daily life has a certain obdurate, taken-for-granted quality to it. The substance of what is taken for granted varies from culture to culture, even between individuals within a given culture, whether one is an artist or a hod carrier. But for all persons, most of their lives have this taken-for-granted quality, which is occasionally interrupted or broken by crises of one sort or another. The effect of such crises is to reacquaint the individual with the precariousness of this taken-for-granted reality. This is a time of heightened self-consciousness, when things and events, previously assumed to have an "objective" character, seem to be merely human in their nature. Individuals who experience this crisis in their daily life commonly begin elaborate reconstructions and reinterpretations of past events and individuals in their lives. Different features of events are highlighted. Individuals previously idealized are now "demonized," as Jack Douglas has termed it, as facts of their (putative) character are fashioned in such a manner as to make sense of their evil victimizing. For some persons, perhaps only a few major portions of their lives are reinterpreted (such as the meanings of one's courtship and marriage, following a subsequent reinterpretation of battering), while for others the reinterpretation may be "global," encompassing all aspects of one's life and identity, which are now cast in a new light and subject to new understandings. Such a global reconstruction rarely occurs quickly. It commonly takes months, even years. But initiation of the process involves temporarily adopting a victimized self as a "master status" (Hughes, 1958), an interpretive frame that overrides all others in importance for the person and provides the foundation for all lesser interpretations. "Being a victim" is a way of relating to the world, a way of organizing one's thoughts and feelings about daily events and persons. Old things are seen in a new way. Old feelings are felt differently now. Old meanings are experienced in a different light. A woman who discussed her marriage while staying at a shelter illustrates this process of reinterpreting the past:

> When I look back on it now, of course, I can see how all along he'd do anything to control me. First it was little things, like wanting me not to wear makeup, then it got so he criticized everything I did. He wouldn't let me drive

> or handle our money. He wouldn't even let me buy the
> kids' Christmas presents. I think he wanted me to be his
> slave, and so he started beating on me to make sure I was
> scared of him.

Achieving a new sense of a victimized self commonly prepares the way for practical action. While it is true that some individuals seem to find solace and comfort in their interpretations of victimization as such, this is not true for most of those who feel victimized. Feeling victimized threatens one's self, one's sense of competence, and this is usually related to practical actions to see that the victimization stops or does not reoccur. The practical actions taken by individuals vary greatly. One battered woman might leave her husband, establish an independent existence, and perhaps undergo counseling to change relationship patterns that had become habitual over the years. Another might return to the marriage, accepting the husband's claims that he has changed and that he will never hurt her again. Some of those who are victimized join together with others for many purposes, such as setting up self-help groups (e.g., Al-Anon), or for social-movement organization and action. The feeling of victimization underlies social-movement participation in many cases and some political actions as well. Wars, revolutions, and many social movements have started with the feelings of the victimized self.

THE EMOTIONAL CAREER OF THE VICTIMIZED SELF

The cognitive aspects of accepting a victimized self, such as rejecting rationalizations and reinterpreting the past, are tied to the feelings that are created by being battered. The emotional career of the victimized self begins with guilt, shame, and hopefulness, moves to despair and fear, shock and confusion, and finally to relief and sometimes even elation. These feelings are experienced by women who first rationalize violence, then reach a turning point, and finally take action to escape. At any point in her emotional career a woman may decide to cling to rationalizations and a violent marriage. Only about half of the women who enter shelters actually progress along this emotional career to the point of feeling relief that they are no longer in danger. The career path, then, should be viewed as a continuum rather than a fixed sequence through which all battered women pass.

When men beat their wives, they usually have some explanation for their violence even if that explanation seems nonsensical to outsiders. Women are told that their abuse is a natural response to their inadequacies. They are made to feel that they are deficient as women, since they are unable to make their husbands happy. Battered women often feel quite guilty about their marital problems. They feel largely responsible for their husbands' violence and make efforts to control anything that might trigger their displeasure. They feel that the violence is a reflection of their own incompetence or badness. Feelings of guilt and shame are part of the early emotional career of battered victims. At the same time, however, they feel a kind of hopefulness that things will get better. Even the most violent man is nonviolent much of the time, so there is always a basis for believing that violence is exceptional and that the "real" man is not a threat.

> First of all, the first beatings, you can't believe it yourself. I'd go to bed, and I'd cry, and I just couldn't believe this was happening, and I'd wake up the next morning thinking, that couldn't have happened, or maybe it was my fault, it's so unbelievable, that this person that you're married to and you love would do that to you, but yet you can't leave either because ya know, for the other 29 days of the month that person loves you and is with you.

These feelings of guilt and shame mixed with hopefulness give way to despair when the violence continues and the relationship loses all semblance of a loving partnership. At the point of despair, the catalysts described above are most likely to influence a battered woman to make a change.

The turning point in the victimization process, when the self becomes organized around a fundamental threat, is characterized by a penetrating fear. Women who do see their husbands' actions as life-threatening experience a fear that consumes all thoughts and energies. It is felt physiologically in general body achiness, a pain in the pit of the stomach, and tension headaches. There is physical shaking, chills, and inability to eat or sleep. Sometimes the fear is expressed as a numbed shock, in which little is felt or communicated. The belief that her husband is intent on inflicting serious bodily harm explodes the prior self, which is built on rationalizations and the myth of a "good marriage." The self is left without a reality base, in a crisis of ambiguity. The woman is no longer the wife she defined herself to be, but she has not had time to create new meanings for her life. She feels afraid, alone, and confused.

> At that point, I was just panicked, and all I kept thinking was, "Oh God, he's gonna kill me." I could not think straight, I was so tired and achey, I couldn't deal with anything, find a place to move and all that. Thank God my friends took me in and hid me. They took me by the hand and led me through the motions for a few days, just took care of me, because I really felt just sick.

The victimized self is highly vulnerable. Battered women escaping violent situations depend on the nurturance and support of outsiders, sometimes strangers in shelters, to endure the period of fear and shock that follows leaving the marriage. In cases where women do not feel the support of others, an abuser's pleas to come home and try again are especially appealing and often effective. People in great pain and confusion will turn to those who offer warmth. If a violent husband is the only person who appears to offer that warmth, a battered woman will probably return to the relationship. However, if she is able to find and accept a temporary refuge with friends, relatives, or a shelter, she will be in a situation much more conducive to the relief that follows in the wake of a crisis endured. Once situated in a safe location, with supportive people, fear for her life subsides. Then, perhaps, she will feel relieved to lay down a burden she has carried for months or years. She will be free of the continuous concern to prevent violence by controlling all potentially disturbing events. This sudden relief sometimes turns to feelings of elation and exhilaration when women who have repressed their own desires find themselves free to do as they please. Women in shelters often rejoice at such commonplace events as going shopping, getting their hair done, or taking their children to the park without worrying about their husbands' reactions.

> Boy, tomorrow I'm goin' downtown, and I've got my whole
> day planned out, and I'm gonna do what *I* wanna do, and
> if somebody doesn't like it, to Hell with them! You know,
> I'm having such a good time, I shoulda done this years
> ago!

The elation that accompanies freedom serves as a wellspring of positive action to begin a new life. The difficult tasks of finding a new home, getting divorced, and, often, finding a job are tackled with energies that had previously been directed toward "keeping the peace." As these activities begin, however, the self moves away from victimization. Active involvement with others to obtain one's own desires is inconsistent with the victimized self. The feelings and perceptions of self required to leave a violent marriage wither away as battered women begin to build a new self in a new situation.

Conclusion

Feeling victimized is for most individuals a temporary, transitory stage. There are good reasons for this. While it is of great importance for victimized individuals to achieve and create new understandings of their present and past, and while this itself alleviates some of the sufferings of victimization, there are certain incompatibilities between feeling victimized and being oriented toward practical actions to change one's situation in the world. Feeling victimized implies, for most persons, significant passivity in accepting external definitions and statuses. To change such a situation involves the individual in active, purposive, creative behavior. Since victimization represents a primordial threat to the self, individuals are highly motivated to change these circumstances, and these actions by themselves diminish the sense of victimization. The specific time frame for this transitory period varies. For most wars, revolutions, and social movements, it may be a matter of months or years. For individuals caught in the throes of a violent marriage for decades, the process may take longer, even the remainder of their lives. It makes little difference, however, whether or not the practical actions achieve "success," whether success is defined in terms of revolutionary victory, the success of a social-movement organization, or moving into a new relationship in which violent or abusive acts are absent. The very process of taking practical action inevitably diminishes the individual's sense of victimization and in many cases even brings the emotional career of the victimized self to an end.

There are both similarities and differences between the form of victimization described here and other forms. Battered children, for example, often reinterpret childhood abuse when they reach adulthood; these reinterpretations thus do not occur as the by-product of a turning point in the course of the abuse, as is the case in violent marriages. Those who are assaulted by strangers, such as victims of muggings or rapes, may experience the existential threat to the self in much the same way as battered women do, but there is no prior relationship to reinterpret as a consequence of assuming a victimized self. The feelings and perceptions of these other victimized selves remain largely unexplored. Future studies, detailing the cognitive and emotional experiences of various types of victims, would make possible a more complete, generalized analysis of the victimized self than can be gained by focusing only on battered women.

Notes

1. We owe a debt of gratitude to David Altheide, Paul Higgins, Mildred Daley Pagelow, and Carol A. B. Warren for comments on an earlier draft of this paper.

2. Data for our respective researches have been gained from direct field observations, depth interviewing, various kinds of official documents, and surveys. More details on the data collection and analyses are to be found in Johnson (1975, 1981) and Ferraro (1979a, 1979b, 1981). An important resource for the research was the personal experience of the authors as cofounders and early leaders (1977–79) of an Arizona shelter for battered women.

References

Davidson, Terry. 1978. *Conjugal Crime.* New York: Hawthorn.

Ferraro, Kathleen J. 1979a. "Hard Love: Letting Go of an Abusive Husband." *Frontiers* 4(2):16–18.

———. 1979b. "Physical and Emotional Battering." *California Sociologist* 2(2):134–49.

————. 1981. *Battered Women and the Shelter Movement.* Ph.D. dissertation, Department of Sociology, Arizona State University.

————. 1982. "Rationalizing Violence." Unpublished paper.

Gelles, Richard J. 1976. "Abused Wives: Why Do They Stay?" *Journal of Marriage and the Family* 38:659–68.

Hughes, Everett C. 1958. *Men and Their Work.* New York: Free Press.

Johnson, John M. 1975. *Doing Field Research.* New York: Free Press.

————. 1981. "Program Enterprise and Official Cooptation of the Battered Women's Shelter Movement." *American Behavioral Scientist* 24:827–42.

Martin, Del. 1976. *Battered Wives.* San Francisco, Calif.: Glide.

Pagelow, Mildred Daley. 1981. *Women-Battering.* Beverly Hills, Calif.: Sage.

Rasmussen, Paul K., and Kathleen J. Ferraro. 1979. "The Divorce Process." *Journal of Alternative Lifestyles* 2:443–60.

Roy, Maria, ed. 1977. *Battered Women.* New York: Van Nostrand.

Walker, Lenore E. 1979. *The Battered Woman.* New York: Harper & Row.

Blood and Money: Exploiting the Embodied Self

Wendy Espeland

> All sense perception is merely one outcome of the dependence
> of our existence upon bodily functioning. Thus if we wish to
> understand the relation of our personal experience to the activ-
> ities of nature, the proper procedure is to examine the depen-
> dence of our personal experiences on our personal bodies.
>
> Alfred North Whitehead

INTRODUCTION

Most people are horrified at the thought of selling their blood for money.
They envision a plasma center as a place frequented by winos who allow
themselves to be tortured and bled only because they are desperate for
their next bottle. The entire business of collecting plasma has seedy over-
tones: What decent, reputable business would exploit the sick and the
outcast for profit? Some people see plasma centers as contributing directly
to the problem of alcohol abuse. A minister told me he believed plasma
centers perpetuated the problem by providing winos with just enough income to keep them from seeking some permanent change in their life-
style. While this view of plasma-collection agencies is widespread, it is
based largely on misconceptions. Actually, winos represent a small proportion of the donor population at most centers. Those who manage and
operate plasma centers are acutely aware of their poor image, and most
work very hard to change it. Much of employees' and donors' behavior can
be understood as attempts to manage the stigma associated with collecting
and selling plasma.

While much of the stigma surrounding the sale of plasma has to do with
the negative stereotypes of donors (most people are embarrassed to appear
too desperate for money) there is, perhaps, a more fundamental basis for
the stigma. It has to do with our ambiguous relationship to our bodies and
our ambivalence about that relationship. Merleau-Ponty's work on perception does much to illuminate this relationship.

Merleau-Ponty's philosophy is rooted firmly in experience. Its focus is

on the relationship of the body and the mind to each other and to the world
as it is lived. Merleau-Ponty rejects the mind-body dualism that is found
in both the empiricist and the rationalist perspectives. Both view the body
as a physical object. In one, the body is the passive receptor of information
about the world; in the other, the body is the physical container for the
mind (which structures the world). Instead of making the distinction between the mind (or consciousness) and the body the premise for knowledge,
Merleau-Ponty makes their integration the starting point for analysis by
positing his thesis of embodiment. He writes (1962:198–99):

> I have no means of knowing the human body other than
> that of living it, which means taking up on my own account
> the drama which is being played out in it, and losing myself
> in it. I am my body, at least wholly to the extent that I
> possess experience, and yet at the same time my body is
> as it were a "natural" subject, a provisional sketch of my
> total being. Thus experience of one's own body runs counter
> to the reflective procedure which detaches subject and
> object from each other, and which gives us only the thought
> about the body, or the body as an idea, and not the ex-
> perience of the body or the body in reality.

Thus, according to Merleau-Ponty, consciousness, because it is embodied, can be comprehended only within the context of lived experience. The
body both expresses and realizes consciousness. It situates consciousness
in time and space. It constrains consciousness with its physical limitations
and biological requirements. It provides for both access to and retreat from
the world of objects and others. Given these characteristics of the body,
Merleau-Ponty, instead of diminishing or dismissing its role, made analysis
of the body the logical place to begin an inquiry into the process of perception and the creation of meaning.

It is the embodiment of our consciousness that makes it impossible for
our experience of the body to be either completely objective or subjective.
The way it is experienced is always ambiguous and depends on what
Merleau-Ponty calls the synergistic experience of "being-in-the-world."

> If I try to think of [the body] as a cluster of third-person
> processes—"sight," "mobility," "sexuality"—I observe that
> these "functions" cannot be interrelated, or related to the
> external world, by causal connections; they are all ob-
> scurely drawn together and mutually implied in a unique
> drama. Therefore the body is not an object. For the same
> reason, my awareness of it is not a thought, that is to say,
> I cannot take it to pieces and reform it to make a clear
> idea. Its unity is always implicit and vague. [Ibid., p. 198]

To conceive of the body as a strictly physical object, as an organism, is to miss what distinguishes the body from other objects, to deny it the potential for subjectivity that is revealed only in experience. To compensate for the narrowness of the strictly objective conception of the body, Merleau-Ponty developed the concept of the subjective or phenomenal body.

The phenomenal body is the habitual, lived body that is oriented toward activity in the world. It is suffused with our conscious intentions. The boundaries of the phenomenal body are not strictly defined. They vary between persons and across situations. For the recent amputee, the phenomenal body will include, for a time, the limb that has been removed. For Martina Navratilova, it includes the tennis racket in her hand.

The phenomenal body also exists for us as a preconscious image. We can know where in space the parts of our body are located without first having to see or touch them. We can reach for an object without thinking about action or watching the movement of our hand. Merleau-Ponty likens the phenomenal body to a work of art because he considers the "expressive unity" of the body, like the thematic wholeness of art, to be greater than the sum of its parts.

Nonetheless, the unity of the mind and body exhibited in the phenomenal body is not constant, nor is it always harmonious. It is ambiguous because the integration is never fixed, never fully constituted. The meaning that our bodies have for us is always dependent on the way the body is situated in time and space and in relation to other objects. For example, sometimes we lose the body to the mind, as when we daydream or meditate. Sometimes the body takes over our consciousness, as when we experience severe pain. Sometimes the body, as we experience it, may betray our intentions rather than realize them; when we are embarrassed, for example, the body, instead of revealing our "true self," may stifle it. At other times our intentions may become clear to us only as they are being expressed by the body. While it is never possible to completely isolate our bodies from our consciousness, they may appear to us, as we experience them, sometimes as object, sometimes as subject, depending on the context. Because the knowledge we have of our body is ambiguous, it follows that the knowledge we have of our self—our self-conception—is ambiguous as well, since the one depends on the other. As Merleau-Ponty put it (ibid, p. 167): ". . . saying that I have a body is thus a way of saying that I can be seen as an object and that I try to be seen as a subject, that another can be my master or my slave . . . ."

As Szasz (1957) has pointed out, in our society most people think that the optimal state of ego-body integration occurs when they are not consciously aware of their bodies—when they are somewhat disassociated from them, or, in Merleau-Ponty's terms, when the body is experienced as an object. Yet, an essential concern for all people is preservation of the body's dignity. Nothing is more embarrassing to people than to lose control of bodily functions. Donating plasma jeopardizes the body's dignity in two ways: it focuses attention on the body, and it requires donors to temporarily relinquish control of their bodies. Selling plasma places the donor in a situation where the body is perceived as an object, both by the staff and, subsequently, by the donor. The emphasis is on the body as an organism, as a producer of plasma. This objective emphasis on the body is at odds with the donor's subjective notion of self. As Merleau-Ponty described it (ibid., p. 107): "in so far as I have a body, I may be reduced to the status of object beneath the gaze of another person, and no longer count as a person for him."

Manning and Fabrega (1973) have shown in their comparative study of health beliefs how the practice of objectifying the body—so characteristic of modern medicine—contributes to a disembodied conception of self, a denial of the integrity of body and self. For plasma-donors the focus on the body as object prevents or inhibits their ability to present the self as it is perceived by them. An initial risk for the donor, then, is the risk of subjecting their self-conception to "being an object" while they sell their plasma. This risk also leaves the donor vulnerable to the even greater risk of being stigmatized by the negative stereotypes often associated with those who sell their blood.

In a sense, plasma-donors betray their bodies because they must grant strangers access to their bodies, and this cardinal invasion of privacy is not based on socially acceptable motives. It is not based on a desire to care for or protect the body, as when we pay a doctor or dentist to treat our body; it is not based on a desire to improve our appearance, as when we pay to visit a hairdresser or a health spa; and it is not based on a desire to be altruistic—to sacrifice self for others—as when we donate blood without payment. Rather, it is based on a desire for immediate cash. Using our bodies in such an obviously opportunistic manner is a highly questionable practice in our society.

People who sell their blood evoke comparisons with prostitutes and mercenary soldiers; selling blood, like selling sex and military service, is an activity whose meaning changes when it is not attached to such stalwart values as altruism, love, and patriotism. Furthermore, selling blood is selling part of oneself. It is no mere service; after donating plasma, part of you is gone. The symbolic link between blood and life is as old as mankind. Selling blood is symbolically equivalent to selling life, and this violates the fundamental principle that life is priceless—beyond monetary value. While most donors are unable to articulate exactly why selling their blood is considered shameful, they are aware of the potential for stigmatization. Most of their mothers would never approve.

The ambiguous way we experience the body is a feature of the more general ambiguity that Merleau-Ponty calls "the essence of human experience." This ambiguity is essential because "everything we live or think has always several meanings" (ibid., p. 169). The ambiguity that characterizes our lives is not an expression of the absurdity or irrationality of existence; rather, it is a reflection of our constant and close engagement with the world. It is a testimony to the complexity and richness of human experience.

It is also a reminder of the pitfalls of abstraction, for those who would prefer to eliminate ambiguity from their explanations of social life are all too often left with precise accounts that ring false. Those who are committed to studying social life in concrete, empirical settings must confront and make peace with the ambiguity of "being-in-the-world." As others have noted, this means acknowledging the tentativeness of our knowledge. It means accounting for the multiplicity of meanings that make up human experience. It means unraveling the various dimensions of context that are inherent in each situation in order to see how each influences the way we order the world. It also means accounting for the feelings of the participants.

A plasma center is a place where the habitual way we experience the body is disrupted. Consequently, it provides a good setting for a close examination of our relationship with our bodies. It is a place where, in Whitehead's words, "the dependence of our personal experience on our personal bodies" becomes explicit.

The purpose of this paper is twofold: it is an attempt to describe in detail an empirical setting in which the risk of being stigmatized or shamed, to the actors involved, is high. The components of the situation will be broken down into various levels of context, all of which come together to influence and define the experience of selling blood. The second purpose is to describe how the participants in this situation, as a means of protecting the self, develop various strategies for overcoming or coping with the risk of stigma.

THE ETHNOGRAPHY OF SELF

While my interest in the process of stigmatization first prompted this research, it quickly became apparent to me that plasma centers provide sociologists with an exceptional setting in which to study a wide variety of topics. Plasma centers are interesting sociologically, first, because they represent a new research area. To my knowledge, plasma centers have never before been studied systematically. Donors and employees constitute an extremely interesting and diverse population. One local center averages 1,500 "bleeds" per week, which means that, within six days, approximately 1,000 different people were confined to beds with needles in their arms for at least an hour. Plasma centers breed strange bedfellows. It is rare to find a setting where so many bored people of such diverse backgrounds interact so frequently with each other. For many donors, the only thing they have in common with the person sitting or lying next to them is a couple of hours to kill and a desire for ten dollars.

Because all plasma centers in the United States are licensed and regulated by the Food and Drug Administration (FDA), they also afford the researcher an excellent opportunity to study rule usage. Previous research on rule usage (Johnson, 1972; Douglas, 1972; Comaroff and Roberts, 1981) indicates that all rules—even those that are codified and considered absolute—are necessarily problematic and must be interpreted in specific situations from the perspectives of the individuals involved. Accordingly, knowledge of how employees and donors learn to manipulate the official rules is fundamental to any understanding of how plasma centers operate.

Besides providing an interesting setting in which to study the effects of stigmatization and rule usage, plasma centers also proved to be a very rewarding place in which to study even more basic processes of human interaction, for they provide rich examples of the ways in which individuals order their experiences, construct meanings, acquire common-sense knowledge, and manage fronts.

Unless one has donated plasma before, the initial experience is likely to be very amorphous. To use Shutz's terms, new donors have no common-sense knowledge about how to act. Donating and collecting plasma requires specific, specialized kinds of behavior that are not part of most people's general stock of knowledge. New donors and inexperienced staff members do not share with the others the same meanings for much of their behavior. Meaningful interaction within this context is thus difficult for them because of their lack of understanding about the situation. They do not share the same perspective as the more experienced employees and donors, and so they frequently misinterpret others' behavior. For example, when seating a donor, an employee will usually ask the donor "Right or left?", meaning, "In which arm do you want to be 'stuck?' " A bed must be arranged with the arm rest and equipment on the appropriate side. A new donor may not understand what the staff member means and will either look quizzical or inform the employee whether he/she is right- or left-handed. In contrast, a regular donor will immediately recognize the intent of the question and respond accordingly. Some check their chart to see which arm was last used so that they can alternate arms. Old donors know which arms contain the best veins and which veins are the "fastest."

As new donors and employees become more experienced, their stock of knowledge about donating and collecting plasma increases. By sharing common experiences, they develop similar frameworks. The experience becomes increasingly less problematic for them as they formulate recipes for behavior—habitual ways of handling specific situations—which serve to typify certain actions, making them more automatic. Their interpretation of others' intentions becomes more accurate, and they begin to rely more on subtle modes of communication.

Whenever someone donates plasma for the first time or a new employee shows up for the first day of work at a plasma center, the experience may be construed as a type of phenomenological experiment, for one's social order is disrupted. The reconstruction of social order that occurs as the experience is repeated and the situation becomes routine or normalized reveals how one's cognitive perspective affects one's subsequent behavior. As individuals become socialized into the setting, changing from novices to regulars, one can watch them acquire reciprocal perspectives, adapt to new roles, and construct elaborate fronts as a means of expediting the donation process and as a method for coping with social stigma. In short, one is privy to the very process of becoming-social.

METHODS

This study is based on experiences I had while working for a year at a plasma-collection center and, later, when I conducted field research at two other centers. The former experience was a critical influence on the latter. Kotarba (1977) describes four ways that the experience of the true participant may be used to increase one's understanding of the phenomena being studied: one's experience becomes a source of data that are especially useful for coming to terms with the affective qualities of the situation; it provides the basis for making comparisons with other people's experience; it generates points of inquiry; and it facilitates the development of a more realistic theoretical perspective for real events, because anyone who has experienced at first hand the complexities of a situation is reluctant to adopt simplistic explanations, which falsify the experience. My experience as a participant, both before I began my research and while I was collecting the data, influenced my analysis in similar ways. Having donated plasma before, and then having worked at the center, I knew what an interesting setting it would be. I used my work experience as a source for ideas and as a standard for checking my current findings. My insider's knowledge of how a center operates allowed me to avoid some of the traditional problems researchers face when entering a setting cold: I was already familiar with the way the business operated; I understood the language and knew the FDA regulations; and, most important, I could empathize.

Because I had donated only twice before I became an employee, and because employees who donate plasma are treated differently from the way the average donor is treated, I felt I needed a better understanding of how it felt to be a new donor. Yet I wanted to develop a close relationship with the staff as quickly as possible so that they would trust me enough to talk with me honestly. I was interested in seeing whether their work experiences were similar to my own. To attempt to get both perspectives, I decided to divide my time between two centers. At one I would pretend to be an inexperienced donor; at the other I would rely on my past experience to try to develop a good relationship with the staff. I attempted to cast myself as an insider at one center and an outsider at the other in order to compare the kinds of information I received at each.

I thought it would be easier to get to know the staff members at the smaller center, so I decided to become a new donor at the biggest center, which was the busier of the two. I was especially interested in the way they treated new donors. In the center where I had worked, new donors were considered a nuisance because they required more work and attention than regular donors. Gaining entrée was easy. I simply made an appointment to donate and then kept it. I was surprised at how apprehensive I felt; however, each donation became easier, and although I never became really close with any of the employees at this center, I could detect changes in their behavior. After three visits, some of the staff began to recognize me, and they began to talk to me more. Soon they began to assume I had acquired some knowledge about the process. One staffer told me, "Let me know if something doesn't feel right," assuming I knew what "right" was.

I didn't think I could justify simply dropping in for a chat at the other center, so, using the same method to gain entrée, I allowed myself to be processed as a new donor. While I was donating, I let several employees know that I had once worked at a plasma center myself and started swapping donor stories with some of the staff. Working at a plasma center is such a unique experience that it frequently creates a bond between people who have it in common. Typically, former and current employees find that they share common perspectives about the work and generally have a lot they can talk about with each other. This special rapport greatly facilitated my ability to establish close relationships with the employees. When I was finished with donating, I asked for, and received, a tour of the center.

I continued to donate there once a week until I became quite good friends with some of the staff and felt I could drop in once in a while just to talk. That's when I got a real break. The manager of the center, whom the staff disliked and I had never managed to get to know, was fired and replaced by a friend with whom I used to work. After Craig arrived, things became much simpler.[1] I eventually told him about my research. While he had a difficult time understanding why a plasma center would be of interest to a sociologist, he proved to be a valuable and reliable informant, and I interviewed him extensively. He answered countless questions and granted me access to all records; he also provided me with a good excuse for coming to the center without donating.

While in the field I used a variety of research techniques in order to increase my confidence in my findings and to acquire as much data as possible. I synthesized and contrasted information gleaned from observation, informal interviews, formal interviews, and analysis of existing documents, such as donor charts, employee records, and logbooks. As a result, I could contrast official records with observed behavior. The records were also an extremely useful source of demographic data on donors and employees.

Occasionally I would conduct field experiments to test an idea or interpretation. For example, in testing the idea (generated from my work experience) that experienced donors and employees were highly skeptical of new donors who tried to act as though they did not need the money, I first talked to as many new donors as possible, asking them why they donated plasma. I recorded as many of their responses as I could and then, to as many other donors and staff members as possible, carefully recording their responses, I systematically presented, as if they were my own, the new donors' reasons for donating plasma. I found that simply telling people that I was donating because I could use the money evoked the most favorable responses. To contrast two accounts:

> ME: [*To an experienced donor lying in the next bed*] You
> know, people often ask me why I donate my plasma,
> and I usually just tell them I can really use the money.
> DONOR: [*Laughing*] Yeah, that's why we're all here, for
> sure.
> ME: [*To an employee*] I really think that donating plasma
> is a good way to help people out.
> EMPLOYEE: [*Laughing*] Well, it keeps me employed, but
> I sure would never donate it if they didn't pay me for
> it.

I also asked some employees directly whether they believed people would actually donate plasma because they considered it a charitable act. Most said they did not. Finally, I tried to ask as many of the originally new donors as I could why they continued to donate, to see if their reasons had changed. Most later admitted to having economic motivations.

Besides relying on triangulation as a mode of verifying results, I also made other tests and used other indicators as a means of assessing the truthfulness of my findings. Douglas (1972) describes what he calls the "member's test" of validity. If the researcher's understanding "fits" with the common-sense understanding of the insider, that itself is an indication of the validity of the findings. Several examples of what I consider to be evidence of such a "fit" are: (1) my understanding of subtle jokes told to me by employees; (2) being privy to, and understanding, complex problems and detailed anecdotes concerning plasma collection; (3) the relative ease with which I could interact with staff members and other donors; and (4) and most important, the fact that, as a former employee, I was an insider before I became a researcher.

Frequent displays of trust by employees increased my overall confidence in the accuracy of my interpretations. On several occasions staff members told me of incidents that, if reported to supervisors, could have led to their dismissal. I was privy to gossip and secrets and was usually included in socializing that occurred outside of work.

As another test of validity, I frequently asked several informants and a sociology student I knew who donated plasma to check my field notes and my interpretations of them for accuracy. Finally, I made it a habit to contrast information received from those who knew of my study with information provided by those who did not, both as a test of my own reactivity and as a check on the reliability of my informants.

HISTORICAL CONTEXT

Central to donating plasma is the process of plasmapheresis. This process was invented during World War II to compensate for critical blood shortages. Many injuries require replenishing only the blood volume crucial for maintaining a stable blood pressure; it is often unnecessary to replace blood cells, and so the problems associated with blood typing are eliminated. Plasma transfusions are universally acceptable; any donor's plasma may be transfused to any recipient, regardless of blood type. During the war, plasma transfusions replaced most blood transfusions. Transfusing plasma rather than whole blood substantially reduces the problems associated with storing, typing, and maintaining a stable supply of blood.

Plasmapheresis entails removing a unit of blood (how much depends on an individual's weight) from a donor's arm and separating the blood into its two primary components, red blood cells (RBCs) and plasma. This separation is accomplished by spinning the blood in a centrifuge (six to eight minutes at about 6,000 revolutions per minute). The RBCs, being heavier than the plasma, drop to the bottom of the container, and the plasma is then extracted off the top and retained. The RBCs are reinfused back into the donor's arm, using the same needle, which, in the interim, has slowly been dripping a saline solution into the donor's arm, thereby preventing clotting. Reinfusing a donor's RBCs enables the individual to donate plasma as often as twice a week. The body replaces the plasma quickly—usually within twenty-four hours—while it would take from six to eight weeks to replace the RBCs contained in a unit of blood.

Plasmapheresis was developed in order to make plasma transfusions feasible. However, most plasma-collection centers are not licensed to sell the plasma they collect for transfusions. Most centers collect plasma solely for purposes of pharmaceutical manufacturing. Plasma consists primarily of water (approximately 94 percent); the rest (approximately 6 percent) is protein. The manufacturing process, called fractionation, consists essentially in isolating and extracting the various protein components of plasma. For example, a blood protein crucial to the clotting process is extracted from plasma and used in the manufacture of the serum injected by hemophiliacs.

The proteins contained in plasma are a critical part of the body's defense system, so that, even though a donor loses a very small proportion of them, it is important that all donors be relatively healthy. Because collecting plasma entails removing and reinfusing an individual's blood, there is always some risk involved to the donor. A donor who accidentally receives someone else's RBCs may die. Consequently, plasma-collection centers are strictly regulated by the FDA in order to protect the health of the donors and the staff and the health of any recipient of the final plasma product. This federal regulation has enormous ramifications for any establishment associated with plasma collection.

NORMATIVE CONTEXT

Anyone familiar with the operations of the FDA will immediately recognize the relevance of that statement. It is almost impossible to exaggerate the number and detail of the regulations imposed on collection centers by the FDA. For example, concerning the maintenance of records, the FDA codebook states:

> Records shall be made, concurrently with the performance, of each step in the manufacture and distribution of products, in such a manner that at any time successive steps in the manufacture and distribution of the any lot may be traced by an inspector.

Translated, this paragraph states that virtually everything that transpires in a plasma center must be recorded. For example, aside from donor charts, which record everything that happens to a given donor, logbooks are kept of donor numbers, bleed numbers, employees' signatures, serial numbers of all equipment used, daily records of testing and standardizing equipment, the temperature of the freezer, donor reactions, donor immunizations—the list is endless. The entire donation procedure is specifically designed to conform to these regulations. While donors are rarely cognizant of the extent of these regulations, most of the staff's activity revolves around working within these rules. The following conversation took place while a phlebotomist was preparing a donor's arm for venipuncture:

> DONOR: Why do you always put that stuff [iodine] on in a circle?
>
> STAFF: The FDA says iodine must be applied in a concentric circle of at least 13 cms in diameter.
>
> DONOR: You're kidding! Exactly 13 cms? Boy, they don't give you much leeway, do they?
>
> STAFF: If you only knew. . . . If some inspector came snooping around and this circle measured only 12 cms, he'd give us a citation.

In order for centers to be licensed by the FDA, they must adopt a manual, delineating the procedures to be followed by employees, that will ensure the center's compliance with federal regulations. This manual, entitled "Standard Operating Procedures" (SOP), must be approved by the FDA before a center can open. In order to be licensed, a center must have passed an FDA inspection after operating for at least six months. This first inspection is the only one the FDA announces in advance. After that, the FDA conducts yearly surprise inspections.

It is widely recognized that any center, on any given day, could be shut down by an FDA inspector. Any inspector with sufficient time could find enough infractions in even the most meticulously run center to justify closing its doors. Company executives, inspectors, and employees all realize this. By scrutinizing enough donor charts, one could find ample mistakes meriting citations: a donor's picture may not be signed, a staff member may have forgotten to initial some procedure, a donor may have been allowed to donate too soon (more than once in forty-eight hours or more than twice in seven days), or a doctor may have forgotten to date a signature. A great deal of folk knowledge circulates among employees concerning FDA inspections. When I asked which factors are most critical in passing an inspection, I received varied replies:

> Nobody is dying while the inspector is there.
>
> The place looks respectable, and the donors appear sane and sober.
>
> The inspector is incompetent or in a good mood.
>
> Someone's paid their bills [*implying bribery*].

Most of these remarks were made sarcastically, but it appears that most employees recognize the arbitrary nature of the inspections. The game is to attempt to appear as though one is following the rules, at least on paper.[2]

To employees, the SOP manual and the FDA codebook represent the official rules. However, employees freely improvise on these official rules. For example, to ensure that donors are generally in good health, they must pass certain requirements before donating. Vital signs and test results must fall within a specific range. It is the receptionist's job to screen all potential donors, making sure that they meet these and other FDA requirements. Sometimes donors who are perfectly healthy may fail to meet specific requirements. One long-distance runner with an exceptionally fine cardiovascular system had a constant problem with his pulse, temperature, and blood pressure; they were always too low (under 50, 97.6 degrees, and 90/50, respectively). Before his vital signs would fall within the designated limits, he would have to drink something warm, run in place, do jumping jacks, and generally exert himself, all at the staff's suggestion. In time, he learned to drink a cup of coffee and then run all the way to the center; that way, he could avoid making a spectacle of himself in the waiting room. This is an example of mutual accommodation, in that the employees recognized the inappropriateness of the rules in this instance and "taught" the donor how to circumvent them. Sometimes the opposite situation occurs, when a donor meets all of the requirements for donating yet does not appear healthy. In such instances the staff may discourage or even prevent a donor from donating. Most employees recognize that health and donor suitability are not mere functions of objective criteria.

Employees manipulate the rules, not only because they are often inappropriate, but also because it sometimes serves their interests to do so. Donors may be accepted or rejected depending on how busy the center is, whether or not an employee likes someone, and for various other reasons. Staff members who donate may process themselves for donation without doing a single test; they simply fill in their chart and other relevant records with the "correct" data. Sometimes employees use their knowledge of the rules to "purge" the clientele. Since most centers—especially those in college areas—are concerned with their image, they try to discourage what they consider undesirable people from donating. Regulations may be strictly enforced or even "fudged" for specific donors, like winos, "crazies," and obnoxious persons.

One "crazy" donor had quite a reputation for bizarre behavior. He wore toothpaste caps in his ears and preferred to donate in a fetal position. The staff, initially amused, soon became irritated with Joel. He was uncooperative, and most wished he would be "P.R.ed" (permanently rejected). Since the manager was reluctant to do this, the staff took matters into their own hands. Joel was suspected of being on psychotropic drugs and tended to have a rather high blood pressure. The receptionist began reading his blood pressure as just over the upper limit, making him ineligible to donate. Joel suspected that he was being had, and one day he accused the receptionist of lying. She defended her reading and offered to have the other receptionists retake it. When they did, lo and behold they got similar readings. I found out later that all three had lied about Joel's blood pressure, for it had been well within the FDA limits. After several more futile attempts to donate, Joel quit trying.

The most extreme case of purging that I heard of occurred when a centrifuge technician became really angry with an offensive wino and intentionally burst his unit of blood in the centrifuge by failing to balance the centrifuge properly. Normally, an occasional bag will break in the centrifuge, especially when a new technician is being trained. When this happens, the donor becomes a "whole blood loss" and is prohibited from donating for eight weeks. Staff members, knowing how Tim felt about this particular donor, suspected that the incident was intentional but kept quiet. Later, when we were alone, Tim laughed off the incident, admitting that he had arranged for the eight-week "vacation." Such an incident is extremely rare because most employees are very conscientious about protecting the donor's health.

Knowledge of official rules becomes an important source of power for both employees and donors. Knowing how and when to bend rules becomes part of their stock of knowledge. Individuals differ in the degree to which they manipulate the rules. Some bend or ignore rules often and in a wide variety of situations; others go by the book. Typically, new employees adhere strictly to official rules until they understand the intent of the rules well enough, and are experienced enough, to feel comfortable in breaking them. Most employees' informal training includes lessons from more experienced staff members on how to manage rules and hide mistakes.

Since managers know the extent to which FDA regulations dictate the operations of any plasma center, they are aware, if they are even minimally involved with the day-to-day activities of their center, that rule manipulation takes place. However, I think that most are unaware of the extent to which rules are manipulated. Most probably suspect, but prefer to remain ignorant of, the extensiveness of rule-bending. Unless rule-bending becomes obvious or produces some serious consequences, they tend to ignore it. In this sense, management's passivity encourages the practice.

Managers, though they understand how manipulating the regulations facilitates the work, would not, I believe, actively encourage the practice. Too much is at stake if they are caught. In general, once employees establish their competence and prove that they are trustworthy and knowledgeable about the entire procedure (not just about their own jobs), their work is seldom questioned. Employees' attitudes toward the practice of "fudging" is quite simple: most assume that everyone is doing it. Usually they are.

DRAMATURGICAL CONTEXT: EMPLOYEES

Besides learning to manipulate rules to their advantage, employees must learn to manage their images, or fronts, as well. Donating plasma is usually a traumatic experience for new donors. Donors who are extremely nervous are more likely to faint or to move around so much that the position of the needle changes, thereby "blowing the stick"; this makes it necessary to readjust the needle (which may be painful) or to restick (which is both painful and costly). One way the staff mitigates donor nervousness is by maintaining a professional appearance. This relaxes donors by increasing their overall confidence in the staff's ability to provide care. It also allows the staff some power to manipulate the donor's interpretation of the situation. Processing a new donor is expensive. Typically, no profit is made on donors until after three donations, making it crucial that donors return. Before they return, they must interpret the experience as rewarding and/or not too unpleasant. If donors perceive staff members as authority figures—as people who are knowledgeable and competent in their jobs—they are more likely to allow employees to aid in defining the situation instead of relying solely on their own (amateur) impressions. It is difficult for a new donor to take umbrage when a staff member says, "Now that wasn't too bad, was it?"

Most phlebotomists (those who do the actual venipuncture) seldom acknowledge a bad stick in front of a donor, especially if the donor is inexperienced and the vein is not a particularly tricky one to reach. Rather than admit to blowing an easy stick, the phlebotomist may say or do things to indicate that nothing is wrong or may even place the blame on someone else, usually the donor. This is both a matter of pride and a practical concern. If donors begin to distrust a phlebotomist, they may refuse to be stuck by that person again, and this could interfere with donor-room scheduling. When I asked an inexperienced donor (two visits) who had been subjected to a bad stick why it took her so long to donate, she explained that "my veins were really rolling bad today." All staff members know that while some people's veins are more subject to movement, or "rolling," they do not roll more one day than the next. Movement depends on the venipuncture and the position of the arm, not on some arbitrary characteristic.

Staff members rely on a variety of techniques in managing their professional fronts. Often staff will try to emulate what they consider the normal behavior of doctors and nurses. At least initially, most will objectify the donor's body. One's appearance is a crucial feature of looking professional. One employee explained:

> First of all, it is important to look like doctors and nurses. That's the main reason we wear white uniforms. Most people will believe anything they're told by someone in a white coat.[3]

It is also important for staff members to appear confident, to look as though they have the situation well under control. Being (or acting) as though they are familiar with the equipment indicates expertise. By using smooth, graceful movements when handling the equipment, employees can foster an impression of competence. One day an experienced staff member was having trouble puncturing the seal that protects the sterility of a bag of RBCs as she was preparing to "hang a bag" to reinfuse the RBCs. This procedure is rather tricky, for the employee must hold the bag of cells, peel back the plastic flaps covering the seal, and then, with one hand, remove the cover from the exposed line and quickly puncture the seal. She made repeated attempts to break the seal before succeeding and was very conscious of how clumsy she appeared. Embarrassed, she remarked, "Shit, I act as though I'd never seen a Y-set before."

As part of presenting a professional front, the staff is careful to appear calm, even in tense situations. They try to keep emotions in check in front of donors and attempt to mask all indications of surprise. One man who had worked in the donor room (as opposed to working as a centrifuge technician or receptionist) told me:

> It's amazing how much trying to look calm helps really calm you. I mean, one day I was just going crazy. It was so busy I was sticking non-stop for three hours. Then Susan [a favorite donor] infiltrates, and her arm starts swelling up like crazy. Some new donor turns green and passes out, and bags were down all over the place.[4] There were only three of us working, but instead of freaking out, I just quickly walked from one bed to another, taking care of things. When I finally got a break, I practically collapsed, and my hands were shaking so bad I couldn't stick the rest of the afternoon. But, I got the job done.

Thus, appearing confident not only relieves donors' anxieties; it also helps the staff to cope with difficult situations. Employees frequently encounter problems with which they have had no past experience. For example, receptionists occasionally have to ask drunk donors to leave, or they must inform someone that they have V.D. In such instances, receptionists rely heavily on their professional front, treating the donor as a problematic body, trying to act in a matter-of-fact and self-assured way, as they would expect a doctor to act. Jill described the first time she processed a new donor with a long history of venereal disease:

> JILL: I was trying hard to act as though it was no big deal to have V.D. I mean, anybody can get it these days. But when he kept telling me about all the times he had had it, and the treatments he'd gotten, I just kept thinking about how I would have to take his pulse and hold his hand for thirty seconds.
> Q: What kinds of things did you do to act as though it was no big deal to have V.D.?
> JILL: Oh, I don't think I looked too surprised. I kept my voice steady and avoided looking into his eyes.

Sometimes employees will drop technical terms as a means of enhancing their professional front. While waiting to be processed one morning, I overheard the following conversation:

> DONOR: Why do you have to poke my finger out here to get a drop of blood, when they're gonna take a whole quart [500 mls] out of my arm in there [in the donor room]?
> RECEPTIONIST: Because we have to run a hematocrit, test for polycythemia and anemia, and record your plasma proteins before you can donate.
> DONOR: What's polycythemia?

RECEPTIONIST: Having too thick blood [abnormally high proportions of RBCs].

As Jill's case illustrates, it is sometimes difficult for employees to mask their feelings. A conflict may occur between what employees "know to be true" and what they really believe. Jill "knew" that she should not socially stigmatize people who have contracted V.D., but her "gut" reaction was to avoid contact with this individual. Generally, the staff's behavior reflects their knowledge, while their attitudes either remain unchanged or change very slowly. Acting like a professional allows an employee to keep the two things separate, while lessening a donor's embarrassment and anxiety at the same time.

Staff members are not the only individuals who learn to manipulate rules and manage their fronts. Experienced donors also become very adept at doing so. Just how donors manipulate the rules and what kind of front they present depend, of course, on the individual. A donor need not be concerned with appearing professional. However, some donors are very conscious of the stigma attached to donating plasma, and so they learn to present fronts that will, presumably, reduce stigma.

DRAMATURGICAL CONTEXT: PLASMA CENTERS

In order to understand why plasma donors frequently feel stigmatized, it is important to differentiate between plasma-collection centers and agencies that collect and distribute whole blood. Whole-blood donors actually donate their blood; they are not paid for their services and must limit donations to once every two months. Donating whole blood is lauded rather than stigmatized. It is widely publicized as an altruistic, philanthropic thing to do. It is hard to imagine Johnny Carson selling his plasma in front of twelve million viewers. People who donate whole blood are pampered, praised, and given a button publicizing their good will; people who "donate" plasma are processed as quickly as possible and are given ten dollars and a large bandage, which most try to conceal. The differences between the two types of donors are primarily economic: plasma donors need money more than social approval.

Those who operate plasma centers are aware of their image problem and of donors' fears of stigmatization. Advertising campaigns to recruit donors often portray donating plasma as a charitable act: "Earn money while you help others"; "Plasma donors save lives"; "Let your plasma help someone who needs it." The advertising, by mimicking the publicity campaigns of the Red Cross, attempts to encourage audiences to associate selling plasma with donating blood. A radio commercial I heard began with a pronouncement about the critical shortage in the world-wide plasma supply and of the desperate need for donors.

Another technique used by plasma centers to combat their image problem is to appear as aseptic as possible. While all centers, if they want to stay in business, must be genuinely concerned with donors' health and safety, it is not enough simply to be safe; a center must look safe. Most centers' decor is based on attempts to make them look like a doctor's office or a hospital. Most have white, pale blue, or green walls. Besides popular magazines, some keep scientific journals or health magazines in the waiting room. Some play taped "dentist office" music. One center encouraged its employees to donate plasma so that the paid donors could see that insiders considered the procedure safe and socially acceptable. (This practice also increases the employees' empathy with donors.)

However, not all donors are fearful of being stigmatized for donating plasma. It depends on the individual and on the location of the center.

Dramaturgical Context: Donors

The donor population of any center depends on its location. Plasma centers rely on a steady stream of people needing immediate cash, so most centers are located near a college or in the center of a large city. The former caters to the poor student, while the primary donor population of the latter consists of the chronically unemployed. The difference between the two centers may be profound. At college centers, donors are apt to receive more personal attention (depending, of course, on how busy the center is), and employees and donors are more likely to interact with each other. College centers tend to be more concerned with their image and therefore spend considerable effort and money on such things as decorating and sound systems. Downtown centers are more impersonal; relationships between donors and employees tend to be brief and businesslike, and the general atmosphere is less cheerful.

College centers are more aware of their image because they are catering to a more discriminating population. Students typically are more wary of the effects of donating plasma on their health than are other donors. They ask more questions about the process and about its long-term effects on their body. If the plasma center did not appear to them to be staffed by competent professionals, and if they thought the procedure jeopardized their health, most would stop donating, regardless of their financial status.

College students are also more concerned with stigma. They are not as familiar with stigmatization as donors who are chronically unemployed, but, if donating plasma did not appear at least somewhat respectable and "normal," students would be less likely to donate.

Those who donate plasma twice a week can earn approximately $100 per month in most places. In college centers, most donors are self-supporting, or partially self-supporting, students. Some use their money for such necessities as food and rent, while others donate strictly for spending money. A few use their "plasma money" to supplement what their parents give them; they relish having an independent (tax-free) source of income that allows them to spend some money without having to account for it to their parents. At college centers approximately 60 percent of the donors are male; at downtown centers more than 80 percent of the donors are male.

One possible explanation for the large proportion of male donors is that it is usually more difficult for females to meet the FDA criteria for donation. For example, women are more apt than men to weigh less than 100 pounds, and they generally have lower hematocrits. Men are rarely prevented from donating plasma because their hematocrits are too low. Another tentative explanation for the sex discrepancy is that women may feel more keenly than men the stigma associated with selling part of the body, since prostitution has been traditionally more closely associated with women.

Besides students, unemployed people make up a large segment of the donor population. Some individuals are only temporarily out of work; they may have recently moved to an area and not yet found work; they may have been temporarily laid off; or they may simply be between jobs. Occasionally, donors who originally were unemployed continue to donate after they find jobs. Once donating plasma becomes routine, it is hard to resist an extra $100 per month. Usually, however, donors quit donating (at least as regularly) once they become employed.

Other donors are perpetually unemployed. Some use the money to supplement their social security or welfare checks, and plasma centers, especially those located downtown, are often busiest on the days just before welfare checks are delivered. For others, selling plasma provides their only income. Besides welfare recipients, donors may include retired people under 65; winos; people in detoxification programs; ex-cons, who have a difficult time finding work; mentally disturbed people ("crazies"), who are incapable of keeping a job; and, finally, people who simply prefer not to work. Some donors are employed and, rather than moonlight, sell their plasma for extra income. College centers will have donors in each of these categories, but they may try to discourage the winos and the "crazies" from donating, since college students are less likely to frequent a place associated with such "low life."

Donors who are concerned with the stigma associated with donating plasma sometimes work hard at constructing fronts they feel will reduce this stigma. New donors often experience a sense of personal powerlessness by agreeing to sell their plasma. They allow total strangers to invade their privacy; they answer embarrassing questions and submit to all kinds of poking and prodding. It is only when donors regain some sense of power, some feeling of control over their body, that they attempt to manage the stigma they feel. Some donors never bother to construct fronts. I think this is either because they accept the stigma as justified or because they are so used to being stigmatized that it no longer disturbs them. Usually it is winos who fall into this category. Some donors are not aware of the stigma involved in donating plasma. One donor told me (in amazement):

> You know, some people think this is a real freaky way to
> earn bucks. It's weird. Like I told this dude, I'd a hell of a
> lot rather make ten bucks laying around a couple of hours
> than for busting my ass at some stupid job.

Sometimes donors who initially aren't aware of the stigma learn of it and
adapt accordingly. A conversation I had with one donor went something like
this:

> Q: Do your friends know you donate plasma?
> A: It's funny. At first I would tell them all about selling
>   plasma. I thought I'd be doing them a favor, since most
>   of them could really use the money. But I'd get the
>   strangest reactions from some of them, so I started being
>   careful about who I told.
> Q: Do your parents know?
> A: Heavens no! They'd die if they knew their little girl was
>   living off her blood. Why, that's almost like prostitution!
>   I try to remember to wear long sleeves when I go home.
>   If they saw my scars, they'd probably assume I was on
>   drugs.

Many donors worry about scarring their arms. Some think of the scars as
a sort of brand; others are concerned with being mistaken for a drug addict.
When I jokingly mentioned this concern to a staff member, he told me not
to worry, because anyone who knew anything about drugs would never mistake my scar for a junkie's scar. He said, with some sense of pride, that no
junkie is that good with a needle. (Phlebotomists are usually very careful to
insert the needle in the same place each time someone donates, in order to
avoid excessive scarring.)

Donors who choose to construct fronts as a reaction to the stigma associated with donating plasma usually adopt one of the following strategies. Some
pretend that they donate plasma for the same reasons that others donate
whole blood: it's a nice, charitable thing to do. The "I don't really need the
money" front is most popular with relatively inexperienced donors, who remember the advertising and haven't yet realized that nobody believes them.
One donor I sat next to in the waiting room went so far as to show me a check
he had for a thousand dollars to prove that he didn't need the ten.

A variation of this front is for the donor to pretend that the money will be
used for some extravagant purpose. Donors may say they donate only to buy
cocaine or that they are saving for an expensive trip. While this may be true,
most staff members are highly skeptical of such accounts. Most donors admit
to needing money, but some take great pains to show that they are not some
ordinary wino or bum. This is easy for students. They merely bring their
backpacks along when they donate and then study throughout the process.

Books become an important prop. The staff used to joke about one donor who brought in *War and Peace* every week for months. He would come in, open the book, and lay it across his chest but then make no attempt to read it. Some donors are careful about the clothes they wear. They actually dress up to donate. The most elaborate front I saw was constructed by a donor named Fred. Fred told everyone he was a lawyer, with a law degree from Harvard. He always wore a suit and carried a briefcase. What really amused the staff was Fred's beeper. It buzzed constantly until Fred was actually lying in a bed with a needle in his arm. He would always ask to use the telephone, pretending to call his office—being careful to keep his finger on the "hold" button—and give instructions to his "secretary." As soon as the needle was out of Fred's arm, his beeper would begin to sound again.

Some donors like to play up their poverty as a method for coping with the stigma. Musicians, poets, and, especially, actors are supposed to "pay their dues" and may actually gain status for "suffering for their art." One man I noticed wore the same T-shirt every time he donated. It said "Unemployed Actor."

As a rule, the longer an individual continues to donate, the less concerned she/he becomes with maintaining such fronts, at least while at the center. Justifications for donating become less important as donors interact with others for whom donating is something taken for granted. Moreover, the gift relationship that Titmuss so carefully documented (1971) is undermined when blood is sold rather than truly donated; in time, those who sell their plasma learn that the moral motives ascribed to those who give blood are unacceptable for those who sell it. Douglas (1977) has noted that new prostitutes rely heavily on their connections with other insiders in the process of overcoming their shame and fear of stigmatization. Interacting with more experienced donors produces a similar effect on new donors; they become less concerned with the social implications of donating plasma. One donor told me:

> I used to worry a lot about being a regular around here. I guess I didn't want people to know how poor I was. Now I don't give a shit. Most people could use a few extra bucks, and this is a convenient way for me to get it. It's not that weird of a thing to do for money.

New donors are outsiders. They do not understand the larger context in which their behavior takes place; they do not understand the language used by insiders, and that sets them apart; they misinterpret others' cues and sometimes completely miss the more subtle kinds of ongoing communication. As donors become more experienced, they are socialized into the donor role; they learn what constitutes appropriate behavior and act accordingly. Donors also learn to differentiate between what is relevant and irrelevant to the situation, between what is typical and what is unusual.

The staff recognizes the regular or "old" donor as someone who shares some of the same meanings, and they will allow such a donor to participate more fully in the setting. For example, regular donors will often help the staff by pointing out a new donor who appears ready to faint or a bag that is "ready to drop" (almost full and ready to be centrifuged). Employees treat these donors more as equals and will share insider knowledge with them. Fronts become irrelevant as they freely exchange jokes about the absurdity of the situation.

Because of the profound influence of the medical model, which sharply distinguishes between the body and the self, the donor's body will probably always remain an object to the staff, distinguishable by good veins, a low pulse, or high blood pressure; however, as the donor continues to interact with the staff, he or she will gradually become a person for them.

When John, a favorite donor, walks in, he is generally given preferential treatment. The staff will attend to him more quickly and will spend more time talking with him. John knows who the most competent employees are and can distinguish between a good stick and a bad stick on his own, so employees drop their professional fronts with him. The staff likes and respects John, so he need not worry about appearing respectable. One phlebotomist joked to John about using that big "vein" in his neck so that he could really get out in a hurry, trusting John to know that he was joking and to understand the joke.

Regular donors like John feel free to ask questions. They become familiar with the rules and may manipulate them almost as much as the staff does. Insiders know when to lie and when to tell the truth. They are usually quite good at assessing the relative importance of the rules. For example, Jim knows that donors who weigh more than 175 pounds are given larger bags, so they end up donating more plasma. His weight hovers right around 175, so he always takes off his shoes and enough other clothes (within reason) to bring his weight under 175 whenever he is processed by a receptionist he does not know well. (The others automatically record 174 pounds.) Part of every insider donor's knowledge is knowing how to manage the staff and how to be managed by them.

CONCLUSION

To summarize: most plasma centers can be classified as either college centers or downtown centers. At college centers, more donors are students or other people who view donating plasma as a temporary way to earn extra money until their status changes permanently (i.e., they get a good job or graduate) and they no longer need the money. Donors at college centers are generally more concerned with stigma because they are still respectable members of society and are more likely to associate with people who do the stigmatizing.

At downtown centers, donors tend to be the chronically unemployed. For them, donating plasma represents a more permanent (if not regular) source of income. Downtown donors are more likely to be desensitized to the stigma. They either ignore it or don't notice it. Some winos are proud when they achieve regular-donor status. To them, donating plasma is evidence of self-control. It is quite an achievement for many to be able to manage their drinking, spruce up their appearance, and meet the necessary health requirements in order to donate plasma.

Donors who are concerned with stigma generally rely on several basic strategies for coping with it. Initially, they may couch their motives in moral terms. They may pretend that they don't really need the money or that they have a very special reason for needing it. They may emphasize the temporary nature of their need. Some hide the fact that they donate plasma from their friends, and some try to convince their friends that selling plasma is an easy and normal thing to do.

Management and staff also try to minimize the stigma associated with selling plasma. Marketing strategies, imitating those devised for blood drives, seek to minimize the profit motive by using the language of altruism. The staff may try to capitalize on the dignity of the medical profession by attempting to emulate doctors and nurses in both their appearance and their behavior.

The distinction between regular and new donors is a critical one. The difference in the behavior of the two and in their interpretations of the experience reflects the donor socialization process. It is also a demonstration of the degree to which all experience is situational. New donors are more likely to be concerned with stigma. They do not possess the shared perspective of the regular donors and the staff. However, as they acquire the specialized knowledge of a plasma donor, their intentions become more meaningful and they regain a sense of power. When donors' understanding of the situation is such that they know the jargon and can manipulate the rules and the staff to their own advantage, the process becomes routinized for them.

Donating plasma, like being ill or physically disabled, increases bodily awareness. Each donation focuses attention on the functions of the body; fingers are pricked, pulses are taken, questions are asked; tests are run, and the results are recorded and made available to the donor.

Plasmapheresis is a fascinating process. Donors actually see their blood coming out of their veins and see the RBCs go back in again; they see what plasma looks like, and they can feel the difference in their temperature after several minutes. They can actually feel movement in their veins. The emphasis on health and this new way to experience the body prompt some donors to closely monitor their vital signs and the results of blood and urine tests.

As a result of this increased awareness of their bodies, many donors acquire a new respect for them. Some redefine their relationship to their bodies as a result of this newfound appreciation. The body's presence is not as taken-for-granted; its role is expanded. For habitual donors, the experience of selling plasma is incorporated into the phenomenal body, as Merleau-Ponty described it. As one donor remarked:

> Now when I look in the mirror, I see more than just a pretty face; I see a plasma machine, a source of income; I see a pulse of about 80 and a hematocrit of 42, and I know just how red my blood really is. And all that is good stuff to know.

Plasma centers offer the sociologist a rich and virtually untapped source of data.[5] They are settings that reveal some of the fundamental social processes. They can provide insights into the relationship between our bodies and our cognitions. They also reveal the dependence of the self on the situation, for the seemingly simple act of selling plasma prompted some donors to protect and reevaluate their self-conceptions. Plasma centers also serve as important reminders of the necessity of, and implications for, firmly grounding research in the empirical, experienced world.[6] As one donor put it:

> Trying to explain what it's like to donate plasma to someone who has never done it is like explaining to a virgin why sex is fun: you keep resorting to lines like, "I guess you had to be there."

Notes

1. All names used are pseudonyms.

2. John Johnson (1972) analyzes this phenomenon—known as "gundecking" in the Navy—as it applies to a U.S. Navy destroyer.

3. In his study of abortion clinics, Donald Ball (1967) discusses how medical uniforms became important symbols identifying the practitioners with medical roles, thereby enhancing their credibility and reducing patient anxiety.

4. Scales are set so that when a unit of blood reaches a specific weight, the scale drops, cutting off the flow of blood into the bag. The bag is then "cut down" and delivered to the centrifuge room.

5. It would be interesting to conduct research on plasma centers now, when the media are paying so much attention to the AIDS phenomenon. Most plasma centers attempt to screen out donors who appear to be members of populations at high risk of contracting AIDS. Such screening might add another dimension (i.e., homosexuality) to the stigmatizing process.

6. Blumer (1969), in his critique of traditional, positivistic methods, has said that the most critical feature of any science must be its grounding in the empirical world.

References

Altheide, David. 1977. "The Sociology of Alfred Schutz." In Jack D. Douglas and John M. Johnson, eds., *Existential Sociology*. Cambridge, Eng.: Cambridge University Press.

Ball, Donald. 1967. "An Abortion Clinic Ethnography." *Social Problems* 14:293–301.

Bannan, John F. 1967. *The Philosophy of Merleau-Ponty*. New York: Harcourt, Brace & World.

Blumer, Herbert. 1969. *Symbolic Interaction*. Englewood Cliffs, N.J.: Prentice-Hall.

Comaroff, John L., and Simon Roberts. 1981. *Rules and Processes: The Cultural Language of Dispute in an African Context*. Chicago: University of Chicago Press.

Douglas, Jack D. 1972. *Research on Deviance*. New York: Random House.

———. 1977. "Shame and Deceit in Creative Deviance." In Edward Sagarin, ed., *Deviance and Social Change*. Beverly Hills, Calif.: Sage.

Douglas, Jack D., and John M. Johnson, eds., 1977. *Existential Sociology*. Cambridge, Eng.: Cambridge University Press.

Goffman, Erving. 1956. *The Presentation of Self in Everyday Life*. Edinburgh: University of Edinburgh Press.

———. 1963. *Stigma: Notes on the Management of Spoiled Identities*. Englewood Cliffs, N.J.: Prentice-Hall.

Johnson, John M. 1972. "The Practial Use of Rules." In Robert A. Scott and Jack D. Douglas, eds., *Theoretical Perspectives on Deviance*. New York: Basic Books.

———. 1975. *Doing Field Research*. New York: Free Press.

Kotarba, Joseph A. 1977. "The Chronic Pain Experience." In Jack D. Douglas and John M. Johnson, eds., *Existential Sociology*. Cambridge, Eng.: Cambridge University Press.

Manning, Peter K., and Horatio Fabrega. 1973. "The Experience of the Body: Health and Illness in the Chiapas Highlands." In George Psathas, ed., *Phenomenological Sociology*. New York: Wiley.

Merleau-Ponty, Maurice. 1962. *Phenomenology of Perception*. Translation by Colin Smith. London: Routledge & Kegan Paul.

Sagarin, Edward, ed. 1977. *Deviance and Social Change*. Beverly Hills, Calif.: Sage.

Schutz, Alfred. 1975. *On Phenomenology and Social Relations*. Edited by Helmut R. Wagner. Chicago: University of Chicago Press.

Spurling, Laurie. 1977. *Phenomenology and the Social World*. London: Routledge & Kegan Paul.

Stone, Gregory. 1962. "Appearances and the Self." In Jerry Rose, ed., *Human Behavior and Social Processes*. Boston: Houghton-Mifflin.

Szasz, Thomas. 1957. *Pain and Pleasure: A Study of Bodily Feelings*. New York: Basic Books.

Titmuss, Richard M. 1971. *The Gift Relationship*. New York: Pantheon.

Whitehead, Alfred N. 1938. *Modes of Thought*. New York: Macmillan.

seven

Leaving the Convent: The Experience of Role Exit and Self-Transformation

Helen Rose Fuchs Ebaugh

One of the most fundamental tasks we all experience is development of a unique self. Self-development occurs throughout our lives and involves two basic processes: discovering who I am to relevant others (role) and who I am to myself (self). Self-identity results from the interaction of role and self.

Traditional theories of socialization and role have emphasized the emergence of the self from the ways that others define us (Mead, 1964; Merton, 1968; Parsons and Shils, 1951). For example, positive reinforcement by parents tends to result in high self-esteem in their children. Similarly, the expectation that doctors value human life and will care rather than harm becomes part of the self-image that a doctor internalizes. Most socialization literature argues that changes in definitions of self result from changes in the expectations that other people have of us.

For most traditional roles, the case is probably well made for the impact of role expectations on self-identity. However, our society is witnessing the emergence of many "new roles"—roles for which few social expectations have been developed. What appears to be happening is that individuals are alienated from or disillusioned with traditional roles and experience a disjuncture between the expectations associated with these roles and who they feel they really are or want to be. If no viable role alternatives exist, these individuals proceed to construct a new self based on personal feelings and desires. They in fact create new roles to fit new experiences of life.[1]

A basic difficulty in this process of developing creative roles is the fact that others tend to have expectations, or at least evaluative feelings, about social roles, regardless of how ill defined these roles may be. We are so accustomed to thinking and reacting in terms of role categories that we tend to invoke role expectations in situations where they are not defined by tradition. As a result, the person who is struggling to express self in ways that are authentic to self-experience but outside of usual social roles has to deal in some way with others' expectations. Such expectations are usually based on lack of knowledge, outdated notions, or habitual preconceptions. The person who is trying to harmonize self and role therefore has the added difficulty of remolding and reformulating others' expectations of his or her self.

The roles of both nun and ex-nun in the Catholic Church have undergone drastic change during the past fifteen years. Role expectations of the Catholic nun that had been consistent for several centuries were suddenly disrupted, and there were no clear-cut, well-defined alternative role definitions. Nuns and laypersons alike were left in confusion and uncertainty regarding what was expected of the modern Catholic nun.

In the midst of the confusion regarding what it meant to be a nun, many nuns chose to leave their convents rather than adapt to the new role that seemed to be emerging. The phenomenon of the ex-nun presented a whole new dilemma in terms of role expectations, both for the women who became ex-nuns and for those who associated with them.

Both of these changes—the change in role definitions of the nun and the evolving role of the ex-nun—resulted when nuns began to search for more relevant and satisfying self-definitions. A disjuncture or lesion developed between the traditional image and expectations of the nun and the feelings of self-actualization that nuns experience.

Several factors explain why role confusion developed within the same religious orders that had been the epitome of stability and consistency for centuries. The Second Vatican Council in the mid-1960s not only legitimated but demanded thorough self-scrutiny of what it meant to be a nun in the modern world. All outdated structures were to be adapted to the conditions and needs of contemporary society. A convent world that was accepted as holy and unchangeable suddenly gave way to challenge and change. The changes effected within religious orders paralleled and were influenced by the trends in the larger society toward greater democracy and self-expression. The fact that convent rules were relaxed to allow for greater contact with the secular world meant that such trends could now impact on convent structures.

The personal dissatisfaction felt by many nuns was caused, in some instances, by the organizational and cultural changes that were going on. In other cases, nuns who were dissatisfied now felt freer to express their dissatisfaction and relate it to convent structures; after all, even the church hierarchy recognized weaknesses and limitations in convent life.

Organizational changes, societal and cultural changes, and personal dissatisfaction interacted to encourage nuns to search for more relevant and satisfying self-definitions. Some nuns found harmony between their self-images, feelings, and desires and the new role of the nun that was emerging. Other nuns could not harmonize their deepest sense of self with the alternative image of nun and decided to leave and discover other roles available in society. In doing so, these ex-nuns were also faced with developing the emerging new role of ex-nun.

What follows is an attempt to describe the process by which nuns decide to leave their orders and begin to create the role of ex-nun for themselves. Throughout, attention is given to the interaction between role and self in understanding the process of disengagement and self-transformation.

DATA AND METHODS

My data are derived from two sources: (1) my personal experience as an ex-nun who, before leaving, had lived for twelve years in the convent and (2) a sociological study of convents and ex-nuns that I conducted in the 1970s. Both types of data were essential in understanding what ex-nuns experienced in the process of identity change.

The sociological study consisted of three parts. I interviewed sixty women who had left three different orders: a liberal order, a conservative order, and a moderate-change order. Each interview lasted approximately two hours and focused primarily on the process of decision-making that led to leaving the order. Special attention was given to interactional and situational factors at each stage of the process and to redefinitions of religious life and the role of nun at each stage. In addition to the interviews with ex-nuns, I interviewed a matched sample of thirty nuns who decided to stay. The present paper, however, focuses primarily on my subjects who became ex-nuns.

As a second part of the study, I conducted intensive case studies of the three orders from which the sixty nuns had departed, including analysis of historical documents, interviews with administrators and key religious personnel, and several days of participant observation while I lived with each group. These organizational data helped me to understand the process of change that was occurring within the orders as they sought to effect far-reaching innovations within a short time. These data were essential for understanding the context out of which ex-nuns were moving, especially in terms of traditional role definitions placed on nuns as well as transformations and reinterpretations of the role over time.

A third part of the research design was a national survey mailed to the president of every active order of Catholic nuns in the United States. In addition to an inventory of demographic items, the questionnaire included questions on the degree and types of change being effected in the order and the number of nuns who had left each year between 1960 and 1970. The resulting data provided a picture of how consistent trends were across the country and enabled me to generalize beyond a few orders.

I am convinced, however, that all these "hard" data would have been of superficial value at best and probably impossible either to obtain or interpret without my personal background as both a nun and an ex-nun. At the time I collected my data, entrée into religious orders by outside social scientists was virtually impossible, due to the cloistered nature of the institution and the prevalent view among nuns that the religious orders were "spiritual" and not subject to scientific analysis. Simultaneously, however, administrators were admitting that organizational problems existed and were looking for solutions. As an insider who was also a social scientist, I was not only accepted but warmly welcomed as someone who might provide answers to the uncertainty developing within the orders.

Being an insider who was very involved in the renewal movement enabled me to establish rapport with interviewees. While I had not yet decided to leave religious life myself, I had been living away from my order as a student for almost four years and was questioning the viability of the life, both as a social institution and, less consciously perhaps, as a way of structuring my life. This psychological distance and personal reflection no doubt enabled me to understand and empathize with the issues and concerns expressed by the ex-nuns I interviewed.

In addition to rapport, my being a nun was crucial to developing an interview instrument. When I was designing the interview questions, several of my professors at Columbia University suggested interesting sociological questions but ones that were totally inappropriate and foreign to an audience of ex-nuns. I am convinced that my personal experience as a nun was essential to understanding the kinds of issues and processes involved in a nun's making the decision to leave.

I collected my data as a nun but analyzed it as an ex-nun. I have often been grateful that the interviews with the ex-nuns were as open-ended as they were and that I taped each interview; for after I had experienced the exit process myself, I had insights that I had never had when I first collected the data. For example, ex-nuns talked about such matters as the struggle and discrepancy between a "head" and "heart" decision to leave, feelings of a void just before they made a final decision, feeling like a stranger in two worlds at the point of leaving, and the social reactions that people expressed when they learned one was an ex-nun. At the time of the interviewing, I tallied these comments as data. I later came to know experientially and painfully just what they meant.

LEAVING THE CONVENT

The process of leaving a religious order was essentially one of a transformation in self-identity. In traditional religious orders, what it meant to be a nun was very well established. When a young woman entered the convent, she became, through a process of socialization, what that predetermined role image dictated. In fact, the whole process of becoming a nun was portrayed as "putting off one's old self" and "taking on a new self." What that meant, essentially, was denying personal desires, wishes, intentions, and needs and becoming identified with the image of nun presented by the order. When a nun decided to give up her role as nun and leave the order, she went through a process of disengaging or relinquishing that image and returning to a more individualized, personalized idea of herself.

How is it that women so closely identified with a predetermined role within an absolutist system—a system that by its very nature discouraged individual thought and self-reflection—could dis-identify with that role and ultimately relinquish it? The fact that it was almost unheard of for anyone to leave a religious order prior to the Second Vatican Council is one indication that the process of leaving is related to changes occurring since Vatican II. For example, when I entered the order in 1960, I knew no one who had left the order. The very idea of leaving after final vows was almost inconceivable. In 1960, 220 nuns left religious orders in the United States. By 1970, one decade later, the number had risen to 2,815. It is not coincidental that the rise in rates of leaving occurred during the decade of rapid change within the religious orders. It is impossible, therefore, to understand the process of exiting religious life without placing it within the context of the changes that were occurring within the religious orders themselves.

STAGES IN THE PROCESS OF LEAVING

While the decision to leave a religious order is a deeply personal and individual decision, there appears to be a series of stages through which women go in making the decision to leave and then actually carrying it out. In reviewing my own experience and that of the sixty women I interviewed, I identified six stages in the exit process.

Stage One: First Doubts

The first stage is that of initial questioning, the time when a nun first begins to allow herself to question the system of which she is a part. Given the fact that religious life is a total institution,[2] allowing oneself to begin to question or doubt that institution is critical to the leaving process. Like that of every total institution, the fabric of religious life was tightly woven. To begin to unravel a single thread was often devastating because of its connections to all the rest. A nun was trained not to think for herself but rather to internalize and accept the theology, the philosophy, and the life given her. She was taught to renounce her own feelings and thoughts and to take on those of Christ, manifested through the order. As one interviewee put it: "I entered along with 150 other girls. The first day we were told not to question our vocation. If we didn't belong, we would be told to leave."

The entire social organization of the traditional convent was built on the goal of death to self and rebirth to God. The three vows, of poverty, chastity, and obedience, were designed to eradicate selfish desires and encourage nuns to be instruments of God's will. To assure total concentration and commitment to these ends, nuns from the twelfth century on were isolated within the cloister. Convent walls and clanging doors kept outsiders out and nuns secure within. However, physical isolation was buttressed by an even more powerful social and psychological isolation, manifested in various rules and customs that preserved strict boundary maintenance between life inside the cloister and "the world" outside.

A series of historical events occurred within the larger church structure that not only permitted critical reevaluation of the system but mandated it. Pope Pius XII's mandate to religious superiors in 1952 to upgrade the professional preparation of nuns—to put it on a par with that of their lay colleagues—and the Decree on Religious Life, promulgated by the Second Vatican Council about ten years later, disrupted the isolation and totalistic way of thinking that had characterized the orders for centuries. As a result of educational experiences and the intensive self-scrutiny and renewal demanded of them by Vatican II, the religious orders emerged in the late 1960s and early 1970s as radically transformed institutions. While the three vows remained, they were reinterpreted, with less emphasis on self-denial and a greater focus on the human and community dimensions of the vows. The hierarchical notion of superior and inferior was replaced by the notion of dialogue between groups and individuals. The stress on cloistered isolation from the world gave way to emphasis on availability and witness in the world. The medieval black habit was discarded for contemporary dress, and nuns were allowed greater choice in types and places of work and in where they lived. In short, the religious orders moved from being total institutions par excellence to being contemporary forms of voluntary organization, committed to providing resources.[3]

Central to changes in structure and life-style within the religious orders was a redefinition of what it means to be a nun. The well-defined image of the pre–Vatican II nun was gone, but the image of the nun in the modern world was still emerging.

When the Vatican Council mandated the religious orders to reevaluate their life-style and structure, every nun was asked to become involved in the renewal process. As a result, the orders set up numerous self-study groups and committees, and every nun was encouraged to be part of the reevaluation proces. Whereas superiors previously told nuns what was expected of them and what was to be done, the stage was now created for democratic processes of discussion, reevaluation, and creation of a new life-style and image. Approximately half of the ex-nuns I interviewed indicated that it was in the course of these group discussions that they first began to question the value of religious life for themselves. In these discussions attention was given not only to daily routines of religious life but, perhaps more important, to the value of religious life, the meaning of religious life in the contemporary world, and the new theology behind the three vows of poverty, chastity, and obedience. In addition, nuns were now allowed to watch television, to read newspapers, and to participate in group processes outside the order, such as social movements, political groups, and discussion clubs. As a result, the changing cultural mores of the larger society outside were brought to bear on the discussions about religious life. These ideas included the reevaluation of the traditional forms of the family, women's rights, and the new emphasis on self-fulfillment and self-understanding.

The atmosphere that permeated group discussions within the religious orders was one that emphasized the processes of reevaluation, discovery, and creation of new forms rather than continued acceptance of forms that had been traditionally accepted both in the culture and in the church. For many nuns, these group discussions within their orders provided them with their first opportunity to question the religious life they had taken for granted up until this point. For some nuns, these discussions provided an outlet for preexisting doubts, but for many they raised new issues and doubts never before raised.

As nuns began to consider the fact that religious life itself was changing, they were also challenged to consider whether they, themselves, wanted to maintain their commitment to religious life. In addition, throughout this process nuns became more and more aware of and in touch with their own personal feelings and needs. As one ex-nun said, "I never should have entered. It took me twenty years to be able to admit that and be true to myself."

Strangely enough, as convent life became freer and less demanding in many ways, more and more nuns found it difficult or impossible to maintain their commitment. Rosabeth Kanter (1972) found a similar relationship between sacrifice and commitment in her study of nineteenth-century utopias: the groups that made intense demands on their members tended to outlive the more lenient groups. One possible explanation offered by Kanter is that sacrifice tends to go along with clearly defined goals and role expectations. In other words, if a cause is clearly seen as worthwhile, members are willing to make extreme sacrifices to serve it. When goals and expectations become more nebulous, members reevaluate the benefits of self-sacrifice.

In addition to the discussion groups and renewal efforts within the religious orders themselves, another major influence that led nuns to doubt their commitment was exposure to advanced education. Going away to study, a nun normally found herself outside the cloistered environment for the first time. While, before, things were secure and well-defined for her, she now suddenly found herself negotiating in a world where her role was not so clearly specified. Among her fellow students she was often an anomaly. She sat in classes where the existence of God was not necessarily assumed. The world was seen not as the result of a magnificent anthropomorphic creator but rather as one that operated by its own natural laws.

My first contact with agnostics and atheists took place in graduate school, where I encountered fellow students who scoffed at the idea of an anthropomorphic god, assumed to be responsible for the existence of the world. In fact, I was frequently asked to defend the Christian position on the existence of God. Having grown up in an isolated Catholic community, where such questions were never raised, such queries were new to me and challenged my thinking. After days and weeks of pondering, I realized that I could not rationally prove the existence of God. For days my very foundation was shaken. Did this mean that my whole commitment to religious life was questionable? When I spoke to my religious superiors about the experience, I was told that such queries represented temptations from the devil. I was counseled to deepen my nonrational faith in the face of such challenges and to realize that the existence of such doubters made my faith all the more necessary in the world.

In my study of social science, I was taught the position of value neutrality, that is, that one could study social phenomena without making personal value judgments about their goodness or badness. Then came my exposure to anthropology and the sociology of religion, in which I learned that many people felt that God was created by man because of man's need to explain certain events, such as death and suffering, or, in Marx's perspective, that man created God because he could not face his own alienation. I was gripped by the idea that perhaps God was invented by man. Once these questions were raised in my mind, I began wondering about the whole structure of religious life and whether it, too, was created to meet human needs rather than given by God himself as a perfect way of being Christian. I did not reject the religious perspective in which I was socialized, but I became aware that it was simply one way among many of viewing the world.

For many nuns the initial questioning of religious life occurred, strangely enough, when they began to study contemporary theology. Many of them realized that theological notions regarding God, the church, the secular world, and religious vocation were changing. As one woman expressed it,

> I entered because I felt it was God's will for me. In a
> contemprary theology course, I learned that God is a loving
> Father and cares about our happiness. Vocation, we were
> taught, was a decision from within, a free response to live
> full human lives and be faithful to our inner selves. When
> my notion of God's will changed, I began to question my
> being in religious life when I felt basically unhappy.

Another woman described a similar experience,

> I always wanted to leave but was brainwashed in the idea
> that God wants me here. What I wanted was not important.
> Then I went away to study and heard a priest in a class
> tell the story of a young sister who didn't want religious
> life but thought God wanted it for her. The priest told her
> she should leave, because God as Father wants what she
> wants. It hit me like a thunderbolt to think that what I
> wanted might be important as part of God's will for me.

Another nun was exposed to modern liturgical changes and began to realize
that traditional forms of liturgy were not necessarily the best and that
liturgy, essentially, was man's response to God and therefore had to be
adapted throughout the ages. Such a sense of relativity and changeableness
led her to question the rigidity with which religious life had been lived for
centuries.

In addition to the intellectual challenges nuns encountered when they
went away to study, they were also exposed to all types of new associations
and social contacts. For the first time in years, many of them were interacting with lay persons, colleagues, and fellow students. In addition to
formal class associations, nuns socialized with male and female fellow
students. For the first time, they were exposed to a life-style other than
"celibate religious women" on a day-to-day basis. They learned that lay-
women with families were living very happy, meaningful lives. Many ex-
nuns commented that during their student days they began to realize the
high cost involved in being a celibate religious. Likewise for the first time
in years, many of them became aware of and admitted having sexual as
well as friendship needs that were not being met in their lives in the
convent. Frequently, nuns were reacted to by male students and male
professors not just as members of religious orders but as women. For many
nuns it had been years since they had been in a dating situation and had
had personal relationships with men. For many of them such male attention
awakened dormant sexual and emotional needs and raised doubts in their
minds about a future life of celibacy.

Being away from the convent and the informal social controls exerted
by religious colleagues provided the occasion for nuns to engage in behaviors prohibited by the order. Nuns, for example, were not allowed to
eat in public places. One of my first experiences of freedom occurred when
I walked down Broadway in New York City eating a candy bar. I felt part
of the human race again and just a "plain person," doing what ordinary
people did all the time. The fact that I was deliberately disobeying official
policy gave me a sense of freedom and self-determination, as well as the
experience of getting away with such behavior without being struck immediately by the Wrath of God!

A more serious stand against authority occurred when I took off my veil
after being away at school for two months. I wrote the superior and said

I couldn't tolerate the stares of people on the subway or of fellow students when they saw me dressed in contemporary clothes but wearing that "funny little veil" on my head. Strangers weren't sure whether I was or wasn't a nun, and their uncertainty created curiosity and often embarrassment. I received a letter of reprimand from the superior and the comment that the veil must be worn or "your vows will be the next to go." I refused to put the veil back on, feeling that I knew my situation better than the superior did. After a personal visit with her shortly thereafter, she gave me permission to go veil-less.

During the several months I wore the modified veil, I also learned how culturally relevant or irrelevant such symbols are. I accepted an invitation from an Indian male student, whom I had just met and who didn't know I was a nun, to have coffee. I learned quickly that in his home province in India available women wore veils to entice marriageable men. My symbol of celibacy thus catapulted me into an embarrassing situation. These first experiences of questioning the taken-for-granted convent system, of becoming aware through social contacts of options, and of being deviant in terms of official norms gave nuns a sense of freedom and self-determination and, at the same time, a sense of anxiety about their role commitments.

Both of the major influences that led nuns to question a total way of life—that is, the discussions that took place within the orders themselves and the educational opportunities outside their walls—came from the church itself, as part of the renewal and adaptation movement formalized by Pope John XXIII in calling the Second Vatican Council. By "opening the windows and allowing the breath of the Spirit to enter," Pope John led the way to what became a major dilemma for convents and the nuns in them. The process of questioning disrupted the totalistic system and the underlying symbolic meanings that sustained the religious orders, and it eventuated in the exodus of large numbers of nuns from their convents.

Stage Two: The Freedom to Decide

The second stage in the role-leaving process comes when the nun begins to realize that she has the freedom to decide to stay or leave. While she may come to this realization rationally in stage one, the time arrives when the nun emotionally faces the fact that she has a choice and doesn't have to stay in religious life even though she may have taken final vows. Nuns handle the issue of redefining final vows in various ways. Some come to realize that the life to which they committed themselves has changed drastically. Their commitment is no longer binding. An even greater number come to redefine the meaning of final vows. Whereas, previously, final vows meant a commitment to live poorly, celibately, and obediently for life, now, in the new system of religious orders, with the emphasis on personal needs and a changing institution, nuns began to feel that such a life-long commitment is simply impossible and that they couldn't possibly have such a "forever" commitment.

My interview data show that many nuns were aware that Rome was quite routinely granting dispensations from final vows, and this further indicated that what one might have promised years ago in terms of one's future might not be binding. The process of requesting freedom from vows from Rome was well-known among these nuns, and the fact that it had become quite routine suggested to them that they now had a choice to stay or not to stay.

My own experience of the freedom to decide occurred after a party with fellow students. There were three men there who were ex-priests in the process of adjusting to a lay life. We discussed their reasons for leaving. Each had become disillusioned with the church and its rigid rule forbidding priests from marrying and having families. After the party I was getting in touch with my own feelings regarding my commitment to religious life, and I suddenly realized that I didn't want to be a nun any more and that for the past two or three years I had been giving increasing signals and clues to that effect. In fact, I had even been doing some dating without admitting that that was a clear indication that I was considering other possibilities. I felt elated and relieved at my sense of freedom in admitting that I wanted to leave religious life and in knowing that, in fact, I could do so.

In stage one, the nun in the process of leaving disengaged herself intellectually from the meanings associated with the role of nun. In stage two the discovery of her freedom to leave resulted in an emotional disengagement from those meanings. This realization was accompanied by a feeling of freedom and elation.

Stage Three: Trying Out Options

After experiencing the freedom to decide, the next stage is trying out the options of a new life. San Giovanni (1978:41) labels this process "role rehearsal," that is, "the process of anticipatory learning and acquisition of social roles before one actually assumes them."

Nuns who were considering leaving their orders tended to try out options in two ways: by imaginary role-playing and by trying out new roles in reality. Imaginary role-playing usually occurred when nuns observed the behavior of friends and acquaintances who had left religious orders. At this stage nuns frequently either made contact with or intensified their contact with friends who had already left the order. By spending time with such friends, one was able to get an idea of what it was like to find an apartment, to learn how to dress like a lay person, to begin the dating game, in many instances to find a man, to get married, and to establish a family life. By making such contact and becoming familiar with what other role options involved, the nun was able to imagine whether such roles were options for her.

Simultaneously, the nun who was considering leaving frequently began to actually try out other options in her life. For example, she frequently began to relate differently to men. By the late 1960s most nuns were in contemporary habit, which usually meant wearing lay clothes and perhaps a veil. These nuns frequently began to wear makeup and in some cases jewelry. They often allowed themselves to take the initiative in introducing themselves to men. When men invited them for coffee or a drink, they would go as a way of testing out how comfortable they felt in a male-female relationship. Other areas in which nuns tended to rehearse options were jobs, living situations, maintaining a home or apartment, and hair styles.

Stage Four: The Vacuum

The period of trying out options brings a nun closer to the actual decision of matching her role with her true feelings. She imagines in her mind and actually anticipates what it would be like if she left. This period, however, is frequently followed by a period of anxiety. It's as though the nun is about to make a gigantic step in her life and takes one glance backward before she actually makes the leap.

Stage four can be characterized as a period of vacuum, an experience of absurdity (Kotarba, 1979:357–58). The person goes through one last weighing of pros and cons before actually taking the definite step to leave. Most nuns who leave realize that the decision is essentially nonretractable because the orders are reluctant to readmit ex-members. The person frequently goes through a final weighing of both sides. Should I stay or should I leave? Staying, in fact, has many pluses. Religious life provides security, a network of friends, and a sense of camaraderie, all of which take very little effort to maintain. The nun who stays in the order is assured of a job and of being taken care of financially. Even in the new system there are broad outlines of what it means to be a nun, so that one has to think quite little about individual adaptability to the role. On the other side of the coin, to remain in the order means, in many instances, denying one's needs, desires, and sense of self-fulfillment. In other words, to remain means not being truly faithful to one's self. For many nuns, there is the question of age, particularly for those who desire to marry and have children. For these nuns, leaving must be now or never.

While it may be relatively easy to weigh the pros and cons intellectually, to do so emotionally is difficult for many nuns. In my own case, I requested an application from Rome to leave. The application came, I put it away in my desk drawer, and for three weeks was unable to look at it. It was not so much a process of intellectually weighing the pros and cons but of becoming comfortable with the idea of no longer being a nun. Those three weeks were a period of deep anxiety. For the first time in my life I found myself going among crowds and having tremors or feeling faint. I had not yet left the order; on the other hand, I *had* left it, in many ways. At that moment I felt like a person without a country, without any footing, without any reason for being. I had no clear definition of who I was or what the future held. On the other hand, I had been away at school for almost four years and had been very active nationally in the renewal movement. I knew exactly where the religious orders stood, and I was very critical of many things going on in them. Intellectually, I could no longer justify my life as a nun. Yet I worried that I had so intellectualized the process that I was not really in touch with my deepest emotions regarding my life as a nun. At the end of those three weeks, I tore up the dispensation application, left Columbia, and returned to my order. I felt the time had come to go back and actually live in the convent for awhile to see if I knew where I was emotionally. For one year I lived in the order again as a nun. That entire year was a kind of vacuum for me. I was outwardly living the routines of religious life, yet I felt like a stranger. I busied myself that year with completing my dissertation and conducting several self-studies for the order. Many of the ex-nuns I interviewed also returned from educational situations to their orders before actually exiting. For many of them this was, as it was for me, a period of reality-testing after their experiences away at school.

The predominant emotion I experienced in considering leaving the convent—and this is true of most of the ex-nuns I interviewed—was that of fear of the unknown. Would I be happy outside the order? Would men find me desirable? Would I find a husband? What meaning and goals would my life have outside the order? At this point, these were unanswerable questions. What resulted was the sense of living in a vacuum without any meaningful points of reference in terms of social identity.

Stage Five: The Turning Point

The fifth stage is a turning point, a time in which the decision to leave is actually crystallized, usually in terms of some event or situation. Very often the event itself is relatively insignificant. It simply comes to symbolize the emotions and thinking that are involved in the decision to leave.

For about 20 percent of the ex-nuns I interviewed, the time for taking final vows was the turning point that prompted them to leave. These nuns had been taking temporary vows every year for one to six years and were now at the point where they were forced either to make a permanent commitment for life or to leave. A small number left because of job assignments that they did not like. About one-fourth of the interviewees, most of them from the very conservative order, left after a major chapter or renewal meeting in the order, at which point they realized that the order was not making the kind of changes they desired and that they therefore could not continue with the order.

For me the turning point in my decision to leave revolved around some financial decisions made by the order. It was customary for nuns who were drawing salaries of any sort to send their entire salary to the mother house. In turn, each local community and each nun turned in a budget. It was community policy that no nun should receive more than $35.00 a month for personal expenses, which included clothing, shoes, toilet articles, entertainment of any sort, and travel. While I was studying, I had a bank account and was trusted to spend money wisely. I felt that nuns should be regarded as mature, independent women who could be trusted to make wise decisions regarding their salary. Then came the day when the community decided that every salaried sister had to request a salary increase the following year. A designated official for the administration came to each local house to negotiate with the pastor or employer regarding the increase. This was the decisive turning point for me. I rebelled at the idea that someone else should negotiate my salary. I called the chancellor, a high church official in the diocese where I was working, and asked him for the quickest way to get out. He dictated a statement, which I then sent to Rome. Within three weeks I had my formal dispensation to leave religious life.

Stage Six: Creating the Ex-Role

The saliency and meaning of an ex-role derive not so much from what one is currently doing but rather from the expectations and social obligations that went with one's previous behavior and life-style. Nowhere does the relation between individual self-identity and self-transformation, on the one hand, and societal expectations, on the other, come more sensitively and centrally into play than in the realm of ex-roles. A person who is in the process of reestablishing herself in a new identity is engrossed in a number of social-psychological processes that are often painful and are undetermined by role models. At the same time that the individual is going through this self-transformation, people in society are expecting certain role behaviors that are based on her previous identity.

There are numerous types of ex-roles, such as the divorcée, the ex-prisoner, the apostate, the heretic, the ex-drug addict, the ex-president of the United States, the ex-president of a corporation, the ex-priest, and the ex-nun. For some ex-roles, society has linguistic designations, such as divorcée, widow, alumnus. In other cases, however, the person is simply known as "ex." Ex-roles that are fairly common and are widely experienced in the society carry relatively little stigma and tend to be institutionalized in terms of expected behaviors. Those that are less well-defined institutionally tend to be what Glaser and Strauss call "emergent passages"; that is, they are created, discovered, and shaped by the parties as they go along (Glaser and Strauss, 1971:85–86). In emergent passages there are few guidelines, precedents, or models to facilitate transfer between roles.

The essential dilemma involved in the ex-role is the incongruity and tension that exist between self-definition and society's expectations. The individual going through the exit process is trying to shake off and de-emphasize a previous identity. She is struggling to become someone she has not been before. An important moment in the exit process occurs when one's friends, family, and coworkers begin to think of one as other than an ex. In fact, Goode defines the process of adjustment (for a divorcée) as one

> by which a disruption of role sets and patterns and of existing social relations is incorporated into the individual's life patterns such that the roles accepted and assigned do not take the prior divorce into account as the primary point of reference. In more common sense terms, the woman is no longer ex-wife or divorcee primarily, but first of all co-worker, date or bride. [Goode, 1956:19]

An ex-nun can be considered adjusted to the extent that she integrates her past experience into her new life-situation in such a way that what is important is the here and now rather than the life she led in the past. She can be considered adapted to the process of leaving to the extent that she feels successful and competent in her present role, whether as woman, homemaker, date, teacher, American citizen, or whatever, rather than in terms of her past life as a nun. Her successful passage to secular life finally occurs once other people relate to her in her new role or roles rather than in terms of who she once was (San Giovanni, 1978:66).

How did it feel in those first days after leaving the convent? My own experience and that of many of my interviewees was one of euphoria, relief, and feelings of freedom, of being released from pressures and expectations. I again experienced the tremendous freedom and release that I had felt in New York when I realized that I was free to choose either to stay or to leave religious life. I was now totally on my own, with no institution backing me up. I felt "normal" again, just an ordinary person with no unusual expectations being made of me because of my status as a nun.

San Giovanni reports a similar experience for most of the twenty ex-nuns she interviewed. These ex-nuns characterized their first days out as "exciting," "crazy," "new," "free," "fun," "peaceful," and "terrific" (San Giovanni, 1978:70). I myself found that in those first weeks I wanted very little contact with the nuns I had lived with. Rather, I found myself seeking out people I knew outside the convent and being eager to meet new friends.

In creating an ex-role, there are three main areas in which the ex-nun undergoes a trial-and-error process of learning social competence. She realizes that all of her previous role rehearsals and imaginations were inadequate in these three areas:

1. The area of intimacies, including friendship and sexuality
2. Presentation of herself, including dress, makeup, hair style, and mannerisms
3. Negotiating and adapting to other people's reactions to her emerging role as an ex-nun

1. *Friendship and Sexuality.* In her first weeks after leaving the order, the ex-nun realizes, perhaps more than ever before, that she is a woman. For years in the convent her femininity was deemphasized; her role as a religious took precedence over everything. Now that her well-defined religious role is gone, she struggles with what it means to be a woman in a secular world.

For many ex-nuns, it has been five, ten, fifteen, even twenty years since they have been in a dating situation. Most entered the convent either during or directly after high school. High-school dating, especially in the 1950s and 1960s, was very different from the dating situation in which they now find themselves. The rules of the game have changed. As one interviewee put it, "Gee! Men have become aggressive and permissive since I last dealt with them. To accept a dinner date almost inevitably means sexual favors in return." Another said, "When I dated twenty years ago, it was considered forward for a man to expect a prolonged good-night kiss at the door. Now men are offended if they are not invited into your apartment after a night out."

While some nuns had been associating with men in educational and social situations prior to leaving their order, and while some had begun dating before they actually left, most interviewees indicated that their situation after they had left was different. They reported feeling very insecure about sexual scripts, that is, what was expected of them in relating to a man in social life. Sexual scripts, as Gagnon and Simon refer to them, had changed tremendously (Gagnon and Simon, 1973).

Most ex-nuns interviewed said they were very nonselective in regard to men the first few months after leaving the order. This stemmed from a fear that they would not be asked out or would be found unacceptable to men.

While few nuns in my sample left religious orders specifically to marry, the majority of them considered marriage as a possible option in the future. To make sure that the option was viable, these ex-nuns realized it was important to be successful in relating to men. Most of them were in their late twenties and thirties and realized that, if they were going to marry and have children, they could not wait too long.

Many ex-nuns soon discovered that most of the eligible men in their own age cohort had been previously married. They then had to decide how they felt about dating a divorcé or, in some cases, a married man who had not yet divorced. In some cases, dating a divorcé also meant coming to know his children. Serious dating relationships brought forth the possibility of being a step-parent. In some instances, then, during the first year or so after leaving the order, ex-nuns faced not only the issue of negotiating male-female relationships but also the possibility of becoming wife and step-parent simultaneously.

Sexual scripts in part involve cues. A man, for example, waits for cues from his date to know how far he can go with her. These cues change over time, and for ex-nuns, who haven't dated for many years, the world of cues is frequently a strange world. Ex-nuns reported misinterpreting these cues and not realizing the implications of their words and gestures. Frequently, then, ex-nuns found themselves in embarrassing situations when the man felt she was saying and doing things she never intended to say or do. For example, several ex-nuns said they quickly learned that accepting an invitation into a date's apartment after being out to dinner or the theater indicated to him that she was interested in sexual involvement.

In the old system of religious orders, "particular friendships" were forbidden. There were numerous structural mechanisms to discourage close personal relationships among nuns. For example, at the beginning of recreational periods, numbers were drawn to determine with whom an individual would walk, talk, or play games. This greatly reduced the probability that an individual nun would often associate with the same person. Fear of lesbian relationships may have been the covert rationale for forbidding particular friendships, but the stated rationale was to encourage universal love among nuns for each other. However, one of the changes in the new system of religious orders has been a greater emphasis on the role of friendship in self-development. By the time a woman left the convent, therefore, she had learned to develop friendships.

Most ex-nuns interviewed indicated that in the weeks and months following their exit they tended to have as friends other nuns or other ex-nuns. These social-support networks and friendships played an important part in the adaptation process for most ex-nuns. Only gradually, my data show, did the majority of ex-nuns develop close friendships with lay people. In fact, the establishment of such lay friendships indicated successful adjustment to an identity other than that of ex-nun.

2. *Presentation of Self.* As Goffman has shown, individuals are actors on a stage (Goffman, 1959), and, as actors, they present their identity to others in a variety of ways. These presentations of self are like masks that indicate specific social roles.

The ex-nun's primary concern on leaving the convent revolves around presentation of self. For example, for many years nuns did not use makeup. When she leaves, the ex-nun faces these questions: Do I use makeup? How do I learn what to do with it? What kind of makeup becomes me? At this point many nuns simply experiment by trying various things available on the market. The use of makeup comes to symbolize an aspect of her presentation of self.

Clothes also become a critical issue. Nuns who left in the 1970s had been in modern habit, but these habits frequently were not in the latest fashion. When dating and relating as a laywoman become a central concern of the ex-nun, clothes become one way of successfully presenting her new self. Many ex-nuns began reading fashion magazines or going to stores to see what was available. It was common immediately after leaving the convent to choose classic styles, such as a basic suit or simple skirt and blouse. To move from the clothes of even the modern nun to sexy bathing suits and low-cut dresses frequently took time for the ex-nun and indicated changes in her self-image. As ex-nuns came to define themselves more and more in terms of new roles, changes in clothing styles tended to express these changes in self-perception.

The length of her hair was frequently an indication that a nun was in process of transition. When a nun began to let her hair grow and became concerned about its management, this often signaled that she was in the process of leaving the convent. The ex-nun faced the task of learning how to wear her hair in a style that did not signal her as an ex-nun.

Especially in the early and mid-1970s, habits such as smoking were frequently taken up by ex-nuns. In my own case, I had never smoked until I left the convent. In the six months prior to my leaving, the order to which I belonged made it a big issue that nuns were not allowed to smoke. Religious significance was given to the issue of not smoking. Smoking for me, therefore, had many symbolic implications. The order didn't like it, so, when I left, I took it up. Smoking gave me a feeling of doing something different from what I did as a nun, and it became symbolic of my new life.

Being a nun becomes so internalized that mannerisms and physical expressions are associated with the role of nun. For example, during my early socialization period in the order, I was made to follow behind a superior day after day in an attempt to undo my "worldly walk." I was told I simply had to learn how to walk religiously. I was also told frequently that my emotional exuberance and expressive mannerisms had to be toned down. Most nuns, therefore, learned ways of behaving and ways of moving the body that were characteristic of nuns.

One day I was sitting in the office of a professor at Columbia University when a young woman walked into the room dressed in modern clothes and wearing makeup. She spoke briefly to the professor and left. When she left, I asked what order she belonged to. The professor was amazed that I could tell that she was an ex-nun. There was a way in which she handled herself and moved that was indicative of her previous life. This example makes it clear that ex-nuns had to relearn the whole world of feminine gestures.

3. *Social Reactions*. Probably the most important aspect of being an ex-nun is learning how to deal with the social reactions of other people. Even if she is partially successful in deemphasizing her past life in terms of her own self-image, she is frequently confronted by other people who remind her that she is an ex. People come to expect different things of the ex-nun. To Catholics, being an ex-nun usually means having certain religious qualities and values. For Catholics who knew the person when she was a nun, seeing her now in lay clothes, wearing makeup, employing feminine mannerisms, and sometimes enjoying the company of a man was often shocking.

For non-Catholics, to realize that a woman is an ex-nun frequently arouses bizarre ideas about what she has previously experienced. Many non-Catholics who have seen such films as *The Nun's Story* or *The Flying Nun* have strange ideas about convent life. It is common, when meeting non-Catholics who realize one's ex-status, to be submitted to a barrage of questions about what one's life was like. For the ex-nun who is trying to move from that life to a new role in society, such questions and reminiscences are often disconcerting.

For the first three or four years after leaving my order, I felt very uncomfortable when people asked me about my former life. I frequently felt in a bind. I wanted to be polite and entertaining, yet at the same time I felt embarrassed to talk about those old experiences. My greatest desire was to be treated as an ordinary person. Goffman states the problem very well when he says that "The stigmatized individual tends to hold the same beliefs about identity that we do. His deepest feeling about what he is may be his sense of being a 'normal person,' a human being like anyone else, a person, therefore, who deserves a fair break. What is desired by the individual is what can be called 'acceptance' " (Goffman, 1963:78).

One area in which ex-nuns frequently find it difficult to handle social reactions is in their new relations with men. Usually an initial item of conversation on a date with a new person is to discuss one's past—where you were born, where you went to school, where you have been during the past year. For the ex-nun, the issue is always: Should I tell him, or shouldn't I tell him? To tell him frequently causes embarrassment. Once men realize that one has been a nun, their reactions frequently depend on their own knowledge of and experiences with nuns. Obviously, it is difficult for an ex-nun to explain where she has been and what she has done during the past year without referring to her former identity.

The fact that people are conscious of one's previous identity as a nun is manifested in ways that frequently cause embarrassment. For example, at my first academic swimming party with colleagues, a woman who had known me as a nun stopped her conversation to apologize to me after using an off-color word. A male colleague apologized after spontaneously whistling when I appeared in a bathing suit.

Success in self-transformation and adaptation to a new role is signaled when the individual begins to think of herself not as an ex-nun but in terms of her current roles and when she projects an image that no longer suggests her ex-status to observers. Likewise, when friends and associates begin relating to her in terms of who she is now, the ex-nun can feel assured that she has made a successful status passage and that her role as nun is now simply part of her personal history.

For some of the ex-nuns I interviewed, the leaving process took many years, while others left within a few months of first questioning their commitment. Regardless of the time span, the majority of the interviewees went through an exit process characterized by the stages I have just described.

SUMMARY AND CONCLUSIONS

Ex-roles constitute a unique sociological phenomenon in that self-definition and social expectations are influenced, and frequently determined, by a previous identity. Usually the person is struggling to disengage from a previous role at the same time that other people take the previous role into account in relating to the person.

Some ex-roles, such as being an alumnus or an ex-president, are fairly well institutionalized in our society, but an increasing number of ex-roles are emerging for which there are few, if any, well-defined normative expectations. Individuals in these ex-roles are having to create role definitions as they live out the roles.

"Ex-nun" is an example of an emergent ex-role that has become more widespread in our society during the past ten years. In this essay, I have outlined the process by which a nun decides to disengage from her role as nun and establish her identity as a laywoman. Throughout the six stages that characterize her exit process there is continual interaction between the issue of who I am to myself and who I am to relevant others. The creation of an identity as an ex-nun results from the process of harmonizing self-definition and role expectations.

The six-stage model of role exit presented in this paper is descriptive of the process of self-transformation as it occurs for one group of people experiencing an emergent ex-role. While the experience of being a nun is unique, I feel the general model of role exit developed here is applicable to a wide range of ex-roles currently emerging in American life. Whether we consider ex-presidents of the United States, ex-academicians, ex-athletes, or ex-astronauts, the process of role exit is similar in all cases.

Notes

I am grateful to Joseph Kotarba for his detailed comments on an earlier draft; they were especially helpful in contributing to the conceptual development of the essay. Jill Alsup's valuable comments also helped me to organize my ideas.

1. Ralph Turner has recently argued that in the past few decades there has been a shift in the laws of self-definition away from institutional role prescriptions and toward impulse (Turner, 1976).

2. Even though religious orders differ from the other total institutions mentioned by Goffman (1961), in that members voluntarily join, the structural characteristics of total institutions that he presents quite accurately describe convents as they existed prior to the mid-1960s.

3. For a detailed description of traditional religious life and of the changes that have recently occurred, see Ebaugh 1977.

References

Abbott, Walter, S.J., ed. 1966. "Decree on the Appropriate Renewal of the Religious Life." *Documents of Vatican II.* New York: America Press.

Ebaugh, Helen Rose Fuchs. 1977. *Out of the Cloister: A Study of Organizational Dilemmas.* Austin: University of Texas Press.

Gagnon, John, and William Simon. 1973. *Sexual Conduct: The Social Sources of Human Sexuality.* Chicago: Aldine.

Glaser, Barney, and Anselm Strauss. 1971. *Status Passage.* Chicago: Aldine.

Goffman, Erving. 1959 *The Presentation of Self in Everyday Life.* Garden City, N.Y.: Doubleday.

———. 1961. "On the Characteristics of Total Institutions." In Goffman, *Asylums: Essays on the Social Situation of Mental Patients and Other Inmates.* Garden City, N.Y.: Doubleday.

———. 1963. *Stigma: Notes on the Management of Spoiled Identity.* Englewood Cliffs, N.J.: Prentice-Hall.

Goode, William J. 1956. *After Divorce.* New York: Free Press.

Kanter, Rosabeth Moss. 1972. *Commitment and Community: Community and Utopia in Sociological Perspective.* Cambridge, Mass.: Harvard University Press.

Kotarba, Joseph A. 1979. "Existential Sociology." Pp. 348–68 in Scott G. McNall, ed., *Theoretical Perspectives in Sociology.* New York: St. Martin's Press.

Mead, George Herbert. 1964. *Selected Writings.* Edited by Andrew Beck. Indianapolis: Bobbs-Merrill.

Merton, Robert K. 1968. "Contributions to the Theory of Reference Group Behavior." In Merton, *Social Theory and Social Structure.* NewYork: Free Press.

Parsons, Talcott, and Edward Shils. 1951. *Toward a General Theory of Action.* Cambridge, Mass.: Harvard University Press.

San Giovanni, Lucinda. 1978. *Ex-Nuns: A Study of Emergent Role Passage.* Norwood, N.J.: Ablex.

Turner, Ralph. 1979. "The Real Self: From Institution to Impulse." *American Journal of Sociology* 81(5):989–1016.

The Media Self

David L. Altheide

Conventional wisdom in social science maintains that who we are, what we think of ourselves, and how we assume others see and regard us are contingent on a complex interplay of social roles, expectations, and structured patterns of interaction. The nexus of the communication that contributes to, and sustains, self-other relationships and identities is in most cases a person-to-person exchange. Another nexus between self-feelings and self-other definitions, expectations, and actual behavior consists of the mass media and attendant organizational, technological, and interpersonal procedures. This essay examines how an increasing portion of daily life is influenced by the acquisition, enactment, presentation, reflection, and feelings about oneself as a focus of media attention. Points will be illustrated with data derived from more than a decade of research on mass-media aspects of political decision-making, professional sports, television, radio, and newspaper journalism, and related personal accounts.

THE SELF AND THE MEDIA IN CONTEXT

Individuals relate to others and themselves through various and diverse media, e.g., voice communication, touch, gestures, etc. These more personal media are essentially invariant and are involved in most forms of communication, although their primacy may be overridden by situational, organizational, or technological constraints and priorities.

Several features inform the likelihood that the above-mentioned essentials of communication will be overridden: proximity of the communicators, the purpose of their communication, the opportunity for and likelihood of response, and the technology employed. In face-to-face communication, for example, two or more people are within hearing distance, are usually exchanging information for a commonly understood frame of reference, can respond to and correct the other, and rely on their own voices, ears, and eyes to fully grasp what is being presented to them. As each of these elements changes through innovations in technology and media formats, the process of communication shifts, usually to a situation in which there are fewer speakers than listeners. It is at this point that "mass communication" begins to emerge. Examples include Greek plays, which presented both philosophical and moral messages to citizens, and the use of the pulpit in Islam (see Fathi, 1978), where both news and direction of conduct are dispensed by authoritative figures.

By far the biggest changes in communication were introduced by technological innovations, first by the printing press, then by movable type, and finally by the advent of radio and television. The latter enabled a few persons to communicate with a multitude—but the multitude could not reply. Moreover, the persons to whom the messages were directed were no longer regarded as individuals in specific situations, known to the communicator, but came gradually to be viewed as members of an "audience"—as an aggregate of attributes defined in economic and commercial terms rather than as a whole people. This audience—envisioned, approached, and studied in this way—was presumed by those who controlled the tools of the mass media to have preferences and, especially, dislikes. In brief, a new mode of communication, with its own logic, arose.

The rise of technologically based forms of mass communication followed the revolutionary impact that mass production and consumption had on daily routines and self-conceptions. More and more of one's identity became tied to products and styles; the increasing relationship between media messages, significance, and personal identity penetrated public life. Ewen's (1976:47) point about media messages and desires is illustrative:

> Increasingly, within the texts of ads in the twenties, these desires are fulfilled in the marketplace. Thrift no longer cohabits with daintiness, but threatens to prevent it. Within the rhetoric of these ads, the accumulation of various products, each for a separate objectified portion of the body, was equated with the means to success.

The effort to "commodify" the self and thereby promote more public styles as individual preferences contributed to the symbolic integration and mass homogenization of ethnically diverse peoples, but other technological and industrial changes, which created affluence, also led to more privatized living. Active participation in public realms diminished, but, as Bensman and Lilienfeld (1979) note, the mass media contributed to this process by becoming a major resource for public stylization, identification, and recognition. *The mass media have become the major public dimension for contemporary social life.*

The unique logic of the electronic media, including their perception of people as audience members, led to the development of, and reliance on, routine patterns of communication. This development included the use of fairly standardized formats, which promoted the portrayal of media types and styles rather than distinct individuals.

In this way, individuals effectively disappeared from public view in favor of media portrayals of patterns of behavior and focus:

> While the mass media increasingly dramatize the inner
> life of their *personae*—their sexual "problems" and
> expression, their inner psychological conflicts, their per-
> versions, delusions, and failures—they do so by projecting
> them in relatively standardized ways. The portrayal of the
> private is thus objectified by the mass media, though their
> subject matter is the subjective existence of their protag-
> onists. To the audience, subjective existence takes on a
> standardized, objective character that nullifies the sub-
> jective character of the subject matter. This is especially
> true when the content of such media presentations is the
> object of repeated discussion by the audience. [Bensman
> and Lilienfeld, 1979:34]

What emerges from standardized presentations is a peculiar brand of
role behavior. These presentations cannot be informed simply by the true
role demands of, say, an occupation, since they must also reflect the logic
of media formats designed to satisfy organizational, technological, and
commercial demands (Altheide and Snow, 1979). The nonmedia reality that
is transformed through media perspectives and work is thereby rendered
unambiguous, interesting, and noteworthy. Indeed, *a very unnoticed feature of mass-media formats is the way that individuals, events, and topics
are presented as though they are noteworthy and important*. This notion,
now essentially taken for granted as part of our cultural stock of knowledge,
perpetuates audience interest in and attention to mass media as *conveyors*
but not *creators* of information and reality.

Being presented in the major media, especially television, marks one as
being noteworthy and exceptional. Not only is this an occasion for one to
be seen by others; it is also a rare opportunity to see oneself not just on
film—home movies make this fairly commonplace—but as a media subject.
With this comes the widespread belief in the "publicity effect" (Douglas,
n.d.), the notion that being presented on the major media is important and
may well have important consequences, either negative or positive. And
it is the perception of self via the mass media that adds a public-other
dimension to one's conception of self. Hyperawareness of one's media
performance, demeanor, and style is evident during initial viewings, hearings, and readings about oneself—for example, "That doesn't really look
like me," "I sound nervous," or "I didn't mean to say that."

In short, the mass media become relevant to current understanding of
self-conceptions and self-indications because of the significance these media have for recognition of self by self and because people become interested in someone they see on television or read about in the newspapers
or magazines. As an assistant to the governor of Arizona put it, "It's great
to read your boss's name in *Newsweek*" (*Arizona Republic* [newspaper],
August 24, 1980). The "ripple effect" of media attention is also apparent

in comments made by one's friends and neighbors, who are quick to remark, "I saw you on television." From my own experience I can report that neighbors I have known for years will offer to shake hands "with someone who gets in the newspapers."

The interest in gaining media recognition seems particularly important for people with little or no media experience. Observing how children behave in front of demonstration video cameras in department stores makes this apparent, as do observations of the studio behavior of children and parents who attend children's TV shows. One of the more extreme examples of the awareness of mass-media attention and its meaning for self was the aftermath of a tragic school-bus accident, one that resulted in the death of one man and caused several children to be badly burned. When one thirteen-year-old-victim was being tended to by the ambulance crew, the sound of shutters clicking prompted the query, "Are they taking pictures of me?" (news report, *Arizona Republic*, September 25, 1980).

The expectations of the "performers"—of any persons presented on television—are greatly informed by their experience as former audience members; in contemporary society we are all media spectators before a few of us are media performers. Thus, individuals interviewed or performing before a television camera for the first time are already knowledgeable about—albeit not proficient at—maintaining a competent media performance; that is, they know about posturing, responding politely to question-answer-question formats, and even acting as though the television studio is not really a studio at all but is part of any routine conversational setting. Most first-timers on TV therefore realize that they should not look or "gawk" at the camera or seem puzzled by the blinding lights surrounding them or even by the pancake makeup when it is applied.

The mass media, then, become relevant for self-conceptions, including feelings about how one is presented or "comes off," because these media are the major presenters of public life to an audience that has little in common except for the media experiences they share. The media-public context has private, personal dimensions when individuals are presented on the mass media and thereby acquire a self-definition, even if this emerges from their reaction—favorable or unfavorable—to their image; the crucial point is that they will reflect on this image, and, in many cases, this will have an effect. The "publicity effect" (Douglas, n.d.) of media reports, even if untrue, can lead individuals to experience deep feelings of shame and in some cases may even contribute to suicide.

Such results can occur because of the cultural significance of mass communication for the assessments that others make of one's moral qualities. In this sense, all media reports are sanctionable as public documents and thereby call for an accounting (Scott and Lyman, 1968).

All of this suggests that self-conceptions are joined to the significance of mass communication in contemporary life and that this is true for members of the audience as well as for the persons who are presented in the mass media. However, the mass media, and especially television, are not passive recorders and presenters of individuals and situations, for they bring their own logic and formats to each media occasion, and these serve as a sort of organizational template for what will be presented. In the remainder of this paper I shall discuss the nature of this template and the ways that it affects what is presented, especially the way that individuals are portrayed and how they assess this experience.

The data for this essay are derived from several studies of mass media that I have conducted over the past ten years. For two reasons, however, I pay particular attention to the relationship between athletes and the media. First, sports are an enormously influential component of our social life and deserve much more sociological attention than they have received. Second, the relationship of self to media is especially apparent in the realm of sports. An athletic career, often short and uncertain, depends considerably for its success on the level of popularity, skill, dedication, and competence the audience perceives in a player. This perception is obtained as much by media portrayals as by direct observation of the athlete's performance on the field.

Media Formats

In general, "format," as used in this essay, refers to the rules for selecting, organizing, and presenting information. All media, including speech, have their own rules of communication, but, as I have already noted, the mass media are distinguished by their unique formats for selecting, organizing, and presenting information. Moreover, communication, or shared meaning, depends on the degree to which the various parties involved in the communication process—the persons applying the format to the content, the persons who are supplying the content, e.g., by speaking or looking into the camera, and the audience members who are receiving the content as presented via the format—share some understanding of the format and its process. But it is common for misunderstandings to occur among the various parties to the communication process—the producers of messages, the persons involved with the messages, and the persons receiving the messages—because expectations and experiences derived from some media, especially daily conversation and personally mediated experiences, are not always applicable to other formats, especially television.

The impact of formats is especially apparent when, say, an individual is interviewed for a television program and is unaware of the unique way that TV formats make use of time, the grammar of visual imagery (film editing), and how certain topics are selected for emphasis because of their presumed relevance for entertainment.

Initial encounters with media formats provide illustrative examples of the contrasting expectations between daily-life experiences and what is regarded as relevant for television. As one reflects on, and even accommodates self-presentation to, these formats and their constraints, an awareness of the distinctiveness of the mass media emerges. An author of a best-selling book on running discussed his experience on television "talk shows":

> I'm not a race promoter, a television personality, or anything like that. But when you write a book that's a popular book in the United States, you discover that there is this whole vast machinery waiting to take you and do what they are prepared to do to you. I can give a very specific example. What I wanted to do was write the book, have it do as well as it could, and then move on to my next book. . . . I wanted to leave this. You go on TV and you're promoting a running book, and somebody says, "When I run or when I used to run I got a black toenail or a blister or something like that." So you find yourself giving advice because you feel you would appear to be stupid if you said, "I'm not in that business. I'm not in the business of giving advice. Go ask your doctor." See, if you're really honest— I mean, if I were completely honest, as I think I'm being with you now—I would just say . . . well, maybe, if you were completely honest, you wouldn't get yourself into doing TV promotion at all; but that isn't right, because you want the book to sell well. What happens is people start asking you questions, and they say, "Come in your jogging suit. We want you to give a demonstration on the show." So I guess the thing to say, if you're completely honest, is, "I wear my jogging suit only when I jog. I don't wear my jogging suit to TV studios." So you find yourself walking around cities like Chicago and standing out there in your warmups, you know, hailing cabs and things like that, and suddenly you realize you're doing a lot of bizarre things. But that is what people want you to do.[1]

Television is the dominant medium in our society today, but other media, such as newspapers, have played a part in the emerging effect of mass media on individual self-conceptions. One way this has occurred is that newspapers have had to adjust to television; in many cases newspapers and even magazines simply add more detail to what has been seen on a television newscast or live coverage of an event. This is especially true of sports reporting. Whereas television provides immediate scores and even visuals of a key play—formerly the province of the morning newspapers— newspapers now must complement the electronic coverage by giving "analysis" and, more recently, "personal player profiles," i.e., what went on behind the scenes. Such coverage is certainly of interest to many sports fans, but it does raise havoc with ballplayers, who may not be prepared for impromptu press conferences following games. A veteran major-league pitcher explained it this way:

> A lot of times a sportswriter will get down on you or something, and you might have a bad ballgame or something, and you don't want to talk to anybody after the ballgame; well, the next time you go out there and you do bad, he'll just rip you. Simply because you didn't talk to him the time before; it's happened to me.
>
> Yeah, after a ballgame when I'd given up a home run in the ninth inning, you know you really don't feel like talking to any sportswriters, so you say, "I just don't want to be bothered right now. I don't want to talk to anybody; please leave me alone." I've done that a couple of times; then, the next time I go out there or something, and you do bad or do good, it is all negative in the newspaper the next day, or they'd write a column about the fact that I didn't say anything to a sportswriter.

Professional athletes are aware that the format of contemporary sports pages emphasizes the personal dimension as well as the unusual, the spectacular, and, more often than not, the negative or controversial aspects of their livelihood. However, these individuals, like politicians and others who bask in media attention, prefer "positive" reporting; not surprisingly, a kind of adversary relationship has emerged between sports writers and many professional athletes. In this relationship, athletes see many writers as enemies waiting—and listening—for something exciting to report. A pitcher who was a Cy Young Award winner discussed this problem:

> Well, sometimes you, . . . once your guard gets down— you're backed, you know—what's terrible is you can't relax around a bunch of asshole writers until it gets to a point where you know who's who and you know what you can say to people that, if things are confidential, will never get in the paper; then there's other guys, you've got to construct every sentence to protect yourself, to cover yourself, or the son-of-a-bitch will just turn it around . . . and, after enough years, you know what you have to do, what you have got to say.

Another major-league player, one who works as a sports journalist in the off season, provided some insight into the problems players face when attempting to communicate to writers their perspective on the game and on related activities:

> There is always a situation where you talk to a guy for a half-hour, and you feel you have communicated the spirit

of what you wanted to say, and you pick up the paper the
next day and one little thing that you said becomes the
focus of the article. We are at a time where people, . . .
where there are a lot of talkers around but there aren't
very many good listeners. To me the primary quality that
a writer has to have is to be a good listener. And there
just aren't many of them. These people, they aren't even
looking at you when you are talking to them. They are
looking around to see if there is another story going on. It
is a distrustful atmosphere, and I am not sure that it has
all been the responsibility of the writers.

In his book, the former New York Yankee relief pitcher Sparky Lyle discussed the suspicious activity of reporters:

The reporters stand around waiting and listening. The
other day I saw Henry Hecht taking a piss and writing at
the same time. You don't know what it is. It could have
been nothing, but why was he doing it back by the pissers?
Henry stands around and listens to what the players say
to each other and writes it down. I've seen him running
around to other writers, asking, "What did he say? What
did he say?" because he doesn't get it himself. [Lyle and
Golenbock, 1979:214]

One sportswriter, sensitive to the media demands on the ballplayers,
observed that the effort to get the "great quote" was part of the problem:

Now I think that we are in a syndrome where we see
something happen and we want to quote about it, and some
of these guys are not good talkers. And you beg them for
a quote, and then you could sit there and say, well this is
what happened, damn it. You don't need the guy to tell it
for you. And we are all listening for that great quote, and
I see too often where a guy is stringing together six, seven,
eight, nine quotes and it is not effective writing. Because
we are taking a guy who hits for a living and asking him
to put it into words, but that is our job.

Moreover, athletes have come to be evaluated by sportswriters partly on
their value as news sources—as "good quoters." Particularly troubling from
the perspective of current media formats are athletes who either cannot
or will not "talk" to the press. One writer assessed a trade involving
basketball players in the following terms:

The dressing room, where most sports journalists spend
most of their life, is a sort of living cliché. It is inhabited
by players who either (1) tell you what the coach wants
to hear, or (2) tell you what you want to hear. . . . Paul

> Westphal is unique. Almost invariably, he provides a dif-
> ferent, often deeper viewpoint. . . . Paul Westphal was,
> in short, a dressing-room delight.
>
> And the Seattle player for whom Westphal was traded?
> Well, Dennis Johnson is called moody. The quality of John-
> son's quotes is not so much suspect, as unknown. . . . He
> wasn't talking to his hometown scribes because of some
> alleged slight.
>
> For press relations, the edge goes Westphal. [Bob Hurt,
> *Arizona Republic*, June 4, 1980]

Providing good quotes in particular, and getting many off-the-cuff statements published, creates a potentially difficult situation not only for the
moment but for a considerable time thereafter; for once they are in print
or on film, statements and acts become "timeless" because they can be
reproduced. A rookie pitcher, unfamiliar with the "rule" that any statement
made around a reporter can be published, made some impromptu remarks
in the off season about the fielding problems of several of his teammates.
Months later his statements continued to appear. He regretted this:

> I said some things early, before the season even started,
> you know, and they can take that quote and they can use
> it as much as they want to. You don't feel that way any-
> more, but they keep using it, they'll bring it up. . . . Yeah,
> there was one time, even my own family said I shouldn't
> have said that. Heck, that hurts, you know. Maybe not,
> but at the time I really felt that was how things were, and
> you go through a period and you're not happy and you say
> things; then two weeks later you feel different about them,
> and you regret saying them. And then people ask you,
> "Why did you say that?" you know. I really wish it didn't
> get written, but just said it.

MEDIA-INDUCED EXPECTATIONS OF THE SELF

Gaining public attention via the mass media has numerous consequences,
including, perhaps, some major social effects we have not fully grasped.
However, a clear consequence of media attention is that one gets recognition by an audience, including individual members who want to develop
and maintain communication with *anyone in public life, including mass
murderers*. Perhaps the most recent extreme case is that of David R. Berkowitz, known as "Son of Sam," the man serving a 314-year prison sentence
for killing six people. Behind the walls of the Attica Correctional Facility
he corresponds with pen pals, including several who apparently seek to
marry him, and newspaper and television reporters, critics, and would-be
biographers. As Berkowitz has reportedly stated, "Son of Sam is big news,

big money, big fame should someone get his inside story" (*Arizona Republic*, September 28, 1980).

The quest for fame—always dependent on media attention—may encourage some individuals to commit certain acts—as though they were playing out a scenario—in order to achieve "publicity"—to see their picture on television and their name in print. From this perspective, the fact that the public not only knows that criteria of media noteworthiness exist but has some knowledge of how they are applied becomes a central component of any effort to understand the numerous false confessions that follow spectacular crimes. But the desire to obtain media attention, to gain a kind of self-validation by reading and seeing oneself as thousands of other audience members would, also contributes to the dramatization of acts and statements for media purposes. A major-league pitcher, widely acclaimed for being a "flake" and "good copy," explained his original goal and his subsequent difficulties with the mass media:

> Well, when I first came up, you know, it was new for me. I wanted my name in the paper because my name had never been in the paper; I was always reading someone else's, and it made me jealous, because I wanted to be in that spot. And then, when I got there, you know—like I say, it was all new—so when I talked to them, the first thing out of my mouth, it was the first time they had heard something coming from me, and it was the first time I had ever heard it myself, you know, like, I was talking. And then, after a while, they started asking me the same questions, and you get sick and tired of listening to the same stuff that you're saying—you know, like you can only think of a few things to say, you can't think of a million things. Everybody wants something different, but you can't give them something different. You start making it up, and that's when you get in trouble.

Another player said essentially the same thing:

> There is no question that there is an impact. We have an example in this club with ——. He became a certain thing for writers. He . . . became the vehicle of the writers . . . it was almost like he was out of control. Not that he didn't cater to the writers at a certain time, but the writers—I am sure it had a lot to do with his popularity in San Francisco—it got to a point where he couldn't say anything without it being blown out of context. Like he said—he might say in passing—"Well, I think I am going to beat the Dodgers," and then all of a sudden he picks up the paper the next day and [there's a headline]: "Can —— Beat the Dodgers?" That type of thing.

The player just referred to did temporarily stop "talking to the press," a decision that was viewed ironically by one sportswriter:

> That is the galling thing about ——. We call him the Fran-
> kenstein of the press. Because he has turned against his
> creators. I mean, he was nothing. He had one good year
> and he was billed as talented. He got a lot of copy in San
> Francisco, and the Giants didn't have much, and they were
> forced to sign him. . . . The thing is, he doesn't even
> realize that the press did so much for him. Since he started,
> it makes me wonder what his intelligence is, to do some-
> thing like that.

The more a person is presented in the various media, the more several things happen. First, other media become interested, partly because the person has, in a sense, become legitimated by having appeared on one. This form of "media incest," whereby the same news sources, topics, and persons are passed around among the various media, has been repeatedly documented in other studies (see, e.g., Altheide and Snow, 1979).

The experience of the author of the book about running illustrates how TV will draw on other media, e.g., print, for its content:

> A week after the New York Marathon they gave me one
> day to rest up; then they sent me to Boston. Then I went out
> and did about ten cities in a big hurry, and that was going
> to be it for a while. Then in January I went out and did
> another five cities, and then you could see, along about
> January, a funny thing happening. I had originally been
> the supplicant—the stations had to be told: "You know,
> there are a lot of people out there who are running, and
> this man has some interesting things to say about running,"
> and they'd say, "Yeah, yeah; well, okay, we'll take him."
> But there wasn't a great keenness. Then you could see,
> early in the year, that there was a shift; I suddenly started
> getting *asked* to be on a show. Like I got asked to be on
> the *Dinah Shore Show* and the *Mike Douglas Show,* and
> things like that. And then the funny thing—and I just let
> this happen, because it was so amusing—I got so busy
> that I would get calls from stations, and I would say, "I
> just can't do it, I haven't got time to do it." A big Boston
> station called me, and I said, "I can't do it." They said,
> "We'd pay your expenses." I said, "I can't do it, I don't
> have the time." They said, "We could pay a couple hundred
> dollars"—which is unheard-of for television stations to pay
> . . . and I knew, when that started happening—I mean it
> happened two or three times, I'm not getting rich from
> being on television—but I knew, when that started hap-

pening, that there was something hot about the subject, because you could see it was like a tide suddenly turning.

One consequence of extensive media coverage is that an individual may become known as a "media personality," an "expert" on some topic, and will subsequently be called on by other media. How one is defined by media people thus has a bearing on how receptive other media may become, and this in turn may affect the way the individual comes to conceive of him or herself. The author of the book on running described how he was "packaged" by his publisher:

> One of the reasons —— gave me for not being able to offer me a good contract [was that the media people] said, "You are not known as a sportswriter, and we are going to have to do a tremendous amount of promotion of you to make you seem authentic. An authentic sort of guy, not a novice." Now that didn't bother —— at all, and we never did anything like that. I never claimed to be any better as a runner than I am.

Even though this author never claimed to be anything more than a talented writer who could make running read like a fun activity, he was cast into other roles by audience members who had read his book.

> [About his transformation by the media:] This morning it happened at this race. People come up to you and they look at you with great reverence, and they say, "I just wanted to shake your hand and tell you how much your book has meant to me." And they say, "I used to weigh 225 pounds, and now I weigh 150 pounds. Your book has changed my life." Now, unless you're completely insensitive, you have to treat something like that with seriousness. You have to thank the guy. I mean, I'm interested in that having happened, but I still somehow feel as if there's a discontinuity.

People who have appeared in the media are thus peceived as "public" persons by audience members who recognize them. But they also develop a sense that they *are* public persons and may even experience a felt recognition, if not an actual desire, to act the way "real" media personalities do. The author of the book about running explained some of his feelings about this:

> I think [that] when something like this happens to you, [if] you know very clearly what you like and what you don't like, you're less susceptible to being changed by something like this. For example, the last thing in the world I want to do is go out and sit around in night spots. It's a burden for me to have to stay up past ten o'clock at night.

So people have said to me things like, "There's this trendy literary restaurant/bar in New York called Elaine's, where Jimmy Breslin and all those types hang out." People are always saying to me, "I suppose you spend a lot of time at Elaine's," and I say "I've never been there." The only thing I've ever done is to run past Elaine's when I'm on my way to Central Park. The funny thing is that one time an interviewer asked me, "Has your life changed any since you had this successful book?" and I thought and thought, and I said, "In one way it did." I've always washed my own car, but one day I drove into the place where I get my gas—and I go there because it's the cheapest gas in town—and they had just put in this new car-washing thing, and they had this introductory offer. For a buck you could have your car washed. I said, "Fuck it, I'm a best-selling author. I'm going to have my car washed!"

Getting a lot of attention and being treated like a celebrity can have an impact on one's expectations about standard operating procedures in day-to-day life. As the author explained:

I feel the only thing that I guess I notice is that every once in a while—if, for example, my wife and I are having an argument about something—I find myself thinking, "Jesus Christ, I go to Phoenix, and people treat me nice. How come at home I have to put up with all this grief?"

MEDIA EFFECTS

In addition to the expectations about fame and notoriety that media attention produces, individuals who are frequently presented in the major media may experience feelings of greatness and/or self-doubt as a result of what the media report about them.

The impact of negative or critical reporting for one's conception of self is evident in professional athletes, many of whom do not have strong ego anchorages beyond their athletic prowess. The sensitivity of some athletes to negative press reports seems paradoxical, since their status as well-paid major-league baseball players would apparently indicate that their expertise, skill, and achievement make them independent of what anyone might say or write about them. However, the very nature of professional athletics is that one's current position is potentially tenuous; it depends on maintaining both the skill one is presumed to have (which is measured by one's batting average or earned-run average, etc.) and the belief in this ability on the part of the team's officials and owners. Thus, critical comments can jar a player. A major-league pitcher and former Cy Young Award winner discussed one critical newpaper article:

> Yeah, it is just like the article today, ——'s column. [He
> said I] was never really any good, never had big-league
> stuff, you know, I guess I have been tripping it for six
> years, and things like that. But you know, you read that
> thing, and those things can really piss you off and hurt
> you and you can get down. Or it can piss you off, and you
> say, "I'll show the son-of-a-bitch" Or you can just stop.
> You know, I read it, and it pissed me off. I got six years
> in, and I'm so shitty?

Another pitcher described his feelings about negative articles in the press
in the following words:

> It makes you really mad. That person [writer], . . . it kind
> of makes you mad at that person for a while. You stand
> in front of the mirror, and you look at yourself, and you
> say, "Hey, you know . . . that guy sure was hard about it.

Another example of the impact that negative press messages have was
reported by a former major-league catcher. This player's career was ad-
versely affected by a newpaper story that was based on the opinions of
the player's former boss:

> I said, "First of all, you didn't have the facts. You didn't
> get my side of the story. . . . The man lied to you about
> a lot of things." I told him that, and he wrote another
> article and gave my side of it. It was good. The first story
> made it sound like I wanted to leave Chicago. . . . Shit, I
> love Chicago; it is my favorite city. And I made it known,
> too, that I didn't want to leave. . . . And then he [the
> general manager] turned around to the paper and said that
> I wanted to leave. That I didn't want to stay there. It made
> me look like a real complete ass.

Professional athletes, while closely attuned to what they perceive as the
fans' interest in and reactions to mass-media accounts, are also aware of
their audience within the organization: their teammates, the manager, and
the "front office." They know that many players have been given "pink
slips" partly because they have the image of being troublemakers and
generally uncooperative, and one way to get this "tag" is to say negative
things to the press about the organization. A veteran pitcher explained:

> Just tell it like it is, but just don't go ripping people or
> saying anything bad, because 90 percent of the time it is
> going to be in the paper the next day. Then you've got the
> manager wanting you in the office, and it's "Why did you
> say this?" and the front office saying "Why did you say
> this?" You don't need that kind of hassle when you're
> trying to play baseball. . . . [If] you watch what you say

> in the clubhouse, you don't have to worry about anything
> else but playing baseball. That's the way it should be.

Another major-leaguer concurred:

> I have said things in a kidding way, but the reporter takes
> me as serious, in a serious way, and then it gets in the
> paper and it makes it look like I am getting all over my
> teammates, which I really wasn't. I was just saying it in
> a laughing way. But our teammates take it serious, and
> they start questioning you about it, and then you don't
> know what to say to them. Plus, and then he will come
> up to you and say, "Well, it was in the paper. This is what
> you said." And you tell the guy, and you say, "Well, I
> didn't say that," and they don't believe you.

The pervasive, though complex, relationship between a situationally based conception of self and media attention and focus may be negative in some cases, but this is because media attention is invariably relevant to the experience of public life. It cannot be ignored by the people involved because others *will* pay attention to it. This is especially apparent in big-time politics, where public accusations of impropriety, incompetence, or illegal behavior are enough to make the voters withdraw their support—which is usually mediated through television and newspapers. This has been shown by Senator Thomas Eagleton's nomination as Democratic vice-presidential candidate in 1972 and his subsequent withdrawal when his history of hospitalization for "mental illness" was revealed. In announcing Eagleton's withdrawal, the presidential candidate, George McGovern, stated:

> We didn't know the impact on the country . . . ; as the
> days went on, it became clear to me that Senator Eagle-
> ton's past medical history—not the state of his health to-
> day, which is excellent, which his doctors say is excellent—
> but his past medical history has literally dominated the
> news. . . . I was of the opinion that this issue would con-
> tinue to plague the campaign. [Quoted by Altheide,
> 1976:141]

That negative statements about an individual in public life can virtually assure his official demise was also apparent in the case of Bert Lance, former director of the Office of Manangement and Budget. Despite numerous charges, heard by a Senate committee over the course of three separate hearings and reported by all the major networks, who also were critical of Lance, plus a two-year investigation by the Justice Department, culminating in testimony and a bill of particulars brought before a grand jury, Lance was acquitted on all counts. The acquittal, of course, was irrelevant, since he had resigned a year earlier, under considerable pressure (see Altheide and Snow, 1979:137–98). More recently, in 1978, Robert

Griffin, the deputy administrator of the General Services Administration, was sacked for alleged impropriety and incompetence. Here, too, the grounds for the charges were not substantiated, only publicized. As Byrne (1980:36) noted:

> When you chip your way through the media imagery, you come to the stark fact that no one to this day has shown that Griffin did that job inadequately or unethically, and the Justice Department has long since concluded that he was not personally involved in any way in the corruption at GSA.

Cultivating the Media Self

The pervasive role that mass-media images play in the careers of individuals in the public sphere has led to great attention to and emphasis on the presentation of self for media purposes. The way that politicians now engage in cosmetic appeals and highly structured activities geared to media logic and interests has been widely documented (see Altheide and Snow, 1979, among others). Not only do politicians employ press agents and media consultants to engineer their media impressions, but a number of professional athletes now employ agents to talk to the press for them or, more commonly, to avoid negative media attention. Not surprisingly, persons who are oriented to mass-media imagery and are skilled in employing it—for example, by making controversial statements—attract media attention and, in so doing, unwittingly set a standard that is then adopted by media workers and by individuals who desire media attention. In politics, John Kennedy comes to mind; President Carter was even better. In religion, Aimee Semple McPherson was good; Billy Graham is better. In sports, Babe Ruth was good; Reggie Jackson is better. Partly because Reggie Jackson plays in Los Angeles, partly because he is a home-run hitter, partly because he is one of the highest-paid athletes in history, and *mainly* because of his flair for media logic, he is, next to Muhammad Ali, the all-time media professional in sports. One former teammate of Jackson's described him this way:

> Let's face it, some writers, there are writers . . . that have their favorite ballplayers, and there are some ballplayers that they are a lot less hot on. You take a guy like Reggie Jackson. Well, he has a nice personality, but that is irrelevant to the writer; it's the fact that Reggie Jackson has a way with words that makes him look good. He can go 0 for 4 and get headlines. I have seen that happen. Or the pitcher will get a shutout, but Jackson will get two hits and he will get the play. He is the type of player who will sit there and, if you ask him one question, he will answer

five. . . . And he knows that he talks, and he knows that
he will get attention by his talking.

Indeed, Jackson, like others who are routinely presented in the mass media, often describes himself in the third person, just as a reporter or broad-
caster or *any other audience member* would. The tendency to see oneself
as, so to speak, larger than life, larger than one's own physical space, is
perhaps inevitable when an individual constantly sees his own public performances on television, reads about them in newspapers, and, in the
extreme case, watches himself being interviewed for television! Such is
the feeling of being an extraordinary, great, and very public person.

Conclusion

The mass media, as distinctively public phenomena, have implications for,
and can directly affect, individuals by adding a dimension of anticipation,
focus, and reflection to their conception of self. In the course of their
ordinary day-to-day affairs most people seldom reflect on their notion of
self, since such understandings are grounded in routines that would have
to be breached or significantly altered before anyone would pay close
attention to these taken-for-granted features of social life. But when we
are presented with someone's interpretation and presentation of who we
are, what we stand for—in short, with an assertion of some character-
ological and status-related statement of our self—then self can become
problematic, *and the raising of self to consciousness is one consequence of
media presentations.*

While most aspects of self remain private and are seldom reflected on,
the growth of the mass media has added a public arena for recognition of,
and socialization for, significant performances, styles, and reactions. Media
life is significant for the experience of public life because the role the
media play in the process, including the use of formats and visual emphasis,
is almost never acknowledged by media subjects or by media workers.
Therefore, the viewing, hearing, and reading audiences cannot meaningfully discount or hold in abeyance the "real-life" images and scenarios
they behold. The issue is not whether people "believe" everything they
see, hear, or read but, rather, how familiar they become with the individuals
and scenarios presented and what they take for granted about the significance and consequence of the fact that these particular individuals and
scenarios have been selected and presented by the mass media.

The upshot is that persons routinely portrayed in the major media are
performing roles, albeit roles significantly altered to favor media logic, as
politicians' campaign tactics are altered, for example (see Altheide and
Snow, 1979). But the fact that these are roles, especially when they pervade
one's daily experience—as when one views hour after hour of television—

can easily become lost in favor of the less skeptical attitude that "seeing is believing." Thus, the audience easily personalizes and reifies the roles that are presented to it and finally substitutes them for the situational and more variant selves of the role-performers. The end result is that media performance, audience experience, and celebration of media attention come to define what is important, real, and a public experience. As Bensman and Lilienfeld (1979:34) observe:

> The boundaries between public and private disappear in the mass media. One of the characteristics of radio and television is the possibility of achieving the illusion of mass participation in the noise they provide, thus achieving some of both the privacy and the public atmosphere of a mass audience when the street scene or mob enters one's living room.

The expectations one brings to his or her first media performance as an actor on the other side of the camera, the microphone, or the reporter's notebook are created by the experiences and expectations one has had as an audience member. But during the actual media experience, the routines of media work become more apparent to the novice "public figure," including the often adversarial relationship between him or herself and the media personnel. *That those who would make you famous cannot also be counted on to make you desirably famous—rather than notoriously infamous—is one of the sudden aftershocks that follow the initial blast of media attention.*

With some experience as a media performer, one realizes that prior expectations gained from being a member of the audience are hardly applicable at a cognitive level to the experience of being in the media. However, one also realizes that being in the media means being before the public, and to be presented in an unfavorable way will have implications—indeed, perhaps disastrous consequences—for both generalized and significant others. Moreover, even as a person matures through experiences as a media performer, his or her conception of self remains tied to the public's conception; no one likes to be disliked or ridiculed by others. For this reason the media presentation of self has implications for conceptions of self.

The emergent relationship between media messages and the idea of the public interest has likewise led to a personalization of roles, with the result that persons in the media began to identify themselves with the public interest. Thus President Nixon, like his predecessors and immediate successors (at least, up to this point) apparently saw himself as PRESIDENT Nixon rather than as President NIXON. From this perspective, his actions were performed on behalf of the American people; they were not the product of the selfish whims and delusions of an ambitious and frightened individual. I suggest that the same misapprehension of their role has taken possession of certain network anchormen and reporters who speak on behalf of the "public" when they are obviously stating their own opinions or imposing a news perspective. Specifically, following a question he had asked of two reporters as to the "winner" in the day's Bert Lance hearings, Cronkite apologized, saying:

> This isn't an athletic contest. . . . We, *the public*, might be excused for losing track of the real meaning and purpose of this inquiry when the committee itself seems to have so much trouble with that matter. [Quoted in Altheide and Snow, 1979:177; emphasis added]

Such contentions and presentations of self are not accidental; they are a logical extension of the ongoing relationship between the self, the public, and the mass media.

Note

1. Unless otherwise indicated, all quotations and examples are from personal field notes. In order to maintain confidentiality, the speakers are not identified.

References

Altheide, David L. 1976. *Creating Reality: How TV News Distorts Events.* Beverly Hills, Calif.: Sage.

Altheide, David L., and Robert P. Snow. 1979. *Media Logic.* Beverly Hills, Calif.: Sage.

Bensman, Joseph, and Robert Lilienfeld. 1979. *Between Public and Private: Lost Boundaries of the Self.* New York: Free Press.

Byrne, Jeb. 1980. "The Persecution and Assassination of Robert Griffin as Performed by Members of the Washington Press Corps." *Washington Monthly* September:33–40.

Douglas, Jack. n.d. "Framing Reality." Unpublished manuscript.

Ewen, Stuart. 1976. *Captains of Consciousness: Advertising and the Social Roots of the Consumer Culture.* New York: McGraw-Hill.

Fathi, A. 1978. "Public Communication in Medieval Islam." Paper presented at the Annual Meeting of the Pacific Sociological Association.

Lyle, Sparky, and Peter Golenbock. 1979. *The Bronx Zoo.* New York: Dell.

Scott, Marvin B., and Stanford M. Lyman. 1968. "Accounts." *American Sociological Review* 33(2):46–62.

The Homosexual Self and the Organization of Experience: The Case of Kate White

Sheldon L. Messinger and

Carol A. B. Warren

This essay deals with the adoption of a "homosexual self" as a strategy for organizing experience and shaping courses of action. It is based on a case study of a married female mental patient, Kate White, who came to believe that she was a "homosexual" and that her husband, too, was a "homosexual." These beliefs, among others, precipitated her confinement in a mental hospital at the behest of her husband, Nelson White.

The Kate White case was drawn from a Bay Area longitudinal interview study of seventeen schizophrenic women (see Sampson, Messinger, and Towne, 1964). Kate White was interviewed approximately twenty-five times between November, 1957, and July, 1958, both during and after her stay in the mental hospital. The interviews were unstructured, in-depth, and open-ended; they were carried out by a male interviewer as part of his duties in the Bay Area study.[1]

The seventeen case studies from the Bay Area files have been used for a number of purposes, from an analysis of the interrelationships between schizophrenia, the marital bond, and the maternal tie (Sampson et al., 1964) to a study of the social situation of the housewife in the late 1950s to early 1960s (Warren and Messinger, 1980). We want to emphasize that our concern here is neither with homosexuality nor with schizophrenia; we have no contributions to make to the study of the etiology of, or societal reactions to, homosexuality or madness. Rather, we seek to investigate, within the general framework of an existential sociology of knowledge, the interaction of self, behavior, and interpretation in everyday life.

Kate White told the interviewer that she sought psychiatric help principally out of fears that her husband was a "homosexual," that she was becoming a "homosexual," and that these facts might have deleterious effects on her children, who might also become "homosexual." It is useful to examine the role of such fearful beliefs in shaping the course of Mrs.

White's conduct, especially the portion of her conduct that came to be identified as "strange," "deviant," and "psychotic."

It must be appreciated that the "homosexual" framework used by Mrs. White is one drawn from everyday life. It is a common-sense typology, variable in its reference to behavior, admitting of the most diverse behavioral events, and consistent only insofar as it usually expresses a moral attitude, disapprobation, toward the experiences or behavior that it organizes. Scientific typologies of homosexuality, on the other hand, tend toward constancy of behavioral reference and absence of moral judgment. Scientific investigations of the "homosexual self" or identity have generally taken two forms: psychiatric and sociological.

Both psychologists and sociologists assume or assert that, objectively, homosexuality refers to wanting or having sexual relations with members of the same sex and that, subjectively, homosexuality refers to a belief that one is the sort of person who has those wants and experiences. When they undertake to explain homosexuality, scientists theorize about the sources of such wants, experiences, and beliefs. They too seldom explore carefully whether someone labeled a "homosexual" by others or by the self wants sexual contact with the same-sex others, has it, or believes that it is wanted. Neither do they explore sufficiently how the label "homosexual" functions for the person using it. Psychiatry frames the homosexual self as a deep-rooted condition that may or may not be reflected in the consciousness or behavior of the affected person. Indeed, Kate White's mental-hospital diagnostic summary labeled her psychiatrically as someone with "intense attachment to her father as a cause of deep-rooted homosexual feelings." Sociological analysis of homosexuality, at least in its contemporary form, suspends moral judgment and the theory of the unconscious but not the empirical linkage of self with behavior or affect.

Symbolic interactionists who have studied "homosexuals" and "homosexuality" have shared those assumptions (see, for example, Humphreys, 1972; Ponse, 1978; Warren, 1974); for them, the homosexual self is one fatefully linked with homosexual longings and emotions (Warren and Ponse, 1977). In a more cognitive tradition, however, Mills (1959), Lyman and Scott (1970), and Lofland (1976) analyze the frameworks people use to interpret their actions and their selves; these frameworks are derived from the intersection of experience and learned social categories. Cognitive frameworks make sense of the world and provide a basis for interaction and for projections of future action. The "homosexual self" as an interpretive framework may be seen as a cognitive strategy for organizing experience.

Sociologists' and psychiatrists' interpretations of homosexuality are both behaviorally consistent and morally neutral. But Kate White's use of the same interpretive framework was neither, despite the fact that it drew on her psychiatric learning that "everyone" is a "latent homosexual" and on her sociological observation that she and her husband had homosexual friends.

Kate White believed and feared that her husband was homosexual and that she was at risk of becoming such. There is no evidence that she believed her husband had same-sex sexual relations or even that he wanted them (although she learned to attribute such wants to him, in their absence, as "latent"). Nor is there evidence that she herself had engaged in, or wanted to engage in, same-sex sexual relations. There is considerable evidence, on the other hand, that she found relations with men troublesome, particularly relations with her husband. Labeling her husband a homosexual and herself one in the making served to explain this experience for her and freed her, morally, to take certain actions based on this explanation. The label also led to difficulty, particularly when she made it public; the culmination of these difficulties was mental hospitalization.

Mrs. White's belief that her husband, Nelson White, was a "homosexual" developed in the context of an extramarital affair. This affair, of at most a few days' duration, transpired approximately three years before Mrs. White sought psychiatric assistance. Her lover, Alan Mann, was an acquaintance of long standing, a married man whose pursuit of Mrs. White prior to her marriage had been interrupted by Mrs. White's father. Alan Mann specifically suggested to Mrs. White that Nelson White was a "homosexual." He also suggested that Mrs. White herself ran the risk of becoming a "homosexual" if she stayed married to Mr. White.

Now, we do not know what Alan Mann intended by his remark that Kate White was becoming a homosexual; that is, we do not know what conduct constituted "homosexuality" for him. Nor is it important for us to know this. For Kate White, we know that homosexuality was a negative category and that it was related somehow to negative familial experiences:

> I had this feeling my husband was a homosexual—at least something was wrong. For a time I wondered if something was wrong with me. I never have had a normal family life myself.

From Kate White's characterization of her "homosexual" husband it may be inferred that for her a "homosexual" was someone who is vacillating and cannot take a stand, someone who is weak, indecisive, and unorganzied in pursuing objectives. A "homosexual" cannot enjoy life; he may remain attached to a hostile and dominating mother, unable to marry or have children. "Homosexuals" lead a half-life; they are objects of derision and discrimination. These negative images and others constituted the category for Kate White. There are two reasons why we cannot be more specific. First, and least important, Kate White was not specifically asked to fill in the content of the category "homosexual." Second, the category had to be loose and vague to perform the functions it did in fact perform for her.

In defining Nelson White as a "homosexual," Alan Mann provided a potential explanation and justification for Kate White's engagement in their extramarital affair. He provided her with a theory of conduct that rationalized her activity for her, permitting her to adjust her conception of herself as a responsible person to the fact of the extramarital liaison. This is not to say that he offered the theory cynically, although that may have been the case. The important thing is that Kate White perceived him as sincere and that he provided her with a theory of conduct that freed her to act in the situation at hand. Such a theory, of course, must not do obvious violence to the facts to be accounted for, but the theory that Nelson White was "homosexual" left much room for interpretation.

The critical link in the theory was that it provided a reasonable explanation and justification for Kate White's current actions. She "needed" the affair because she was frustrated in her marital relationship. She was frustrated in the marital relationship because her husband was a "homosexual."

> I had this feeling my husband was homosexual. . . . I felt something was wrong with him. I seem to have to keep myself from growing. I had to do this to stay on his level. I did not have much sexual experience until Alan. I know one gets adjusted to it. It isn't everything in life. I felt that he wouldn't grow. Something was wrong. I guess you could sum it all up by saying there was some kind of lack of communication between us.

The theory of conduct thus organized and explained certain troubling affects generated by the marital relationship. Kate White felt unable to "get through" to her husband, she felt "unfulfilled" and continually pressed into an "active"—and, to her, "masculine"—role. It organized these affects, furthermore, in relation to Nelson White's conduct, i.e., *he* became responsible for her feelings. Thus, Mr. White did not focus his energies, he hesitated in making an occupational commitment, he made friends—especially male friends—easily and attended to them, while neglecting Mrs. White.

When the typology was used by Kate White to refer to Mr. White's conduct, she organized such diverse qualities as indecisiveness, inability to commit himself, friendliness toward males to the exclusion of herself, and a supposed unreadiness to communicate. All of these features or supposed features of Mr. White's have a common reference, namely, Kate White's experience of alienation in her marital relationship—her sense of incompleteness, of inability to "get through," to feel "close." The facts she organized with the typology had only the vaguest reference to "homosexual" conduct in the sense of sustained intimacies with members of the same sex. This plain fact was accommodated by the notion of "latent" homosexuality she had learned in therapy.

It should also be noted that, when the typology had reference to her own conduct (i.e., to her fear was that she was becoming a homosexual), it did not refer to any conduct that indicated a desire on her part to enter into or maintain a sustained intimate relation with a woman. Rather, the core reference was to a sense of alienation from male figures, particularly her husband in the then-current situation.

Mrs. White, disturbed by her feelings of alienation in her marriage, was afforded an explanation of these feelings that placed the onus of responsibility on another. Troubled by her apparently powerful desires to initiate intimate contact with males other than her husband, she was provided with a reasonable explanation of these desires and a justification for satisfying them. This last was extremely important. The point was that Mrs. White could enter an extramarital relation for her health, as it were. This was perhaps the crucial significance of the notion that she might become homosexual through constant association with her husband.

An additional significance of the "homosexual" frame of reference was that it provided Mrs. White with a rationale for her inability to separate from or divorce her husband. She developed the idea that she was engaging in a heroic act by staying married, a responsible act. To leave would be to abandon Nelson White to the half-world of homosexuality; she stayed to prevent this.

Why did Kate White accept the "homosexual" framework? The primary reason has already been suggested: it provided her with a theory of conduct that permitted action in a painful situation, action that temporarily reduced the pain. But the theory also permitted Kate White to integrate many past experiences she had had, and it related these experiences to moral judgments she had made about them. During her college years, and perhaps earlier, Kate White felt that she was "insufficiently attracted" to men. She had attributed this to the "immaturity" of the men she had met, but it is apparent that this theory left a residual question in her mind about her own emotional makeup. That she might, especially in contact with inadequate males, feel alienated from men she accounted for by the "homosexual" framework. She had been upset over the prospect of marriage, over becoming engaged, and over getting married.

Kate White had an abiding ambivalence about intimate relations with males. Her experience of alienation waxed and waned with pressures to enter into and sustain intimate relations with men. In college there was pressure to date. She had coped with this by limiting dating when she could (this, for example, was one function of her "involvement" with a boy who went off to join the RAF), and, when she couldn't, she rationalized her discomfort by defining males as "immature." Later she felt pressure to marry. This pressure came in part from Nelson White, who pressed the issue, and in part, no doubt, from general cultural definitions of the appropriateness of certain actions at certain ages.

Once Kate White was married and living with her husband, the pressures for intimacy increased and, with them, her sense of discomfort and alienation. She maintained what distance she could from Mr. White by working, among other things. Both of the Whites in fact spent a considerable amount of their time in extra-family pursuits. Mr. White went to school while Mrs. White worked. Later he took on two jobs and went to school while Mrs. White concerned herself with a newborn infant. She spent a summer away from her husband while he was going to school in another city. It was during this summer that the brief sexual liaison with Alan Mann, mentioned above, took place. Alan Mann provided both an attractive heterosexual experience and a reminder of its rarity. Thus their illicit liaison both undermined and underlined her "homosexuality."

> It was all such a strange business with Alan, he coming so near the time of my father's death; I was always attracted to him, not as much when he comes as before, but I still was attracted. Also I had never been very much attracted to men, so few men had been attractive to me.

Given the "homosexual" framework, Kate White had no difficulty in adducing further evidence to support it. The framework continued to serve her pressing needs, including one that was probably unintended by Alan Mann, who had offered the theory. This was her need to maintain her marital relationship—indeed, to maintain fidelity to it. Throughout the interviews with Kate White, she expressed extreme fear and denial of the possibility of divorce.

In time this "homosexual" theory of conduct had difficult consequences for Kate White. It gave specific focus to an identity, namely, that of "homosexual." Any increase in her experience of alienation from her husband came to be taken by Kate White as evidence that she was becoming a "homosexual." This was in line with the second postulate of the theory, that continued association with Nelson White would lead her into "homosexuality." As this "homosexual self" was formed, Kate White faced this dilemma: to give up her marriage was to run the risk of becoming a homosexual; to remain in the marriage was to run the risk of becoming a homosexual.

There is no evidence that, prior to her affair with Alan Mann, Kate White entertained the notion that her husband was, or that she might become, a "homosexual." Prior to the suggestion, Kate White used alternative frameworks to handle the same affective experiences. After the suggestion, Mrs. White both reassessed these disturbing experiences of alienation and interpreted ongoing events within the new framework. The framework, thus, had both retrospective and current or prospective significance for her.

Because of the way the label "homosexual" is used in everyday life, the belief that one is a "homosexual" or that another person is indicates disapproval of one's own or another's conduct. The conduct referred to is extremely variable; perhaps "vague" would be a more accurate term. The "vagueness" of the category seems to be intrinsic to its function, which is *not* primarily to order events for the sake of ordering them (i.e., for the sake of understanding them); its function, rather, is to order events *for the sake of taking action in terms of them.*

In order to understand the belief—or the theory of conduct, as we have called it—one must look to *its* sources, functions, and consequences. These are only indirectly related to the facts of conduct that are organized by the theory. And in order to understand the *conduct* at issue, clearly one must first determine just what conduct *is* at issue. The sources of the belief that certain experiences indicate "homosexuality" must be distinguished from the sources of the experience itself. The experiences at issue may be differently defined: in Kate White's case there is evidence that, prior to a specific learning situation, she defined these experiences in one way and that afterward she defined them differently: as evidence of "homosexuality."

Kate White's defining her feelings of alienation from men and from her husband as "homosexual" is *not* explained by tracing the sources of these feelings; it is independent of these sources. This is not to say that she could not have defined her feelings differently. She in fact proffered as an alternative to his "homosexuality" the idea that her husband was "less sexual" than she; or she may have achieved the view that she was "frigid" or that her husband was "frigid." Moreover, the issue is not whether the feelings are labeled correctly in the scientific sense. Rather, the issue is whether the label permitted the necessary action, saved valuable liaisons, and so on. Some explanation of the facts was called for, to be sure, but not necessarily the one she achieved. What *can* be said is that *whatever* explanation or theory is achieved will have to perform certain functions to be acceptable, and, once it is accepted, it will have certain limiting consequences for further conduct.

Thus, for Kate White the theory had to account not only for her feelings of alienation from men in general and from her husband but for her feelings of attraction to Alan Mann. It also had to explain the lack of communication in her marriage and her husband's passivity and neglect of her; it had to justify her current actions of engaging in extramarital sex and in not seeking a divorce; and, ideally, it should have organized into a single pattern a multiplicity of affectively toned experiences, primarily those dealing with the marriage and with sexual relationships.

Another interpretive framework that could, in principle, have organized all these experiences is the equally loose and vague one of craziness or "mental illness," and, indeed, Kate White was labeled as crazy by her neighbors and relatives before she was hospitalized—particularly when she began to assert her and her husband's "homosexuality"—and she was officially labeled a schizophrenic in the course of that hospitalization. Given the adequacy of the label to organize her experience, together with the presumptive power of audience labeling, it would have been quite surprising for Kate White to deny that she was mentally ill.

But in fact Kate White was, of the seventeen women interviewed for the Bay Area study, one of the two or three most highly resistant to accepting the labels "mentally ill" or "schizophrenic." Giving an ironic twist to the Freudian theory that homosexuality is a defense against paranoia, one might argue that Kate White found the "homosexual" label preferable as an organizing category to that of "mental patient."

Throughout the interviews with Kate White it was apparent that she thought something was "wrong" with her and that there had always been something "wrong" with her, both from others' point of view and from her own.

> Mrs. White felt that in many ways she did not have the same goals and ideals that her neighbors had. This awakened in her the old conflict she had talked about in the past, about whether she had to conform or not and whether not conforming meant something was wrong with her.
>
> After her first child was born, Kate White said she would go "crazy" if confined to a diaper-formula routine . . . ; she felt guilty if she spent time away from household routine, and isolated after her second child's birth; her aunt lectured her for wanting to be a "career woman."

Prior to her hospitalization, Kate White had apparently toyed with the idea of interpreting her experience within a mental-illness framework.

> In the past she felt that all her nonconformist behavior, all her rebellion, were signs of mental illness; now she didn't think this was necessarily so.

This framework could encompass all the diverse experiences already noted and also provide an explanation of her dislike of many aspects of household care and child-rearing and her longings and ambitions to be a writer. At the same time, the mental-illness framework would accord with her neighbors' and relatives' evaluation of restless and ambitious housewives like her as "crazy" (Warren and Messinger, 1980).

But Kate White rejected the mental-illness interpretive framework and, instead, embraced the "homosexual" theory proffered by Alan Mann. To her, we can thus assume, the identity of homosexual was preferable as an organizing device to the identity of mental patient, and it had the additional advantage that it could interpret Nelson White as well as herself (although, presumably, she could also have interpreted her husband as being mentally ill or schizophrenic).

Thus she rejected the hospital's labeling of her. During the mandatory follow-up period after discharge, she was further labeled "maltherapeutic" as well as "inefficient, unfriendly, impersonal, and confused." She stated that she did not want to see the hospital outpatient staff because "I would have nothing to bring to them." Because he reminded her of the hospital experience, even the interviewer was no longer particularly welcome (see also Warren and Messinger, 1980):

> She did not feel any particular strain in getting back to the normal flow of things. . . . She feels entitled to feel normally, in a normal situation. In this situation, I [the interviewer] also felt some sort of pressure to be placed in a more equalitarian role with the patient.

Continued references to self-doubt about her mental state in the post-hospital phase, however, shows that her identity as a "mental patient" was not totally discounted:

> She indicated again that her problem was not knowing what she was entitled to feel. If she felt critical or angry at doctors . . . she felt that this might just be interpreted as a symptom of her mental illness, and as a matter of fact it might be.

We might surmise that to Kate White the idea of being homosexual was more appealing as an identity than being schizophrenic. Perhaps it was more appealing precisely because it enabled her to retain a sense of herself as essentially and legitimately ambitious, striving, and, in the context of the 1950s, "masculine." Acceptance of the "crazy" label, preferred by neighbors, relatives, and experts, would organize the same experiences that the homosexual label organized, but it might also make of her nonhousewife side something ephemeral, to be cured or taken away. This was, at the time, a common response to such "masculine" strivings.

Ironically, Kate White's use of the homosexual interpretive framework had consequences of precisely the kind she would need to avoid to escape classification by others as mentally ill: mental hospitalization. Categories used to frame the world can have external as well as internal consequences for the framer's further experience of the world. In Kate White's case, it led her to experience severe anxiety, which, in turn, she conceived it a medical function to relieve. And it led her husband to have her hospitalized for proclaiming an obvious unreality; for him, her attributing "homosexuality" to them both was so aberrant as to seem a disorder of mind.

Once hospitalized with the diagnosis "schizophrenic," Kate White was also constrained to give up what was now medically framed as her "delusion" of homosexuality. In the posthospital interviews, she in fact seems to have done so, although in one of them she remarked, "It's hard for me to believe that there wasn't something in what I felt that was true."

What hospitals intend to do is to replace "delusional" identities with "mentally ill" identities and—paradoxically—to restore the patient to a normal self through that acceptance. In this the mental hospital succeeded only in part with Kate White. It succeeded in eradicating her belief in the truth of her homosexual interpretive scheme (or at least the experience of hospitalization convinced her that she should not use it in conversation with others). But it did not succeed in replacing it with a schizophrenic framework. The combined assertions of the hospital staff and of the outside world of disapproving neighbors and relatives were not enough to convince Kate White that she was mentally ill. It appears that for her there were referents of *that* label that made it intolerable; although it could organize her experience, it could perhaps also cause her to lose her own sense of some more central aspect of her being.

We learn something about the character and functions of labels like "homosexual" from Kate White. The labels are specifically vague; like the master label "mental illness," they refer not to particular experiences but to frameworks for interpreting experiences. They are normative frameworks of quite general reference, used as they are in everyday life, rather than value-free frameworks of specific reference. For the everyday user, such labels serve to "explain" conduct and feelings, in part by distributing responsibility and in part by providing a connection between conduct and feelings and a sense of self. Finally, these frameworks or labels must be examined in their interaction contexts. It is there that they do their work; that is, it is there that they permit their users to take certain actions under the umbrella of perceived legitimacy and personal authenticity.

The points made in this paper can and should be generalized. It is important to distinguish between the categories—like "homosexual" or "mentally ill"—that persons employ as elements in their everyday theories of conduct and the experiences these categories serve to summarize, explain, and rationalize. Too often we end up analyzing "homosexuality" or "mental illness" without any firm sense of the referents these categories have within the vocabularies of those who employ them. A cognitive theory of self-conceptions is a necessary adjunct to an interactional and existential-emotional theory.

Note

1. See Sampson et al. (1964) for a summary of the larger project's research methods (pp. 15–18) and for a summary of Kate White's case study (pp. 50–59).

References

Humphreys, Laud. 1972. *Out of the Closets: The Sociology of Homosexual Liberation.* Englewood Cliffs, N.J.: Prentice-Hall.

Lofland, John. 1976. *Doing Social Life: The Qualitative Study of Human Interaction in Natural Settings.* New York: Wiley-Interscience.

Lyman, Stanford M., and Marvin B. Scott. 1970. *A Sociology of the Absurd.* New York: Appleton-Century Crofts.

Mills, C. Wright. 1959. "Vocabularies of Motive." In Mills, *The Sociological Imagination.* New York: Oxford University Press.

Ponse, Barbara R. 1978. *Identities in the Lesbian World.* New York: Greenwood Press.

Sampson, Harold, Sheldon L. Messinger, and Robert D. Towne. 1964. *Schizophrenic Women: Studies in Marital Crisis.* New York: Atherton Press.

Warren, Carol A. B. 1974. *Identity and Community in the Gay World.* New York: Wiley-Interscience.

Warren, Carol A. B., and Barbara Ponse. 1977. "The Existential Self and the Gay World." In John M. Johnson and Jack Douglas, eds., *Existential Sociology.* Cambridge, Eng.: Cambridge University Press.

Warren, Carol A. B., and Sheldon L. Messinger. 1980. "Intensive Interviewing and Human Subjects' Protections: The Selves of Ex-Mental Patients." Paper presented at the annual meetings of the American Sociological Association, New York.

———. 1980. "Women and Mental Illness: The Ambivalence of Housework." Paper presented at the annual meetings of the Society for the Study of Social Problems, New York.

Creating the Competent Self: The Case of the Wheelchair Runner

Dwyne R. Patrick and

John E. Bignall

INTRODUCTION

To the extent that we are free individuals in an open society, we are able, through the activities in which we choose to engage, to create a self. The self that each individual creates interacts with the self that others see, which they in turn project back to the individual during interaction. In this process, daily life may be seen as a dialectical confrontation between the self-I-think-I-am and the self-they-think-I-am. Goffman has examined one side of the dialectical tension when it involves the deviant individual:

> The stigmatized individual can also attempt to correct his condition indirectly by devoting much private effort to the mastery of areas of activity ordinarily felt to be closed on incidental and physical grounds to one with his shortcomings. [Goffman, 1963:10]

In this view, deviant and stigmatized individuals engage in activities that lie outside the realm of what the others they encounter have come to expect of them. The self-I-think-I-am claims identity as something different from what the self-they-think-I-am reflects. The individual-personal self and the social-role identity are in conflict. It is within the tension generated by this confrontation of self and identity that these individuals can create the selves by which they are known.

Within Goffman's "mastery of area of activity" lie the keys to the individual's creation of a self. Individuals master, or become competent in the performance of, activities that reflect both the identities they wish to become known by and the selves they in essence want to be. We become racquetball players, golfers, bridge-players, and mountain climbers both for the personal satisfaction we derive from these activities and for the social interactions based on them and the identities that are created by competent performance of them. When we claim competency in a particular area of endeavor, we also establish an identity as one of "them." In this manner, the marathon runner not only derives satisfaction from running marathons and from his interactions with others who do; he also establishes a personal self and a social identity as a marathoner.

When the individual who runs a marathon is a person whom others generally do not expect to be capable of running, the act of marathoning can be defined as deviant. Since this particular deviance is not seen as generally wrong, immoral, or bad by the observers, it is not an act of bad deviance but of what Douglas (1977) calls creative deviance. Such deviance creates for the deviant a more comfortable identity than his previous one.

When individuals are injured severely enough to require the permanent use of a wheelchair, they are removed from many of the reference groups they have used for creating a self. For a time after they are injured, they engage in a reevaluation and reestablishment of both self and identity in terms of the realities of their new physical being. This process has been characterized by Kerr and Thompson (1972:94–95) as a "regression" followed by a "rebirth of self." More is changed than the individual's means of mobility. The individual has effectively regressed back to infancy and must relearn many things previously taken for granted: self-care, independence, and social skills. Upon their reemergence into the social world, "wheelers"[1] also begin to engage in activities that are reflective of their interests and self-identity.

In general, the others whom wheelers encounter have an image of the disabled individual that they apply to the disabled as a group. This a priori image of the wheeler may or may not be congruent with the identity by which an individual wheeler wishes to be known. While the specifics of this a priori image of the disabled vary somewhat from person to person, it generally involves feelings of pity and the expectation that the disabled individual is not as competent, able, or active as "normal" individuals.

The widespread existence of this a priori image of the wheeler raises the question of what happens when wheelers lay claim to identities that are not congruent with the expectations embodied in this image. In this paper we explore the implications of athletic involvement for the self and identity of wheelers. We examine the ways in which the identity is forged by participation in marathon racing and the role that acceptance by others plays in this process. We know what brings able-bodied individuals to marathoning and what keeps them there, and we are familiar with the insider's description of the subjective experiences of running.[2] What we examine is the comparability of the wheeler/marathoner's experience.

METHODS

The data for this study are derived from six months of intensive team field research. The basic data come from a series of in-depth interviews, supplemented by participant observation. In addition, we brought to the project individual biographical factors that aided the research. Since one of the authors is a wheeler and the other is a runner, we had an intimate understanding of the two social worlds that are combined in this study. We were able to use our backgrounds as checks on the validity of what was being told to us and what we saw occurring. These diverse backgrounds provided a route around the problems embodied in the multiperspectival experience of wheelchair marathoning. In addition to the in-depth interviews, conducted with eleven of the top wheelchair marathoners active at the time, representing around 12 percent of all active wheelchair marathoners, we read extensively in three publications: *Runner* and *Runner's World*, two authoritative publications for runners, and *Sports 'n' Spokes*, the only publication devoted to wheelchair sports. Each of these was a source of member-insider perspectives on issues that were central to the study.

We worked individually in interviewing wheelers for this project. When the transcripts were analyzed, a very distinct pattern emerged. In the interviews done by the researcher who identified himself to the wheelers as a runner, running was a central topic; what the day-to-day implications of running were for being a wheeler were less so. For the researcher who was identified as a wheeler, the reverse was true. This differential way in which the researchers were perceived generated overlapping, yet distinct, bodies of data. For example, the interviewee's display of competence as a runner was strongest in the interviews done by the runner; competence as a wheeler was most clear in those conducted by the wheeler. In each case, the display of competence was an affirmation of membership, fraternity, and identity.

A second group of interviews was conducted with able-bodied runners. The purpose was to gain their perspective on the presence of wheelers in the running fraternity. These interviews also served as a check on the impressions that wheelers had of able-bodied runners' attitudes. We also attempted to interview officials, both in person and via long-distance telephone, when we learned that they had a degree of control over the legitimacy of wheelers' participation in marathons; unfortunately, no interviews could be secured. We were thus prevented from checking on the impressions that wheelers have about officials and about official actions that had had strong impact on their participation in a number of marathons. This lack does not, however, compromise the member views of either the wheelers or the runners. Officials form a third faction in marathoning; both runners and wheelers had opinions about them and described their actions. Their refusal to grant interviews leaves the officials with no response to these opinions and descriptions and no view, in turn, of the other two groups. Interviews were refused by both local and national officials of the Amateur Athletic Union (AAU), which is the national governing body for marathoning and road racing in the United States.

The Historic Context of Wheelchair Marathoning

Both athletics in general and wheelchair athletics in particular have experienced large-scale growth in the past thirty years. The two kinds have, however, grown in parallel, not together. Until the 1970s they existed in complete isolation from each other.

Wheelchair athletics did not exist before the end of World War II; the most significant reason for this was the lack of potential participants. Then the medical advances achieved just prior to and during World War II produced the skills and technology necessary to keep a spinal-cord-injury victim alive and, aside from paralysis, healthy.[3] Because of the higher survival rates, longer life-expectancy, and the boost in the population of wheelers occasioned by the war, large numbers of active young men in wheelchairs were housed together in veteran's hospitals. Proximity and biography impelled them into becoming a close-knit group. At this point (1946) the fortuitous convergence of several of these men and a basketball at the Van Nuys (California) Hospital led to the creation of wheelchair basketball, the first organized wheelchair sport. Since then the world of wheelchair sports has come to include not only more and more events—bowling, archery, mountain climbing, track and field competitions, and scuba diving—but also greater numbers of participants. The greatly increased participation in sports by the able-bodied has paralleled this growth in wheelchair sports. Each world has seen the emergence of more highly individual events in the past ten years. Long-distance running, or marathoning, is the culmination of this movement, and marathoning was the first sport in which these two sports worlds converged.

Becoming and Being a Runner

The individual process of becoming either a marathoner or a wheeler/marathoner can be examined through the analytic concept of the "career." Becker (1963:24) states that this concept "refers to the sequence of movements from one position to another in an occupational system made by an individual who works in that system. Furthermore, it includes the notion of 'career contingency,' those factors on which mobility from one position to another depends." Becker goes on to transform the concept for use in the analysis of deviant careers. A similar transformation is made here in order to examine the notion of the recreational career—specifically, that of the runner and the wheeler/runner.

Running is a career in which individuals begin with a simple interest and proceed to gain more knowledge and competence through participation. Although the experiences and meanings attributed to running vary with the individuals, the able-bodied and wheelers, as groups, demonstrate distinctive career patterns.

For the able-bodied, running begins as an interest stimulated by publications or acquaintances and by the perception of the rewards to be gained by participating. Individuals place an initial "side-bet" in favor of running and proceed from there. A side-bet is an investment of time, money, or other personal resource small enough to be abandoned with no discernible loss to the individual (see Becker, 1960). Given the smallness of this "stake," individuals can either cut their losses or increase the bet. In the first instance, the interest in running is forsaken, and the individual goes on to other pursuits. If the bet is increased, the individual proceeds with additional side-bets, each small enough to abandon but cumulatively large enough to form a significant investment of individual resources. Such an investment forms the basis for the creation of a self as a runner and an identity as such. Neophyte runners begin by running around the block. Soon they are running farther and longer, and, as they venture farther afield, they encounter other runners, who reinforce a new self and identity as a runner by fraternal interactions.

At this juncture, a career contingency emerges. Individuals may continue the neighborhood/local running they are engaged in, or they make an additional bet that causes a career change: they may begin social running; that is, they begin to run with other individuals, not just alone. The runner's goal at this point shifts from individual to social rewards, though the individual rewards remain. For the social runner, another career contingency appears. Social runners can begin to compete in races. The 10, 12, and 15K (kilometer) races, as well as half and whole marathons, are held on a weekly, if not almost daily, basis across the nation. Some are no more than large social, or fun, runs; others, however, are serious competitive events. Serious races provide the final career contingency for runners. They may elect to run and race just for the pleasure, both social and individual, of participating, or they may attempt to become serious competitors in the world of distance racing.

For the wheeler, the career pattern of running is different. There is not, generally, a casual entrance, via jogging around the block. Wheelers tend to enter marathoning as serious competitors. The enticing publications that lure the able-bodied into running are not relevant to the nonrunning wheeler. Likewise, able-bodied acquaintances who run do not seem like realistic role models.

Long-distance running emerged as a possibility for wheelers primarily through Bob Hall's competing in the 1975 Boston Marathon in a wheelchair. By this time, running at the sprint and short/middle distances of track competition had been popular in the wheeler fraternity for more than twenty years, but competition was restricted to wheelers. The structure of wheelchair track and field events included, and still includes, local, regional, national, and world-level competition in these distances. Prior to Bob's galvanizing run in 1975, no long-distance running for wheelers existed.[4]

When they became aware of Bob's action, other wheelers began to enter and compete in marathons. Clint, a student, father of two, and holder of the world record for the wheelchair marathon, sums this up:

> I came down here to the —— area to go to school and ran into a fellow who played [wheelchair] basketball on the team here. I got enrolled on the team and literally ran into a fellow from Denver while going down the court on a fast break, and he told me to harness some of that speed and told me about the track and field competition that the wheelchairs had [regional and national games] . . . ; from there I came into contact with Bob Hall, who so to speak founded marathoning, and from there went to Boston [the Boston Marathon] in 1977.

It is clear that, while Clint was already an athlete and even a competitive participant in wheelchair sprint races, he had not entertained the idea of running a marathon in a wheelchair before his exposure to Bob Hall. This career entry pattern is common to nine of the twelve wheelers we interviewed. All of them became marathoners because of personal contact with Bob Hall. For this reason we call them the first-generation wheelchair marathoners. Two of the remaining three are also first-generation participants; the difference is that they began marathoning through exposure to *reports* of Bob's run in *Sports 'n' Spokes*, the wheelchair-sports publication. The last individual became a marathoner through contact with a runner who had had direct contact with Bob Hall. This individual is thus a second-generation runner; however, the career-entry pattern is in all other respects exactly the same. In addition to opening up the personal possibility of marathoning to other wheelers, Bob's run also helped open institutional barriers. For example, James, a teacher and first-generation runner, experienced the disappearance of an institutional barrier in this way:

> I went down to the [newspaper] office and entered, and they were kind of surprised but thought it was all right. Then a few days later they called me up and said the committee had met and decided they wouldn't let me do it because it was an able-bodied race and [my participation in a wheelchair] would make it unofficial. Then, the night before the race, they called me up and said that they had heard about a fellow who had run the Boston Marathon in a wheelchair and that it would be okay for me to run if I still wanted to.

As an entry point, wheelers move directly from either segregated, short-distance wheelchair competition (nonrunning) to competitive, long-distance, integrated running. The pattern of gradually increasing one's involvement and escalating one's side-bets, which characterizes the career of the able-bodied runner and takes place over a period of months or years, is either absent or lasts for only a few days or weeks for the wheeler.

For the able-bodied, running can become an obsession. The daily run is often given priority over other concerns. Lunches are sometimes forfeited in order to get in that all-important run. For those who are most involved, running often becomes a business as well as an avocation. In this case, a career in business begins as centered on running. In any case, running often assumes a place in the daily life of both wheelers and able-bodied runners that is well beyond that normally given to a simply recreational activity or hobby. As Sanny, a lawyer and a wheeler, notes:

> I had to put running first; most other things I had would take care of themselves . . . running wouldn't. . . . When I was in [law school], I always put it ahead of going to class . . . schedule it first, then work on the other things. . . . I even got my boyfriend to build a sort of treadmill device so I could run indoors when the weather was bad.

With this, running has moved from the status of avocational activity to central concern. If it does not always supplant all other activities, it is clearly equal in importance.

The able-bodied individual first has a peripheral involvement in running; then, through an increasing investment, via side-bets, it becomes a central part of daily life. In some cases, running becomes *the* central focus of daily life. In contrast to this, the wheeler enters running at a seriously competitive level. After becoming a competitor, the wheeler begins to discover the experiential elements of running that woo the able-bodied into increasing involvement. The wheeler starts as a competitive marathoner and moves "down" to the pleasure and addiction of daily running; the able-bodied runner discovers the pleasure and addiction of daily running, then moves "up" to the world of competitive running.

THE SOCIAL EXPERIENCE OF RUNNING

When able-bodied individuals begin to run, they do not enter a realm of uncharted experience. Neophyte runners enter into a rich new social world, replete with folklore, legend, heroes, traditions, and travelogues that are told to them by the old-timers. Runners talk of "hitting the wall," "doing the distance," and "running the Boston." Special terms are used, and topics that to the nonrunner may seem extremely trivial assume great importance. Becoming a runner involves more than simply beginning to run. New runners acquire the language, culture, and ideology of running. As they go on in their careers as runners, these cultural artifacts of the social world of running become second nature. Such items assume the taken-for-granted status that the cultural artifacts of the general society have in everyday life. What was once new and curious becomes ordinary and comfortable.

Wheelers enter this social world with as little expectation of its hidden richness as the able-bodied. They enter a fraternity of the like-minded, intent on the same goals and using the same tools and analytic concepts. It is an entry into a *social world*, a world intent on the pursuit of running. When they become marathoners, wheelers find that they have entered a world of shared experience with the able-bodied that is unavailable in the segregated world of wheelchair athletics. David, a world-class wheelchair athlete, sees this function of integrated marathoning:

> What doing a marathon is, if it is something you can do both in a wheelchair and on your feet, the essence of your experience has to be the same for both. . . . Whatever it is that runners and pushers [wheelers] both share, that's what a marathon is, and the rest is just a question of technique.

The entry of wheelers into this social world creates new ties between the wheeler and the able-bodied. The disabled/able-bodied distinction of everyday life is replaced by the transcendent identity of "runner." Runners are a very fraternal and cohesive group, and, in this world, the wheeler is accepted as a legitimate runner. Tom, a veteran and second-generation runner, says:

> The others cheer you on. You know, its pretty positive between me and the rest of the runners . . . everybody is friendly; you're all out there running.

The wheelers all felt that other runners were highly supportive of their presence in the marathon. This is confirmed in their interactions with the majority of the runners they encounter and by the attitude of the well-known runners. As Clint notes:

> Most runners are really supportive, too. Bill Rodgers came out with a statement in this public hearing for the New York City Marathon. Someone asked him, "What if wheelchairs were in the Olympics, what would you think about that?" And he said, "I'd be willing to take a silver to a person in a wheelchair." And most runners have the same attitude.

Only one of the wheelers we interviewed mentioned encountering negative reactions on the part of able-bodied runners. He stipulated, however, that these came from a single individual, who was not supported by other runners.

If able-bodied runners are very open and accepting of wheelers in marathons, this is not true of the second group of individuals concerned with the wheelers' presence in marathons, the officials. It is the officials, individually and as a group, who have the power to stop wheelers from participating in marathons and to legitimate or disqualify the performance of any participant, whether wheeler or able-bodied. Officials work at two levels in controlling marathoning. The officials of a particular race may grant or deny permission for wheelers to enter it. At the same time, the regional and national officials of the AAU may desanction the results of a race if wheelers have participated in it. Times for performances in unsanctioned races cannot be used to qualify for special races, such as the Boston Marathon or the Olympic trials. Likewise, a faster time in an unsanctioned race is not officially a record. Officials have barred wheelers from participating in several marathons on this basis. Clint's experience reflects that of the majority of wheelers:

> Bob Hall and I ran in the New York City Marathon, and there is no way to describe it. We had trouble getting into it. Finally the mayor said, made a declaration, that wheelchair competitors would not be eliminated or excluded from the race. Now it's gone back to public hearing to see if they ever will again [exclude wheelers].[5]

Not every race or every official has been problematic, and several workable solutions have been used, though these are still not accepted by the AAU. The rift between the runners and wheelers and the officials has been a very erratic problem, changing from race to race and from official to official. There are some consistencies, however, as Sanny notes:

> When the officials are runners themselves, and people coming from that background, and are younger, they seem a lot more open to us than the people who have been around for thirty years and are established in their way of thinking.

The third group that the wheelers encounter as a consequence of their entry into marathoning is the spectators. Spectators tend to view the wheelers as "magicians," who display great competence, given their obvious disabilities:

> His once most ordinary deeds . . . are no longer ordinary. He becomes an unusual person. If he performs with finesse and assurance, they excite the same kind of wonderment inspired by a magician who pulls rabbits out of hats. [Chevigny, 1962:140]

The appearance of a wheeler in a marathon is outside the expectations generated by commonly accepted, a priori definitions of disability. The crowd always cheers the runners, and they cheer for the wheeler too. Sanny describes this: "I know that—like at Boston—I was the first woman in a chair that the people saw, and they went absolutely wild over me."

THE SUBJECTIVE EXPERIENCE OF RUNNING

There are segments of the experience of long-distance running that are highly subjective and individual; yet these segments show a remarkable degree of consistency in content from person to person.[6] The runner's "high," and the intense feelings of freedom and competence that are described as occurring in the latter stages of extended-distance runs are two of the seemingly transcendent experiences of running. Such experiences are reported by runners who do long distances, i.e., over ten miles. These runners describe feelings of total freedom, both physical and mental, and of pure, unrestrained ability.

For wheelers, such feelings seem to take two forms. The first is described by James:

> I spend so much time working and working, physically exerting myself with the chair, and I found at a point I became lost. It brought back a lot of memories and that kind of freedom of the way the arm and the wheel became one unit, the chair and the body were all one, it's like the chair became flesh. . . . I worked out a lot of things about being handicapped . . . ; it's a good way to get in touch with yourself and your body.

This is the freedom to turn inward and explore the self in depth, to review the past and seek the inner meanings of individual existence. It is a freedom that allows the individual to begin to explore the status in which he or she exists and to recreate that status. The melding of chair and individual creates a unity where, before, a pair of discrete entities existed. A body-in-a-chair becomes, at that time, a unified self: a *body/chair*. The physical and mental demands of running a marathon act as the catalyst for a catharsis that unites the two selves—the mechanical "self" of the wheelchair and the organic self of the individual—in a single entity. The injuries and diseases that require wheelers to use wheelchairs become almost epiphenomenal.

At first the new wheeler realizes that he or she must master certain essential skills—like mobility—that able-bodied runners can take for granted. Ultimately these skills are mastered through the use of a tool. The unified self that emerges over the course of becoming competent at racing, however, provides the impetus for learning these skills creatively and resourcefully. The wheelchair, as a tool, not only compensates for the wheeler's physical limitations but can become a source of competitive and artistic advantage in constructing a performance during a marathon. Thus an element of personal *style* allows the wheeler to move beyond the level of basic competency and functional equivalency. David elaborates on this experience:

> It's like when I hit a little downgrade, and I can weave in
> and out between the ab's [able-bodied individuals] out there,
> then I can move and flow and feel really graceful in the
> wheelchair. I'm not clumsy and clunky any more.

When the bimodal self fuses into a new self, the wheeler gains feelings of
physical competency, gracefulness, and skill.[7]

The second form of freedom that wheelers experience in the marathon
is described by Clint:

> Running is hard to explain. It's like feeling that euphoria
> type of feeling, and you're out there giving your all, and
> you are enjoying the freedom of being out here in the
> mountains . . . it's just a whole feeling you can't get inside
> a basketball court or on a tennis court or somewhere like
> that. It's just not the same, you can't catch that feeling.

From the marathon comes a feeling of freedom-in-the-world—the ability
to be who you are and to do what you please. The marathon provides a
challenge to individuals, something that can be accomplished through the
use of personal abilities. The intense sensations and emotions that accom-
pany the ability to "do the distance" on your own create a feeling of personal
freedom. The individual feels able to handle anything that the world has
to offer.

The most widely heralded of the subjective experiences of running is
the runner's "high," experienced in the final stages of long-distance runs.
It has been described by able-bodied runners as a feeling of "contentment,"
of having both "enormous power" and moments of "exceptional perceptual
clarity."[8] It is, above all, a subjective and unshared experience, essentially
undescribable in language. Runners do communicate about the runner's
high to each other, but they insist that the experience cannot really be
communicated in words; it has to be experienced to be understood. When
they enter the world of marathoning, wheelers are exposed to this experience in two ways: through the inadequate verbal descriptions offered by
others and experientially, in the course of running. The nature of this
subjective experience is different for each individual. Sanny says:

> It's not like nirvana or anything. I get real cheerful, and
> I feel strong.

Clint amplifies this:

> [It's] an especially great feeling. I go out early in the morn-
> ing, and there's nothing else on the road. I'm breaking my
> own path through the snow. I get this physical exertion
> and freedom feeling—it's really an excellent feeling.

According to Tom, the "high" is one of the reasons he continues to run:

> I get it [the runner's high] all the time. The only reason
> I'm in it [running] is what I get from it, and when the
> adrenaline pumps, it's really great.

There is one element of running that the able-bodied do not seem to
share with the wheelers who have joined them. This has been dubbed the
"anti-stereotype effect" by Sanny. To Sanny and other wheelers, what is
"magic" about the wheelers' participating in an event that, in the a priori
imagery of many individuals, is closed to disabled people is its power to
spread a message. This message is not just about the individual wheeler
but about all wheelers:

> Anything disabled people do is anti-stereotype and creates
> a more positive image—*anything*. It plants a seed in some-
> body's head, like, you know, "Disabled people don't just
> sit in a corner. I saw one run a race!" or something like
> that. Every little thing we do helps. I don't like to think
> of myself as an example, but we are, you know . . . we
> do something different, and it creates a more positive image
> for the disabled.

Runners, Wheelers, and the Self

The wheeler faces the world enmeshed in a "master status" (see Becker,
1963:32–34) that is both deviant and unchosen. Wheelers are unwilling
deviants in society. While the visibility of the wheeler's condition often
makes the status "disabled" a common master status and frequently makes
it the core of self-identity, this does not have to be the case. Individuals
can lay claim to selves and project identities different from the ones that
others attempt to impose on them. Given the right skin tone, individual
blacks can "pass" for white. They can claim an identity other than the
one generally imposed on them by others. In becoming marathon runners,
wheelers lay claim to a self based on the transcendent criteria of running
and project an identity based on this new self. This claim sets aside considerations of disability and the wheelchair, both of which are transcended
by claims to the ability and achievement that are part of being a runner.
Wheelers "do the distance," they "speak the language" of running, they
accept its goals and obey its rules. In the world of running, by the actions
they engage in and by their comportment, wheelers claim identity as runners, irrespective of their physical condition. This claim to both a self and
an identity as a runner is generally supported by the able-bodied runners
who run races with the wheelers. They accept wheelers into the fraternity
of running, along with all others who meet the important criteria. David
expresses this philosophy of the irrelevance of disability to running:

> You are going to be in pain and discomfort, and it's not
> going to be something that you can deal with tomorrow or
> the next day; it's going to be something that you have to
> deal with now, as an integral part of the experience, while
> it is happening. That's what doing a marathon is. It's some-
> thing you can do both in a wheelchair and on your feet;
> the essence of the experience has to be the same for both.
> Whatever it is that runners and pushers [wheelers] share,
> that's what a marathon is, and the rest is just a question
> of technique.

In this view, it doesn't matter that runners do the distance on their feet
while the wheeler does the distance in a chair powered by a pair of arms.
It is the ultimate decision of the individual to do the distance that makes
him or her a runner.

The wheelers and runners thus share a transcendent definition of running
and of being a runner, but there is opposition from the officials. Even
officials who accept the claim of wheelers that they do the distance will
counter with the claim that they do it with the aid of a mechanical con-
trivance, "like a skateboard or a bicycle" (from the AAU rulebook, 1980).
The claims to a transcendent set of criteria that define runners and running
are brushed aside in the face of this contention that the use of the wheelchair—necessitated by the physical impairment—is equivalent to the use
of skateboards and bicycles and that the use of such "devices" is unfair
in a footrace. The wheelers' response to this is typified by Sanny:

> I don't like the idea that we can't be in there competing;
> at least I don't feel that I am competing against a runner
> except mentally. I don't think that it is fair to compare a
> wheelchair to a runner—or to a skateboard.

Since Bob Hall ran the Boston in 1975, marathoning has been the athletic
arena in which the selves of the able-bodied and the disabled were potentially subsumable under the same identity—that of runner. Other sports
have held a similar promise of competitive equality and identity-subsum-
ability in the past—most notably, archery and power lifting—but the sought-
after transcendence of the status "disabled person" by the status "athlete"
has never taken place. There is a bottom line described by Clint: "I like
to consider myself an athlete; that's important to me."

Note that Clint does not say "disabled athlete" or use some other evasive
label. He moved from being disabled to being a wheelchair basketball
player, to being a wheelchair track star, to being a marathoner. It is only
with the final term of this series that his self-concept and identity are free
of the prefix "disabled." The movement from each of these reference
groups and self-concepts is clear. By becoming a marathoner, Clint has
claimed and held an identity and a self that are not segregated from those

of the able-bodied. Marathoning is the only athletic arena in which the able-bodied and the wheeler meet the same criteria, share the same experiences, and fill the same role.

CONCLUSION

The creation of a new self, amenable to one's own desires yet effective in the social world, is an extremely complex and difficult task. If we operate on the assumption that the relationship of self to society is inherently confrontational (see chapter 11), it is clear that an individual seeking a more rewarding experience of self must contend with "society's" prejudgments, presuppositions, and, in the case of wheelers and other deviants, moral stigmas. Thus, interpersonal resources are required for successful self-transformation. A coalition of people experiencing the same anxieties, for example, helps the individual to achieve the ability to convince "society" of the validity of claims to a new self. Another often critical resource is the availability of an already established and morally legitimate identity, such as "marathoner," to which the individual can anchor the emerging self.

One of the greatest felt rewards of the creation of self is an increased sense of control. In becoming a wheeler, the initial object of control is performance or behavior (i.e., acquiring the ability to run); this leads to control over one's self (i.e., becoming a wheeler), and it culminates in control over "society" (i.e., being identified and accepted as a marathoner). Our examination of wheelchair running raises an important and more general theoretical question that should be explored further: To what degree does the urge or need to control one's existence provide the impetus for the process of becoming?

Notes

1. "Wheeler" is a common self-referent used in the community of the wheelchair-bound disabled. Other similar terms include "pusher" and "chair."

2. See Fixx (1978) for an excellent member's description of the experience of running.

3. See Bignall (1980) for an elaboration of the consequences of medical technology for the development of wheelchair and special athletics.

4. In reality, Bob and several other wheelers had run a National Wheelchair Marathon in Toledo, Ohio, in 1974. No wheeler we interviewed knew of this event. Our mention of it in the course of the interview was the first time any of them had heard of it.

5. This issue eventually found its way into the courts. Ruling specifically on the New York City Marathon, the judge held that the exclusion of wheelers constituted unlawful discrimination. At this point, the AAU revised its rule book to categorize wheelchairs with other "mechanical devices," such as skateboards and bicycles,

which were barred from footraces. This had the effect of letting officials bar the wheelchair but letting the wheelers enter, albeit without a means of mobility!

6. The similarity of content from runner to runner speaks to either a learning effect from the running subculture or a true equivalency of the raw experience. The similarity of content is well documented in the literature on running. The reason for it is of no concern to this essay.

7. Our current work indicates that this phenomenon is not limited to the arena of athletics; rather, it occurs in other places and at other times for other handicapped individuals.

8. From "Runners' Highs: Who Gets Them and Why," *New American Runner,* 1978:15–18 and 92–93.

References

Becker, Howard S. 1960. "Notes on the Concept of Commitment." *American Journal of Sociology* 66(1):32–40.

———. 1963. *Outsiders: Studies in the Sociology of Deviance.* New York: Free Press.

Bignall, John E. 1980. "Wheelchair Athletics: Competent Deviance." Paper delivered at the meeting of the Pacific Sociological Association, San Francisco.

Bignall, John E., and Dwyne R. Patrick. 1981. "The Bimodal Self: Wheelers, Wheelchairs, and Self-Concept." Paper delivered at the meeting of the Western Social Science Association, San Diego.

Douglas, Jack. 1976. *Investigative Social Research.* Beverly Hills, Calif.: Sage.

———. 1977. *Nude Beach.* Beverly Hills, Calif.: Sage.

Fixx, James. 1978. *The Complete Book of Running.* New York: Random House.

Goffman, Erving. 1955. "On Face Work." *Psychiatry* 18:213–31.

———. 1963. *Stigma.* Englewood Cliffs, N.J.: Spectrum.

Kerr, W., and M. Thompson. 1980. "Acceptance of Disability of Sudden Onset." *Paraplegia* 10(1):94–102.

Patrick, Dwyne Rhodes. 1980. "Victim or Accomplice: Some Considerations on the Mutual Occurrence of Physical Disability and Alcoholism." Paper delivered at the meetings of the Pacific Sociological Association, San Francisco.

eleven

A Synthesis:
The Existential Self in
Society

Joseph A. Kotarba

There is a movement within sociology today toward renewed interest in the concept of the self. While it is true that the primary thrust of our field, as judged by the contents of our major scholarly journals, has been in the direction of highly technical research protocols, a growing number of sociologists are rejecting the value of processing seemingly lifeless variables and indicators in favor of seeking to understand the actual *experience* of both social life and individuality. One may well argue that this renewed interest in the concept of the self is somewhat anarchical at this point, for there is little agreement among sociologists regarding either the ontological status of the self or the proper methods for studying the self (see chapter two). Nevertheless, many influential works on the self have been published in the past five or six years, reflecting what I consider to be a healthy diversity in analytical goals and perspectives. Some writers have rejuvenated the discussion of George Herbert Mead's classic philosophical analysis of the self-concept, especially his interpretation of the socially learned as opposed to the creative aspects of self-definition (e.g., Carveth, 1977). Others have attempted to apply more recent insights from phenomenological thought to understanding the cognitive structures of the self (e.g., Kovit, 1980). We have also witnessed the emergence of new models of the self, such as Turner's (1976) "impulsive" self and Zurcher's (1977) "mutable" self, which attempt to account for the strategies used by people today to anchor their personal sense of being in a rapidly changing social world.

An interesting question for the sociology of knowledge is why this renewal of interest in the self-concept is occurring today. Although a complete and meaningful answer to this question is undoubtedly complex and worthy of detailed study in itself, I will discuss briefly two of the more important factors involved. First, this renewed interest parallels and to some degree results from the dramatic surge of interest in self-actualization and development that is occurring within popular culture—a development that is not only monitored but nurtured by the media. The "me" generation of the 1970s was marked by numerous best-selling books extolling the virtues of dropping out, looking out for number one, fulfilling one's most personal sexual needs, finding God in the depths of one's consciousness, conducting an open marriage, and in general gearing one's life toward self-gratification. The apparent pervasiveness of this cultural shift toward accenting the good of the self—as opposed to the good of the group—led one acute if perhaps overly pessimistic observer, Christopher Lasch (1979), to conclude that we are living in a "culture of narcissism." Lasch argues that our civilization, engulfed in political and economic despair, is doomed if we continue to pursue immediate gratification and forsake the rugged sense of competitiveness and achievement needed to build a viable future. The cultish excesses of the 1960s and 1970s upon which Lasch bases his argument, however, have waned as we enter the 1980s and begin to witness more people seeking admission to prestigious graduate schools of business than to cosmic communes. Indeed, beneath the rhetoric of gross individualism highlighting the recent cultural turmoil we find less rejection of society than the institution of new kinds of social groupings designed to augment self-actualization. Nevertheless, "real-world" interest in the self was and continues to be a phenomenon that sociologists, as the gatekeepers of social life, could not ignore for long.

Second, researchers and analysts in several academic disciplines have been finding that traditional modes of conceptualizing the self are inefficient and have been seeking new methods for understanding the self. Social psychologists who study the self-concept by means of objectified measures and scales, for example, have found that these highly quantitative methods cannot account for the immense complexity of the self. One of the important aspects of the self in social psychological research over the past twenty years has been the measurement of self-esteem. In fact, many researchers view self-esteem as the dominant motive in a person's life (Kaplan, 1975), all but equating it with the self. Consequently, they have developed a number of measurement tools, such as the Coopersmith Self-Esteem Inventory and the Rosenberg Self-Esteem Scale, to gauge objectively how good a person feels about him or herself. Self-esteem has been correlated with a wide range of variables, including emotional disturbance, IQ, delinquency, and minority status. In spite of the many studies conducted on self-esteem, this narrow approach to the study of self has led to relatively little understanding of the ways we experience our individuality. Morris Rosenberg, one of the most scholarly researchers of self-esteem, recently reviewed the literature in this area and found that self-esteem research "seems to be spinning its wheels, unable to get untracked. All the important sociological variables that might be expected to account for it . . . are found to explain remarkably little variance in it" (Rosenberg, 1979:286). Thus, instead of focusing on a single aspect of the self, such as global self-esteem, Rosenberg suggests that researchers in his genre widen their perspective to include the analysis of certain neglected aspects of the self, such as the specific content of self-esteem, the notion of the desired self, and the presenting or dramaturgical self.

Rosenberg's counsel is encouraging because it not only grounds the study of self-esteem in a more realistic awareness of the true complexity of the modern self but also provides a preliminary bridge between two quite diverse traditions in the study of the self, which I call the *positivistic* and the *ethnographic*. The positivistic tradition is heavily steeped in psychological and behavioristic metaphors and assumes that the self is an entity that can be *measured* by means of objective instrumentation. The responses of subjects to structured interview questions are viewed not as reflecting the self directly but merely as indicators of an underlying "true" self, of which only the researcher is aware. The ethnographic tradition, within which most of the authors assembled in this collection conduct their research, is more concerned with the *empirical* content of the self. The object of study is the experience of individuality—through the perspective of the subject—as it unfolds, adapts, and copes in concrete, everyday-life situations. There has been remarkably little cross-referencing between these two traditions, to the mutual detriment of both.[1] Rosenberg's insightful analysis can lead only to an increased appreciation within the positivistic tradition of the value of open-ended and creative research methods, and, within the ethnographic tradition, it should lead to an increased appreciation of the value of rigorous conceptualization. In any event, the rethinking of the self-concept in social psychology is matched by a similar movement in other disciplines, especially the helping disciplines involved with psychoanalysis (see Yalom, 1980).

Popular and professional interest in the self undoubtedly has contributed to the emergence of the existential model of the self. But those of us who conduct social research under the rubric *existential sociology* have felt the need for a new model of individual experience, primarily as a result of what we have been discovering about contemporary social life. Existential sociology is the study of human experience-in-the-world (or existence) in all its forms (Douglas and Johnson, 1977:vii). As I have argued elsewhere (Kotarba, 1979), this definition is necessarily broad and open-ended because modern life is most notably marked by unceasing flux, change, and uncertainty. The constant, and occasionally dramatic, changes occurring in our social rules, values, institutions, and life-styles encourage exploration of the contrasts and innovations in social life and make the search for conceptual universals seem, for the moment, premature.

Since existential sociology is designed to monitor closely the tone of and trends in contemporary life, our attention has been drawn especially to the many people in all walks of life who are dissatisfied with both their own sense of who they are and society's demands of who they should be. Furthermore, *we have been finding that new social forms, whether they are entirely innovative or simply reconstructions of existing social forms, are reflections of new and innovative ways in which members of our society are coming to think and feel about themselves.* The conceptual relationship between innovative social forms and changes in our selves is complex, as I will illustrate below. But it is clear that many members of our society are actively seeking new ways of fulfilling and expressing themselves. The papers in this collection represent the diverse forms that this search for self can take.

The following *working* definition of the existential self is intended to display the relative fluidity of the modern self and to account for the internal as well as external manifestations of the process of making sense of one's being. *The existential self refers to an individual's unique experience of being within the context of contemporary social conditions, an experience most notably marked by an incessant sense of becoming and an active participation in social change.*[2] I will now discuss the major components of this definition, since they provide the central themes for the papers in this collection.

THE SENSE OF BECOMING

The notion of "becoming" is one of the most important ideas in existentialist thought. Sartre, in his philosophical and literary writings (e.g., 1945), argued dramatically that we are condemned to be free, condemned to choose continually who we are because existence in itself is empty and meaningless. Merleau-Ponty (1962) takes a more moderate view, and one more conducive to the sociological perspective, by insisting that our becoming must be grounded in the real (read: social) world if we have any intention of being effective in coping with the given world. The individual is encouraged by the brute reality of life to acquire some distinctive *style* of self-actualization:

> The very notion of freedom demands that our decision [on how to approach the world] should plunge into the future, that something should have been *done* by it, that the subsequent instant should benefit from its predecessor and, though not necessitated, should be at least required by it . . . a decision once taken and action once begun, I must have something acquired at my disposal, I must benefit from my impetus. [Merleau-Ponty 1962:437]

Freedom, therefore, is viable only to the degree that it allows us to *control* the goals of our endeavors and to utilize them for our own personal growth. Put differently, existentialism presents an image of the self-to-society relationship that is quite apropos to today's world: the image of the self *confronting* society. We constantly attempt to shape and manipulate society—that is, society as we experience it—in order to have it as a resource for fulfilling our most basic needs and desires.

To conceptualize becoming as the necessity to create the self continually runs counter to the dominant view of self-emergence in sociology. In this view, which we can summarize as socialization theory, the self is largely passive in relation to the world; it emerges as either a mirror reflection or learned product of society-as-experienced. Accordingly, we go through life acquiring the roles that society provides for us. It is easy to understand how the research that supports socialization theory is conducted largely with children and adolescents, the groups most susceptible to imposed definitions of the self. (The exception to this rule can be seen in some of the more recent work in life-cycle studies, such as Blau, 1981.) Socialization theory tends either to ignore adults or to assume that the experience of self is lastingly shaped early in life.

The papers in our book clearly demonstrate that the self not only is in a state of constant becoming throughout life but is actualized only through social roles that must be shaped and even created to meet the needs that emerge as the self confronts itself (see Yalom, 1980). As Douglas argues (chapter three), the inner self (i.e., the deepest, most personal sense of being) is always problematic. Children experience insecurity as their increasing independence is confounded by "faulty" understanding of the world. Adolescents become extremely conscious of their need to resolve anxieties over their sense of self, as is indicated by the great amount of time they spend thinking about themselves and often writing about themselves in their diaries. And adulthood is not marked simply by occasional biographical crises that bring questions of self-identity to the fore; it is, on the contrary, permeated with anxieties over competency in dealing with love, intimacy, sex, dominance, and other powerful feelings.

The most obvious reason why the self is grounded in a constant state of becoming is the *embodiment* that forms the core of our existence. The body is not only the source for unending and ever-changing feelings and emotions and the criterion by which we evaluate the objects in our world; it also provides life-events that may either threaten the self or open the way to self-fulfillment. The act of selling one's blood plasma does both, as Espeland (chapter six) indicates. The primary motive for engaging in this practice is to get money, but the "respectable" donor must develop intricate strategies for counteracting the stigma associated with prostituting the life-stream of the body. Messinger and Warren's case study of Kate White (chapter nine) illustrates the necessary intertwining of cognitive and physical inputs in the process of attributing meaning to a self. The term "homosexual" was not for Kate White a direct reference to her sexual preference or behavior; it served, rather, to summarize, explain, and rationalize her uncertain feelings about herself and to make sense of the suspicious behavior of others. Her "homosexual" self was a normative strategy or framework that she utilized to account for her alienation from her husband, the lack of communication in their marriage, and her husband's neglect of her. The authors' analytical argument is relevant to all students of the self: it is important to distinguish between the categories employed in members' common-sense theories of conduct and the bodily experiences these categories serve to summarize, explain, and rationalize.

Since the experience of becoming is inherently problematic (i.e., unpredictable), we are liable at various times in our lives to encounter discrete yet critical episodes that severely threaten the security of self and often require massive reconstruction of one's sense of being. The dramatic experience of meaninglessness has been a recurring topic of interest among writers as they attempt to come to grips with it by means of concepts like *reflexivity* (Mehan and Wood, 1975) and *absurdity* (Lyman and Scott, 1970). The affective result of meaninglessness can be either pleasurable or painful, depending on the social context within which it occurs. Robert Lifton (1976:3–34) elegantly describes the pleasurable encounter with meaninglessness as "experiential transcendence," which is

> a state so intense that in it time and death disappear. When one achieves ecstasy or rapture, the restrictions of the senses—including the sense of mortality—no longer exist. Poetically and religiously this has been described as "losing oneself." It can occur not only in religious or secular mysticism but also in song, dance, battle, sexual love, childbirth, athletic effort, mechanical flight, or in contemplating works of artistic or intellectual creation. This state is characterized by extraordinary psychic unity and perceptual intensity. But there also occurs, as we hear described in drug experiences, a process of symbolic reordering. One feels oneself to be different after returning from this state.

Many of the modalities Lifton mentions for achieving pleasurable meaninglessness have been important components of the self-actualization movement. One cannot ignore the irony of people seeking the ultimate experience of personalized being by constructing and participating in mundane albeit innovative social forms, such as the phenomenon of organized running described by Bignall and Patrick (chapter ten).

The experience of meaninglessness can be quite painful when an individual becomes the victim of external, harmful forces, which destroy the security of self. In this situation, the person will seek social forms that can assist in reconstructing the self and in eliminating the threat. The notion of being a victim and the interpretive basis for it is the theme of the Ferraro and Johnson paper (chapter five). The self-definition "victim" is not automatically adopted by an individual who is suffering intense physical abuse. A married woman, for example, may be battered by her husband for years but not come to define herself as a "victim" until certain events elicit introspective redefinition and a confrontation with self; for example, a sudden change in the severity of the beatings may denote a threat to her very life. At this point, the content of the woman's previously secure sense of self as a "happily married woman," "good Christian," or "deserving of punishment" is destroyed, and she may become willing to let third-party interveners (e.g., shelters) help her restore her sense of self-integrity and protect her from further abuse.

Finally, a somewhat benign force that impels us to redefine the self is one that most of us experience at one time or another: *the fear of boredom*. A smoothly functioning social system, one that provides for the members' material needs and offers excessive levels of security for the self, can lead to what Simon and Gagnon (1976:361) refer to as the "anomie of affluence" that occurs "precisely when the objects or experiences that have symbolized achievement become part of the easily accessible and therefore unspectacular, everyday quality of life." The anomie of affluence can lead to a stagnant sense of self, which the person can attempt to alleviate by rejuvenating the search for self-fulfillment through overconsumption, withdrawal from competition for culturally approved goals, pursuit of the unconventional, etc.[3]

It would seem that the formal organization is a likely setting for disillusionment with success, since organizational goals, such as efficiency, tend to be imposed rationally and impersonally. But as Smith (chapter four) demonstrates, the organization is best conceived in terms of the members who compose it. The feelings, perceptions, decisions, and priorities of all members are the real determinants of organizational life. The viability of an organization is closely tied to its ability to respond constructively to these ever-changing member inputs.

THE SELF AND SOCIAL CHANGE

The two concepts most commonly used for discussing the relationship between social change and the individual are *culture* and *role*. We can define social change as the significant alteration of the content of a culture (see Moore, 1963). Numerous theories have been proposed to explain social change; some are based on the natural evolution of society, others on the advancement of science and technology or on the diffusion of economic resources and other processes in the social structure. All of these theories view the effects of social change on the individual as essentially a reordering or elimination of traditional expectations of individual behavior or social roles and the institution of new role expectations. Thus, the individual is viewed as the dependent variable in the process of change—as one who must adapt to the requisites of an ever-changing world or suffer what Toffler (1971) refers to as "future shock."

Whenever the concept of the self is discussed in the literature—which it rarely is—it too is placed in the position of dependent variable. Based as it is on the assumption that self-definition is derived from a person's position in the social structure, the answer to the question "Who am I?" is largely determined by whatever personal identity is currently culturally fashionable for any particular social stratum (see Lifton, 1970). While there is some obvious truth in this claim, the papers in this collection point to a different model of the relationship between social change and the individual—different and potentially more exciting theoretically. *From the existential perspective, the self can be seen as an active agent in the process of social change.* My intention is not to swing the pendulum of causality in the opposite direction, by asserting the preeminence of the Meadean "I" over the "me," but only to view the process of social change *reflexively.*[4] The facticity of social change, and therefore its perceived consequences, is grounded in the person's interpretation of events in the world as changing. Furthermore, the interpretation or definition of "social change" or similar common-sense typifications is elicited largely by the person's concern for the becoming of self within the context of what are perceived to be uncertain social conditions.

By focusing on the self, we can arrive at the following tentative model of social change. The individual perceives an uncertainty or change occurring in the segments of the social world that impinge on his or her existence. This uncertainty, whether it is "real" or imagined, can occur at the level of technology, attitudes, values, rules, or any other realm of social life. What is crucial is that the individual view these changes as *critically relevant* to maintaining a coherent and satisfying self. This relevance can take two forms. The individual may decide that uncertainty in social conditions leaves existing modes of self-actualization obsolete. Or the individual may perceive new possibilities for self-actualization emanating from changing social conditions. In either case, the individual will seek new means for self-actualization, usually in the form of new social roles. This search is likely to be a *collective* endeavor, for the individual will either actively cooperate with others who are experiencing similar concerns for self and are therefore instituting new social forms or he/she will passively share in new social forms created by others. The process is then perpetuated when these new social forms provide still other individuals with a new basis for perceiving uncertain social conditions.

Ebaugh's analysis of the plight of the ex-nun is a fine illustration of the way this process operates (chapter seven). Many nuns feel tremendous anxiety over perceived changes occurring within the Catholic Church, particularly those associated with the Second Vatican Council. The call for upgrading the professional status of the religious and for reevaluating the status of women in the church, among other events, led many nuns to seriously question the traditionally unquestionable role of the nun. Surrounded by a church that seemingly no longer supported the role of the nun and by a newly discovered secular world that preached liberation, these women came to doubt the viability of the "vocation" as an anchor for the experience of self. By leaving the convent, these women sought different ways for actualizing the self, including experimenting with existing social forms (e.g., the role of wife, mother, or lover) and the need to create a radically new social form, the role of the ex-nun. The construction of the social role "ex-nun" is a collective enterprise involving the social-support networks in which ex-nuns engage as well as other significant people in the ex-nun's life who provide assistance in the re-creation of self. The function of the ex-nun phenomenon for social change is to add substance to the more general categories of uncertain social conditions, such as "uncertainty in the Catholic Church," which may lead other women to question the viability of their own experiences of self.

The importance of the media in fostering social change must be mentioned. As Altheide (chapter eight) indicates, the media not only provide a format for people in public life to present a convincing self to their audiences but also create a version of reality that must be dramatic and "newsworthy" in order to attract audiences. Thus, the media are inherently biased toward presenting social conditions as uncertain and changing. As the media, especially television, become an increasingly pervasive element in modern life, we can expect increasing numbers of people in our society to tie their experiences of self to a social world that, at least on the screen and in print, seems to demand an almost constant revamping of our answers to the question "Who am I?"—which leads to the question "Who do I want to be?"[5]

CONCLUSION

One of the key purposes in assembling these essays was to demonstrate that the existential study of the self is an exciting enterprise because the experience of self today is so exciting. As these essays clearly indicate, answers given to the hypothetical question "Who am I?" are as varied and complex as the biographical possibilities that are present in modern life. Some of the topics covered in this book refer to relatively new social phenomena, like the impact of the media, the role of the ex-nun, and organized running by the physically impaired. But most of the topics— including family violence, compromising the body's integrity, intimacy, homosexuality, and organizational life—are not so new. The one theme that weaves its way throughout these essays and serves to unify them is the fact that modern life provides many individuals with the opportunity, if not the necessity, to evaluate critically his or her personal biography and to seek change when possible and to cope with it when necessary.

There is little question that we have not achieved the theoretical synthesis alluded to by Lester (chapter two) regarding the self. Meaningful concepts of the self can emerge only as we increase our *empirical* understanding of the varied forms the self assumes in everyday-life situations. Therefore, the mandate of existential sociology is clear: we must continue to study transformations in the experience of self in order to understand the process of change. But it is equally important to study experiences of self that remain constant even though the social conditions surrounding them change. A fascinating example is the tramp or hobo's experience of self, which Harper's recent (1982) ethnographic study found largely the same as that described by Anderson (1923) sixty years ago.

As the research questions directed to the self become more and more refined, we must seek innovative methods with which to answer them. In-depth personal involvement with changing social forms, which is the primary method utilized in these essays, will continue to be an important method, especially as an organized team endeavor, for it allows the researcher to elegantly describe the nuances of the experience of self in its natural settings. Another extremely promising method is the *life-study*, which Douglas utilizes in his analysis of love, sex, and intimacy (chapter three). The life-study method is an interview technique that involves the in-depth probing of the subject's entire biography. This method not only facilitates the close monitoring of the process of change in a person's life; it also helps the researcher to determine to what degree biographical experiences of self are cumulative and to what degree they are situational.[6]

It seems reasonable, therefore, to assert that future studies of the existential self will not (and should not) lean in the direction of searching for definitive statements, for the essence of the experience of being precludes that. Instead, we should engage in works that are *relevant* to the lives of the people we study and conducive to our goal of remaining true to the actual experiences of those lives.

I will conclude this essay, and our book, by reiterating Douglas's optimistic thoughts on the exploring and creative nature of the self (chapter three). While existential sociology has in general adhered philosophically to the major premise of existential thought—that the world and our selves are essentially meaningless—we reject the commonly accepted consequences of this assumption (e.g., dread, fear, alienation etc.). Our observations of contemporary life clearly lead us to celebrate the self, for a primary, if not the primary, project in life seems to be the insatiable need to discover viable meaning in order to make life work. We share our optimistic view of the self with other humanistic thinkers, ranging from Polanyi (1967) and his philosophical work on spontaneous social orders to Rychlak (1977) and his work on the psychological preeminence of agency as the ultimate motivating force in human behavior. The future of existential sociology, then, rests largely on our ability to explore interdisciplinary interest in the primacy of the self.

Notes

1. The symbolic interactionist strategy of studying the self-concept by means of the TST (Twenty Statements Test) lies somewhere between the positivistic and ethnographic traditions (see Kuhn, 1964). The TST lies somewhat within the ethnographic tradition insofar as it is based on subjects' personal responses to the open-ended research question "Who am I?" However, this inventory can be criticized for seeking nonsituational definitions of self or, at best, the ways that college students experience the self in the classroom, where the TST is usually administered. I would argue that the individual rarely if ever frames his or her natural experiences of self in such clear and rational terms as "Who am I?" But the TST belongs in the positivistic tradition insofar as it is administered in a standardized format, and the responses to it are readily codable. Nevertheless, the coding schemes used in analyzing responses are probably best seen as tools for generating summary statements rather than techniques that treat responses simply as indicators. Probably the most useful application of the TST can be seen in ways that several researchers (e.g., Snow and Phillips, 1982) have used it to monitor changing global self-attitudes among various cohorts of college students.

2. Tiryakian (1968) provides an insightful analysis of the existential self, based on the philosophical premises of existentialism, but it is complementary to my own more empirically based analysis. He discusses the differentiation between ontological and ontic existence, the significance of the openness of the self, the distinction between the person (in a psychological sense) and the existential self, and the concept of situation.

3. The reader may well argue that Simon and Gagnon's thesis (1976) is outdated in light of current economic conditions in our society, marked by high unemployment and low growth rates, which may limit the chances of many people to reach affluence. The authors anticipated this historically-specific criticism of their argument by insisting that the experience of affluence they describe is grounded in the long-term, cumulative, and continuing technological revolution occurring in industrialized societies. In other words, the authors implicitly view recession as cyclical and transitory.

4. Put simply, to analyze social life reflexively is to begin with a common-sense belief in the facticity of a social form (e.g., social change) and then to proceed to explore the ways in which members continually recreate that social form by means of intensive cognitive and interactional work (see Freeman, 1980).

5. Becker (1982) provides us with an analysis of the relationship between social change and the individual that is quite complementary to mine. In examining the world of art as a network of interacting people and a set of normative conventions, he argues that change in this system (e.g., styles) originates with the individual artist:

> Change takes place . . . because artists whose work does not fit and who thus stand outside the existing systems attempt to start new ones and because established artists exploit their attractiveness to the existing system to force it to handle work they do which does not fit. [Becker, 1982:136]

6. See Denzin (1978:214–55) for a comprehensive discussion of the history and use of the life-study method, including strategies for insuring validity and reliability through comparative research.

References

Anderson, Nels. 1923. *The Hobo*. Chicago: University of Chicago Press.

Becker, Howard S. 1982. *Art Worlds*. Berkeley: University of California Press.

Blau, Zena Smith. 1981. *Aging in a Changing Society*. New York: Franklin Watts.

Carveth, Donald L. 1977. "The Hobbesian Microcosm: On the Dialectics of Self in Social Theory." *Sociological Inquiry* 47:3–12.

Denzin, Norman K. 1978. *The Research Act*. New York: McGraw-Hill.

Douglas, Jack D., and John M. Johnson, eds. 1977. *Existential Sociology*. Cambridge, Eng.: Cambridge University Press.

Freeman, C. Robert. 1980. "Phenomenological Sociology and Ethnomethodology." Pp. 113–54 in Jack D. Douglas et al., *Introduction to the Sociologies of Everyday Life*. Boston: Allyn & Bacon.

Harper, Douglas A. 1982. *Good Company*. Chicago: University of Chicago Press.

Kaplan, Howard B. 1975. *Self-Attitudes and Deviant Behavior*. Pacific Palisades, Calif.: Goodyear.

Kotarba, Joseph A. 1979. "Existential Sociology." Pp. 348–68 in Scott G. McNall, ed., *Theoretical Perspectives in Sociology*. New York: St. Martin's.

Kovit, Leonard. 1980. "The Phenomenology of Self." *Reflections* 1:23–37.

Kuhn, Manfred H. 1964. "Major Trends in Symbolic Interaction Theory in the Past Twenty-Five Years." *Sociological Quarterly* 5:61–84.

Lasch, Christopher. 1979. *The Culture of Narcissism*. New York: Warner Books.

Lifton, Robert J. 1970. *Boundaries: Psychological Man in Revolution*. New York: Random House.

———. 1976. *The Life of the Self*. New York: Simon & Schuster.

Mehan, Hugh, and Houston Wood. 1975. *The Reality of Ethnomethodology*. New York: Wiley.

Merleau-Ponty, Maurice. 1962. *Phenomenology of Perception*. Translated by Colin Smith. London: Routledge & Kegan Paul.

Moore, Wilbert. 1963. *Social Change*. Englewood Cliffs, N.J.: Prentice-Hall.

Polanyi, Michael. 1967. *The Tacit Dimension*. New York: Doubleday.

Rosenberg, Morris. 1979. *Conceiving the Self*. New York: Basic Books.

Rychlak, Joseph F. 1977. *The Psychology of Rigorous Humanism*. New York: Wiley.

Sartre, Jean-Paul. 1945. *L'Age de la raison*. Paris: Gallimard.

Simon, William, and John Gagnon. 1976. "The Anomie of Affluence." *American Journal of Sociology* 82(2):154–76.

Snow, David A., and Cynthia L. Phillips. 1982. "The Changing Self-Orientations of College Students: From Institution to Impulse." *Social Science Quarterly* 63(3):462–75.

Tiryakian, Edward A. 1968. "The Existential Self and the Person." Pp. 75–86 in Chad Gordon and Kenneth J. Gergen, eds., *The Self in Social Interaction*. New York: Wiley.

Toffler, Alvin. 1971. *Future Shock*. New York: Bantam Books.
Turner, Ralph H. 1976. "The Real Self." *American Journal of Sociology* 81:989–
    1016.
Yalom, Irving D. 1980. *Existential Psychotherapy*. New York: Basic Books.
Zurcher, Louis A. 1977. *The Mutable Self*. Beverly Hills, Calif.: Sage.

Contributors

DAVID L. ALTHEIDE is professor of Justice Studies and director of field research, Center for Urban Studies, at Arizona State University.

JOHN E. BIGNALL is in private-practice counseling of the physically handicapped in Phoenix, Arizona.

JACK D. DOUGLAS is professor of sociology at the University of California–San Diego.

HELEN ROSE FUCHS EBAUGH is associate professor of sociology at the University of Houston–University Park.

WENDY ESPELAND is a graduate student of sociology at the University of Chicago. Her essay is a revised version of one that won the Herbert Blumer Award of the Society for the Study of Symbolic Interaction.

KATHLEEN FERRARO is assistant professor of Justice Studies at Arizona State University.

ANDREA FONTANA is associate professor of sociology and director of the Gerontology Program at the University of Nevada–Las Vegas.

JOHN M. JOHNSON is professor of Justice Studies at Arizona State University.

JOSEPH A. KOTARBA is associate professor of sociology at the University of Houston–University Park.

MARILYN LESTER, who resides in Los Angeles, California, is conducting research and writing on the social dimensions of intimate experience.

STANFORD M. LYMAN is professor of sociology at the New School for School Research.

SHELDON L. MESSINGER is professor of law at the University of California–Berkeley.

DWYNE RHODES PATRICK is assistant director of Management Services at Saint John's Hospital and Health Center in Los Angeles, California.

RONALD W. SMITH is associate professor and chairperson of sociology and codirector of the Survey Research Center at the University of Nevada–Las Vegas.

CAROL A. B. WARREN is associate professor of sociology and senior research associate in the Social Science Institute at the University of Southern California.

Index